New Directions in the
Sociology of Health

New Directions in the Sociology of Health

Edited by

Pamela Abbott and Geoff Payne

Explorations in Sociology No. 36

RoutledgeFalmer
Taylor & Francis Group

LONDON AND NEW YORK

In conjunction with the British Sociological Association

First published 1990
By RoutledgeFalmer, 11 New
Fetter Lane, London EC4P 4EE

Transferred to Digital Printing 2004

British Library Cataloguing in Publication Data
New directions in the sociology of health. (Explorations
  in sociology no. 36)
  1. Man. Health. Social aspects
  I. Abbott, Pamela II. Payne, Geoff III. Series
  362.1042

  ISBN 1-85000-786-1
        1-85000-787-X (pbk)

**Library of Congress Cataloging-in-Publication Data is
available on request.**

Jacket design by Caroline Archer

Typeset in 11/13 Bembo by
Chapterhouse, The Cloisters, Formby L37 3PX

Contents

Chapter 1

Introduction: Developing the Sociology of Health

Pamela Abbott and Geoff Payne

The sociology of medicine has come a long way from its origins in epidemiology and clinical practice. Like all specialist areas of study it has developed its own internal debates, its preferred core of research topics, and its own professional infrastructure for their analysis. Over the years, there has been a shift from a sociology *in* medicine to a sociology *of* medicine, and from a sociology of *medicine*, towards a sociology of *health and illness*. It is to the development of this latter perspective that the present volume is addressed.

Within what is a large and active field of study there are inevitably several competing paradigms. Medicine and medical science continue to play a substantial part in setting the agenda. This is reflected not only by a concentration on illness and illness behaviour, but also by the relative neglect of paramedical workers such as nurses, or the wider settings in which health behaviour is determined. The narrow focus of much earlier research means that we are still today in the process of discovering more about the ways in which ordinary people act to promote their own, and other people's, health. The structural and cultural factors that hinder them in so doing have been under-researched, as have the roles played by the State and other agencies in these processes. To take one example, the health promotion work of the non-professional health worker and of the unpaid worker have virtually been ignored.

In selecting papers for this volume, we have therefore looked for those which address these under-researched areas and set a new direction for the sociology of health. The articles were all originally presented at the 1989 Annual Conference of the British Sociological Association, held at Polytechnic South West in Plymouth. The theme for the Conference, 'Sociology in Action', was chosen to demonstrate how current work in the discipline was directly related to issues in contemporary society: Health and Illness was one of the main 'streams' and provided a rich resource of contributions from among which the contents of this conference volume were chosen.

At first sight, the papers here might seem to be disparate, because they raise a number of wide-ranging issues, and deal with them in rather different ways. However, they share more than just a common concern with the sociological understanding of health and illness for the 1990s. There are two interconnected central themes. First, we wanted to broaden the perspectives, and to connect research in the specialist field of health and illness to developments and approaches in other cognate areas of current sociology. Second, we wish to foster the promotion of a 'sociology of health', as distinct from a sociology of medicine, or even of 'health and illness'. A broader perspective leads us to see the advantages of escaping from the medical model: the rejection of the medical model opens up new perspectives for study.

The first of these themes manifests itself in several ways among the articles. On the one hand, there are papers such as those by Sara Arber (Chapter 3) and by Gary Littlejohn and colleagues (Chapter 2), which take a well established tradition and carry it forward through more sophisticated and systematic analysis. Arber applies to health statistics perspectives on women and social class that have been recently advanced in the context of social mobility, labour markets, and class analysis. Littlejohn *et al.* use improved standards of empirical research to disentangle individual, household and community level effects in the familiar field of social epidemiology. On the other hand, George Giarchi and Lorna Warren (Chapters 4 and 5) expand the idea of health care by looking at parallel, non-medical services, while Ursula Sharma and Nicki Thorogood (Chapters 9 and 10) offer us insights into the world of alternative therapies. Other papers draw on work in the sociology of deviance and the sociology of the media, to explain public reactions to initiatives aimed at dealing with alcoholism, tranquillizers and AIDS.

The second theme in this selection, a concern with ways that sociology can enhance our understanding of health by placing health maintenance at the centre of things, also presents itself in a number of ways. Warren shows how Home Helps in practice go beyond their formal duties and carry out work with the elderly which could be seen as nursing, and certainly resembles the informal health support which they do in their domestic sphere for their own families. Norma Daykin (Chapter 11) shows how occupational health research has focused on male workers, ignoring many work hazards that affect women. Giarchi, Sharma and Throrogood have already been mentioned as setting the problem of health maintenance in specific cultural contexts, far removed from the world views of the medical practitioner. Thomas Acton and David Chambers (Chapter 12) address questions of public health policy (as do several of the papers), but again, from a new angle.

The papers, then, contain a coherence at a level which reflects recent movements in the field, while equally spanning a range of work that builds bridges to other fields. Our choice of title is deliberate: as editors we see the need to draw attention to new directions, and in particular, we have selected the title 'the sociology of health', rather than 'health and illness' to emphasize where we believe the focus should lie. It is not our claim that we are being totally original in this; rather it is a case of adding the weight of part of the BSA's annual conference — an opportunity to report on work in hand — to reinforce a fresh perspective in the field.

The sociology of under-researched groups

It is certainly also not original to add that several groups in our society have not received the research attention that they deserve. This collection includes new work on four of these groups with, most obviously, the health situation of women not only receiving specific attention (Chapters 2, 3 and 11, for example) but being a recurrent element in many of the other papers. Within the conventional boundaries of the sociology of health and illness, the particular health concerns of the elderly, of Black Britons, and of rural dwellers have also largely been marginal, whereas there has been a growing literature on other aspects of their life experience in associated fields of sociology. To a large extent, the earlier narrow perspective that we now wish to replace is a product of a medical model, in which medicine, maleness, metropolitanism and middle class membership have been equally constraining.

The potential of breaking this mould can be seen in Arber's examination of women's health in Chapter 3, in which she points out that despite the fact that the Black Report on Health Inequalities was published a decade ago, inequalities in women's health remains a largely unresearched area, because research in the area has been dominated by male-oriented class analysis. She argues for two kinds of refinement here, drawing on her background as a member of the Stratification and Employment Group at the University of Surrey. On the one hand, Arber is identifying the need for more sophisticated indicators of material deprivation, differentiation and inequality than the conventional catch-all of social class. This takes us away from sterile 'left versus right' debates and accusations of political bias; but, more important, it redirects us towards a more informed picture of what we wish to know. Too often in the past, sociologists have tended to see health inequalities only as particular symptoms of class, the latter being their real interest. The way forward must be to take health patterns as an interest in themselves, and to explore them using a larger battery of variables and indicators. (Ironically, this may cause more problems for the medical professions than for sociologists; what often passes for 'scientific' research among the former is frequently typified by simplistic statistical analysis, and the new complexity implied in Arber's paper could be a daunting challenge for many medics!)

On the other hand, Arber is not abandoning the question of class structures and structuration, although she does suggest that the concentration on structural/materialist explanations has deflected researchers from seeing the ways in which women's familial and employment roles need to be analyzed within a structural context. She concludes that, as with men, structural factors have a major impact on women's health status, but that also women's health status influences women's roles. This suggests that the material disadvantages of some households may be compound by the poor health of female members as they are unable to take on paid employment in addition to their domestic work. Indeed it could further be suggested that the poor health of women in disadvantaged households may reduce the 'health promoting' work that they are able to perform in the household, compounding the disadvantages of children and other household members. Women's health status is of vital importance in determining their ability to promote the health of other members of the household — including children, and their own parents.

For the elderly who cannot draw on health support from their own families, an alternative may be found in the Home Help, although this is neither the prime function of the service, nor the original motivation of those who start as Home Helps. These are, as Warren's study shows (Chapter 5), on the whole unqualified women who become Home Helps because the hours are convenient. However, the work that they do as Home Helps is much the same as they perform for their own families. The care they give makes a valuable, often vital, contribution to maintaining the health of the elderly. Furthermore, as Warren points out, they often go beyond their defined duties and carry out work that could be seen as nursing. This echoes Graham's point (1984) that much of the unpaid work that women routinely undertake in the domestic sphere is health promotion or health monitoring work. Yet it is rarely acknowledged as such, not least where the medical model narrows our focus on to disease *per se*.

A parallel case of health promotion which is largely invisible to the formal medical world is the use of traditional treatments by West Indian women. Thorogood (Chapter 10) argues that we need to understand the cultural attitudes of Black Britons to health and health care if adequate provision is to be made to meet their needs. She focuses on the health work of West Indian women in London. While she is specifically concerned with the traditional 'bush' medication used in the West Indies, she develops her analysis to argue that class, gender and race shape the ways in which West Indian women make use of traditional and western medicine. On the one hand, a decision to use 'bush' remedies may be influenced by experience of racism in the NHS, both as patient and as worker. On the other 'bush' represents one element within a (largely female) cultural tradition. Thorogood suggests that among West Indian women in her study, 'bush' was used in the West Indies (and still is used amongst older West Indian women) to maintain health as well as to cure specific illnesses/diseases. Perhaps it could be seen as akin to the taking of vitamin pills and other 'health preparations' as a way of maintaining health, an increasingly common practice in Britain.

In contrast 'alternative medicine', also of increasing popularity in contemporary society, is more frequently used when conventional medicine 'fails'. Sharma (Chapter 9) suggests that when people turn to alternative medicine, it is generally because they are seeking alternative ways to restore and maintain their health when conventional medicine is unable to meet their expectations. Frequently she found this is in respect to chronic illnesses. Thorogood and Sharma both illustrate how the medical model influences wider perceptions of 'problems'. The medical profession has a claim to the monopoly of skills in the treatment of disease and judgments of successful treatment. This is not always accepted by those suffering from disease, who may choose to consult and follow the treatment prescribed by 'alternative healers'. Most medical practitioners are critical of 'alternative medicine', at once trying to incorporate elements within their own domain, and challenging others to 'prove' their efficacy by scientific methods (generally controlled clinical trials). Sharma argues that this lack of scientific 'proof' of efficacy may not be seen as problematic by those who use alternative medicines, because they are generally suffering from complaints that conventional medicine cannot cure. There are also alternative measures of 'satisfactory outcome' to that of positivist science. For example, Thorogood suggests that 'bush' is based on tradition and presumably empirical knowledge, that is knowledge built up through a perceived 'successful' experience of use.

Before one can use such remedies, one must be in a position to exercise choice, based on knowledge and availability (or access). George Giarchi (Chapter 4) points to the neglect of rural deprivation in dimensions of health inequalities. He argues that the rural poor 'suffer' all the deprivations of the urban poor, plus additional ones because of living in rural areas — making not only access to services difficult, but also adequate knowledge of services difficult to obtain. In his Cornish study, reported in his article, he shows how the problems of the rural poor were also compounded by age and social isolation. Not only are many of the rural poor elderly, but also many have moved to the area after retirement, leaving behind family and long established community ties. This means that many are not integrated into communities and cannot rely on community support. This is an even greater problem for those who live in isolated dwellings or small hamlets where there are few people available to provide 'community care'.

Giarchi's article raises two key issues for the sociology of health, knowledge of available services, and provision and access to services. Both are political. In recent years there has been a tendency to centralize services — exemplified in the development of the centralized District General Hospital. Knowledge of the availability of a service is necessary, as is an ability and willingness to travel to use it. Giarchi argues that the further from services people live, the less likely they are to have or to be able to obtain knowledge of them. He identifies 'knowledge deprivation' as a new dimension of general social deprivation. This extends Graham's (1984) argument that the centralization of services may cause severe difficulties for women in carrying out their health maintenance work in the domestic sphere. Problems such as cost, time and transportation may deter women from making use of available services for themselves and their children. Transport may be the greater problem, despite higher levels of car-ownership, because women rarely have access to 'the family car' (Graham 1984).

These people are consumers of the available services, even if their 'choices' are constrained by availability, knowledge and cost. While Stacey (1976) may be correct to argue that patients are health workers and that the consumer analogy is a misconception, people do make decisions about service utilization. This still applies even in circumstances such as those that Giarchi found in Cornwall, where these choices are heavily constrained.

Research on these four under-researched groups goes beyond providing substantive information about the groups in question. As this brief review demonstrates, the papers are also a rich resource of concepts and approaches — such as the interaction of structures and processes, cultural systems, and individual action on constrained choices — which can fruitfully be brought to bear on health from other fields of sociology. This enrichment follows naturally from the refocusing on health, rather than on illness, as the central issue.

Focus and Framework

The sociology of health is centrally about the ways in which people strive to maintain their health. This is a different model from one that starts with ill health, or that contained within the medical model. It starts from the assumption that people are concerned, in their everyday lives, to maintain their health and that in doing so they carry out health work and make decisions about and choices between the available services. It also recognizes that members are using their own social definitions of health and illness, and their own knowledge of how to promote, maintain and restore health. They do so within a material framework that not only constrains and limits the choices available to them, but is the major factor in shaping their health status. Class, gender, age and ethnicity all play a major role in structuring our abilities to maintain our health.

We would, however, want to distinguish between a structuralist perspective *per se*, and its application to health and the process of health promotion. This is not to reject structuralist research, but to call for further developments. It is of course true that the sociology of medicine has contributed to the analysis of structures, in the senses of class structures, and of Government policies. Obviously, the Black Report (DHSS, 1980) has prompted considerable research on health inequalities (see e.g. Townsend *et al.*, 1988 (a) and (b); Abbott *et al.*, 1988), some of it undertaken by sociologists. The major conclusion from this work is that health inequalities are structural and that as in the past, future improvement in health will come from improvement in diet, housing and such. Recognition has also been given to cultural factors and particularly the ways in which they articulate with material disadvantage (see, e.g., Graham, 1984). In this way individualistic explanations of health inequalities have been challenged, despite their continuing popularity with Government.

As Acton and Chambers (Chapter 12) demonstrate, such structuralist research has had singularly little impact on Government, while at the same time, this problem has been exacerbated by sociologists' choice of research topics. For example, public health, and the role of Environmental Health Officers in particular, have been virtually ignored. Yet this is an area where sociologists could make important contributions to the development of public policy. While it has been commonplace to point out that we have an 'ill-health service' rather than a 'health service', little attention has been paid to the preventative arm. This neglect is, of course, not just one of sociologists: for instance, the recent Government White Paper on the Health Service, *Working for Patients* (DoH, 1989), made no reference to preventative or public health policies. Government remains not only committed to individualistic explanations for health status, but also to the traditional emphasis on a curative rather than a preventative health policy, and an emphasis on chronic rather than acute illness. In this sense health promotion exists in a framework of public policies oriented to illness.

This does not mean that Government has not played a role in health promotion policies. However, campaigns have generally been directed at the individual, with a view to changing individual behaviour — often with little success. When such campaigns have been successful it has generally been because there are strong motivating factors and individuals are able to make choices. This is probably best illustrated by cigarette smoking. There has been a sustained campaign for a number of years to get people to give up smoking. Middle-class and, to a lesser extent, working-class men have reduced their consumption of cigarettes while the proportion of working-class women smoking has actually increased. Graham (1984) has argued that this suggests that it must have something to do with the situation that these women are in. Her analysis of the budget of poor single-parent women, as compared with those of women in more advantaged households, indicates that the disadvantaged women who smoke see it as an essential item of expenditure. She argues that these women see cigarette smoking as their only pleasure and the thing that enables them to get through the day. For them giving up smoking is not a realistic choice.

A parallel example is the mid-1980s health education campaigns against heroin, which were designed to persuade young people not to try heroin. Graham Hart (Chapter 9) argues that the campaigns had negative as well as positive effects: they were so targeted to heroin that other drugs appeared relatively benign, and the drug-addicted sallow youths appearing in the posters were considered attractive enough to be put up on bedroom walls. The campaigners were concerned when heroin addiction was seen as having a debilitating and dependency-inducing effect on 'youth' and the solution was seen as persuading individuals not to take the drug, or to give it up. The campaign ignored the wider social and economic problems of young working-class people which led them to consider taking heroin in the first place (Parker, Newcombe and Bakx, 1987). However, while drug use was seen as causing individual physical deterioration and as having negative social consequences such as crime and unemployability, it was not until the late 1980s that drug use and in particular the intravenous injecting of heroin became seen as a major health problem. Indeed it became seen as such an important issue that the Government put relatively large sums of money (in health education terms) into campaigns. The new threat was AIDS: injecting drug users became recognized as one group who were responsible for the spread of HIV, the causative agent of AIDS amongst the heterosexual population. Concern developed about a group of people enjoying an elicit and health-threatening addiction who were seen as threatening the health of the heterosexual population. Despite not being enthusiastically endorsed by all members of the Government, the response was to move from campaigns designed to persuade individuals to give up their (illegal) drug-taking to ones to educate them to take their drugs safely and to engage in 'safe sex'. One of the policy initiatives was needle exchange schemes, designed to encourage heroin addicts not to share needles and to use sterile equipment for 'fixing'. Graham Hart reports on one at University College Hospital which has been relatively successful.

While the approach is still individualistic, the change in tactics has come about, at least in part, because of the recognition that the health of one individual group can affect that of others. Another important factor has probably been the high cost of treating and caring for patients with AIDS. In other areas, high costs have resulted in Government legislation. e.g. the car seat belt legislation, although in general the Government is reluctant to intervene. For example, the current administration has refused, despite lobbying from health groups, to raise taxes on cigarettes or alcohol and has resisted demands from the EEC to put new, stronger health warnings on cigarettes (although it has now been forced to do so). There has been recurrent criticism of Health and Safety at Work legislation, both in terms of its coverage and enforcement. It is also suggested that even when firms are brought to court and fined, the fines are too low to act as a real deterrent. The more recent concerns over food poisoning have resulted in the Government issuing advice to householders on hygiene in the home, and to pregnant women and other vulnerable groups on food to avoid. Health education is persistently aimed at the individual, assuming correctly that most people want to maintain their health, but ignoring the cultural and structural factors that mitigate against this. Individualistic programmes are, of course, much less expensive than structural reforms, as well as passing the blame for their own problems on to the victims. While it may be more true of the New Right administration headed by Mrs Thatcher, it has been a common factor of health education under Conservative and Labour Governments in the past. It is trapped within a simplistic, psychological model of attitude formation and change.

Robin Bunton (Chapter 8), however, points to a new direction in public health campaigns on alcohol. While the health education is still directed at individuals and at changing individual behaviour, he suggests that the target has changed. In the past, health education targeted the alcoholic — the 'alcohol dependent'; the target is now the 'problem drinker'. We have moved, he suggests, into a post-addiction period, into an alcohol misuse period. The focus is now on what is a safe amount to drink, based on units of alcohol. Health is a key concern, and an unhealthy amount to drink is contrasted with what is an acceptable level. There is similarly new attention paid to anti-social behaviour such as drinking and driving, vandalism and rowdyism associated with drink.

This concern with health is not confined to the health education profession. It has been taken over by the media, into the public domain, where consumerism and programmes as units of consumption go hand in hand. In Chapter 6, Michael Bury and Jonathan Gabe point to the role of the mass media both in expressing consumer concerns about health and health issues, and in constructing consumer concern. Looking specifically at tranquillizers, they suggest that recent television programmes on the addiction problems suffered by long term tranquillizer users are both an outcome of consumer anxiety and a 'creator' of that anxiety. They argue that some programme formats are more likely than others to sensationalize long term tranquillizer use, and to be one-sided in their criticisms of tranquillizers, so causing unnecessary concern to many who rely on them. However, they also conclude that these programmes, by criticising drug companies for manufacturing the drugs, and individual doctors for prescribing them, deflect attention away from the socio-economic factors that cause many people to experience the problems for which tranquillizers are prescribed in the first place. Tranquillizers are frequently prescribed to enable people to carry on as 'normal' when they feel unable to do so. The major group of tranquillizer users are women, who are often prescribed tranquillizers to enable them to carry on with their domestic roles (Roberts, 1984). It could be argued that while women provide an emotional support for the members of their immediate family, they themselves have to turn to the doctor when they need similar help. Women's domestic roles and the conditions under which they carry out domestic labour may be the cause of depression in the first place (Brown and Harris, 1976).

At the same time, women may also be exposed to unnecessary risk when they are in paid employment. In another example of an area which has not received its full attention due to the medical model, Norma Daykin (Chapter 11) argues that Occupational Health Research has focused on areas that affect male workers and has ignored work hazards that affect women. This is because the focus has been on the more dramatic industrial accidents in occupational environments dominated by male workers, while chronic ill health and stress have been ignored. Given that the majority of women now work for the majority of their employable years (Martin and Roberts, 1984), work conditions are of vital concern to women if they are to remain healthy. This, as Daykin shows, is not a static problem: changes in unemployment and youth training, changes in Government policies, and the prospect of Europeanization in the 1990s go hand in hand with other non-work trends in society.

Health in the 1990s

The call for a sociology of health is not just a symptom of the greying of the sociology profession, and still less a response to current fashionable obsessions with the environment and 'healthy living'. It is of course true that there is now a booming industry in health, health clubs, fitness for health, dieting for health as well as large chains of supermarkets advertising particular foods as 'healthy'. More people are concerned about their health, about eating healthy food, adopting a healthy lifestyle, avoiding addiction and pollution and so on. Their concerns have been taken up and amplified by the media and health education campaigners. In turn this has resulted in a growing interest in alternative therapies, and more conventionally in pressure on Government to improve health prevention measures, such as providing for cervical smear testing for all women at regular intervals. However, both the 'consumer movement' and the Government response is individualistic. In addition the 'consumer movement' is middle-class in inspiration and orientation: it is dependent on people being able to make individual choices with the minimum of constraint. While all of us are constrained in our choices, the socially-deprived are more constrained than others.

Just as at the turn of the century the main response to the perceived problem of the health of the working-class was the appointment of Health Visitors to teach working-class mothers infant care and hygiene in the home (Abbot and Sapsford, 1988), so now the solution is seen as being to encourage healthy lifestyles. Ill health, then, is seen as a problem of an unhealthy lifestyle (or occasionally bad luck or misfortune). However, not everyone can choose a healthy lifestyle. As Cornwell (1984) points out, her respondents were well aware of the 'causes' of their ill health over which they had no control — unhealthy work conditions, poor housing, poverty — and, given this, were reluctant to give up pleasures such as smoking and drinking, even if they had an associated health risk. As Gary Littlejohn and his colleagues (Chaper 2) show in a study of respiratory problems in four mining areas, there is an interaction between occupation, material deprivation, health related behaviour and gender. These cannot be separated out but are integrated aspects of individual lives that are related to the likelihood of developing respiratory problems. While it may be possible to predict which groups in the population are likely to suffer poorer health than other groups, there are limits to the extent to which individual behaviour on its own can alter the outcome.

The sociology of health is not so much a new concern as a reorientation, based on an essentially sociological perspective. Just as 'health' needs to replace 'illness', so we would argue that social processes must replace the individual as the focus of attention. Process helps to integrate the actor into the structure. This observation is not offered as some kind of neat solution to questions of general sociological explanation. Rather, in keeping with the core theme of the BSA Conference at Plymouth, we maintain that good sociology — by which we mean clear analysis, progressive conceptual clarification and careful empirical research — is not dependent on the 'givens' of the external world but rather interacts with it. 'Sociology in Action' implies that our work not only draws from society but can and should modify that world. The goal of a sociology of health, then, is not only better sociology, but also better health.

Chapter 2

Socio-economic Conditions and Aspects of Health: Respiratory Symptoms in Four West Yorkshire Mining Localities[1]

G. Littlejohn, M. D. Peake, D. Warwick, S. Allen, V. Carroll and C. Welsh

Introduction

In this chapter we wish to explore the background to a specific health question relating to the mining and former mining districts of West Yorkshire. Why are standardized mortality ratios for respiratory diseases in these districts double those in the rest of the UK? This question links with the aims of this volume in that we hope to challenge purely medical interpretations of its answer, and we will stress the significance of socio-economic conditions, which predispose the population to chest diseases. Further we shall break with a tendency, found particularly in the study of mining districts, but not only there, to concentrate upon the men, and we will point to the situation of both men and women.

In epidemiological studies, there have been many debates about the interrelationship of environmental, occupational and personal factors in the explanation of variations in health and illness. We would assume that these cannot in any real sense be separated from each other as factors in explaining the cause of respiratory disorders. Sociological analysis has always pointed to the importance of recognizing the interaction of factors in a social context of institutions and processes. The variables that we have studied are no more than indicators of the complex which makes up that social context.

It is to be recognized, of course, that our study is based on a small sample of households and therefore is not a basis for sure generalizations. It does, however, offer data and discussions about health conditions in a specific regional context, something called for in the Black Report (Townsend *et al.*, 1988). We present our data in the hope that others may consider and compare it with their own findings, and we begin with a description of the socio-economic conditions of the mining localities where we interviewed our household members. Following this we shall consider a number of indicators of variables that have potential explanatory power with reference to the respiratory symptoms identified by the Medical Research Council as defining chronic bronchitis (see end-note). In conclusion, we shall point to the significance of involvement in the mining industry along with other social conditions in explaining the prevalence of respiratory disease.

Socio-economic Conditions of Four Mining Localities in West Yorkshire, 1986/7

The four mining localities in West Yorkshire, within the City of Wakefield Metropolitan District, were chosen by a research team from the University of Bradford and the University of Leeds. They are referred to as Localities One, Two, Three and Four, for reasons of confidentiality, though they are in the neighbourhood and to the south of Featherstone. This was the place featured in the classic study *Coal is Our Life* (Dennis, Henriques and Slaughter, 1969). Funds were obtained from the Economic and Social Research Council to employ one full-time research assistant for two and a half years and interviewers to contact members of two random samples of households in each of the four localities, in 1986 and 1987. Table 2.1 indicates the number of households sampled. The 1986 survey represents approximately a 2 per cent sample, and the 1987 survey, a 3 per cent sample.

Table 2.1 Number of households surveyed in the 1986 and 1987 surveys

	Loc. 1	Loc. 2	Loc. 3	Loc. 4	All
1986 survey	30	32	31	31	124
1987 survey	50	50	50	50	200

Note: In all tables the four localities are labelled as above.

For the 1986 survey, households were chosen randomly from the 1986 electoral register and our interviewers contacted women householders, but in a quarter of the households we also interviewed a male, normally the partner of the woman. In one case we interviewed a single male, and there were thirteen women who had no partner. In the course of the interviews, averaging two and a half hours, we asked about their work situation, work histories, education and leisure interests, family background and links in the locality, domestic arrangements in the household, their attitudes to and experience of the miners' strike of 1984/5, and the future prospects of their localities. During 1986, we also contacted and interviewed former members of women's support groups about their experience during and after the strike.

In the 1987 survey, fifty households were chosen in each locality, some of which had been interviewed in 1986 (forty-six households overall), and the rest randomly chosen from the 1986 electoral register. The interviewers were asked to interview the 'householder' and his/her partner, provided they were of 'working age', that is 64 years or under. In the two hundred household interviews, lasting on average just over two hours, we collected responses from 170 men and 154 women. The interviews covered household structure and living arrangements, work histories, records of children's employment, household decision-making and division of labour, use of and attitude to state services, voting intentions, income, details of general health and indicators of respiratory disorders and related factors.

> LOCALITY ONE is a spread out settlement based on an old village, which grew in the nineteenth century as a result of nearby mining and quarrying. At the 1981 census it had a population of 5,836, 23 per cent of its male labour force in mining, and 28 per cent of heads of households in the Registrar General's Social Classes I and II.

> LOCALITY TWO grew up in the early twentieth century around a new colliery. This closed in the 1960s but a new drift mine was opened with the prospect of twenty-five years mining in 1979. In 1981 it had a population of 4,931, 56 per cent of the male labour force in mining, and 5 per cent of the heads of household were in R. G. Social Classes I and II.

> LOCALITY THREE is part of a mining town, but as a consequence of pit closures and new land use, including open cast coal working, is now physically separate from the main urban area, which in 1981 had a population of 10,726. There were two large collieries nearby, and 41 per cent of its male labour force was in mining. Ten per cent of heads of household were in R. G. Social Classes I and II.

> LOCALITY FOUR consists of mainly twentieth century housing which grew around a pit opened in the 1920s between two small villages. The pit closed in the 1960s but a large proportion of its male labour force continued to travel to other pits. In 1981 its population was 5,284, 59 per cent of male workers were coal miners and 8 per cent of heads of household were in R. G. Social Classes I and II.

The localities are within one parliamentary constituency and fall in an area of some eighty square miles of small towns and villages. Localities One and Three are in the north of the area and the other two to the south. They had had historically different experiences of the coal mining industry, but in the 1980s they have all been affected by pit closures which have reduced the number of jobs in mining in the area from about 7,000 ten years ago to less than 2,000 at present (O'Donnell, 1988). This means that there have been considerable changes in the labour market for men (at least) in our four localities. Not one of them now has a working pit within its boundaries. The historical link of these localities with coal mining still, however, gives them a strong sense of being different from communities which have other salient local economic activities. Nevertheless, even within our four localities, there are obvious differences between Locality One which has the lowest proportion of households where men have ever been employed in mining, and the other three where the proportion rises from over a third to over a half. It is difficult to speculate what the 'critical mass' is, that is in terms of the proportion of mining households to all households, which gives a locality its distinctiveness as a 'mining community'. Some authorities have suggested that it might be about 25 per cent, but this is probably a question that cannot be resolved, except through a much wider study. Table 2.2 is a summary of indicators of the socio-economic conditions of the four localities from the surveys.

Significant differences can be observed between the localities in our collected data and are related to the percentage of mining households, the economic position of men, household income, and the educational indicators for both men and women. All men we interviewed in 1987 were less than pensionable age, and the rate of unemployment among the whole sample was 15 per cent, compared with the official national rate of about 12 per cent at that time. Among those in mining households it was 27 per cent, but with the variations which can be seen in Table 2.2. Locality Two was the one with the highest levels of unemployment. It was also the locality with the highest proportion of households whose net monthly income was below the national average of £850. In terms of educational indicators, most of our sample were over 30 and had completed their schooling before the school leaving age had been raised to 16. The highest proportion of 'early leavers' were found in Localities Two, Three and Four among both men and women. Consistent with this was the relatively small percentage of respondents with O levels or above, in contrast with the situation in Locality One. The variations noted in other indicators do not mark out Locality One as significantly different from the others in statistical terms. There is little to alter the general picture, however, that socio-economic conditions are more advantageous in Locality One, which we could call the more middle-class locality.

In the case of women's paid work, there is a tendency for more women to be in employment and on a full-time basis in Locality One than in the other localities, but the myth that women in mining communities are all full-time housewives tied to the kitchen sink and the cooker, tends to be dispelled by the data in Table 2.2. Historically, as coal mining has declined the participation of women in the labour market has increased, but in many cases this is low paid, part-time work. The opportunities for

Table 2.2 Socio-economic conditions of four mining localities, 1986/7

Indicator	Percentages			
1987	Loc. 1	Loc. 2	Loc. 3	Loc. 4
Mining households	21	56	35	49
TENURE				
Owner-occupiers	83	56	67	75
Council tenants	17	42	33	25
AGE				
Women aged 41–64 years	44	60	36	56
Men aged 41–64 years	45	45	43	62
PAID WORK				
Women in paid employment	61	50	55	65
Of women in paid work: % P/T	42	65	40	50
Unemployed women	0	6	8	0
F/T housework and non-employed	38	44	36	35
Men in paid employment	95	59	68	69
Unemployed men				
in mining households	13	35	24	25
in non-mining households	4	18	10	0
Household monthly net income				
less than £850	44	78	65	73
more than £850	56	22	35	27
1986				
Mean household size (persons)	(3.3)	(3.5)	(3.5)	(3.2)
Single households	13	13	6	13
EDUCATION				
Left school by 15 yrs (women)	43	69	84	70
Left school by 15 yrs (men)	50	86	88	75
Educ. Quals: O level + (women)	37	6	6	17
Educ. Quals: O level + (men)	25	0	0	0
Attended school locally (women)	48	78	57	23
Attended school locally (men)	50	67	50	63

Note: Figures in brackets are not percentages.

casual work or second jobs, too, seemed to follow the pattern shown in other research. That is, participation in the 'hidden' or 'informal' economy is greater where there is wider access to jobs in the 'formal' labour market. So there was a higher participation in second or casual work in Locality One than in the others.

In many studies especially concerned with health, type of housing tenure and age are seen as indicators of significant differences. Locality One has a higher proportion of owner occupiers than the other three, though not significantly higher than Locality Four. Among tenant households, 87 per cent had average net monthly incomes of less than £850, compared with 55 per cent of owner-occupiers. Not surprisingly many more tenants than owner-occupiers told us in the interviews that they felt 'worse off' in 1987 compared with 1986. Locality One also tends to have a younger population, judging by our sample, than Localities Two and Four. These variations will be explored later in discussing the very high incidence of respiratory symptoms in our research area. There is also variation between our localities in terms of the extent to which respondents were 'insiders' or 'locals' as distinct from 'outsiders' or 'incomers'. In Table 2.2 this is suggested by the percentages who had been to local schools. This variation is one which suggests different probabilities of these localities being 'occupational communities', where not only is one industry very salient, but also there are locally strong traditional social networks with shared values. Locality Two is different from the others in having a high percentage of 'locals' among both men and women, but the variation does not reach statistical significance. Generally it is the case that Localities Two, Three and Four have the characteristics of working-class communities, based historically in the coal mining industry (see Warwick and Littlejohn, forthcoming). Locality One tends to differ markedly from the others.

In sum, though there are variations between the more affluent locality (One) and the three others, where the salience of the coal mining industry used to be much greater, we observe socio-economic conditions which are poor. The decline of the mining industry is likely to make things worse, unless access to new labour markets for both men and women is provided. The very significant differences to be observed between tenants and home-owners in general are also indicative of the general problem of uneven distribution of resources and paid employment. It is perhaps too gross a generalization to suggest that the dichotomy between tenants and owner-occupiers corresponds to the distinction which has been noted in contemporary societies between an 'underclass' and those involved fully in the class system (Gallie, 1988) but something of the meaning of the term 'underclass' — experiencing high rates of un-employment, very low incomes and dependency of various kinds — seems to attach itself to what we see as the social conditions of the tenants in our samples. There is also evidence that tenants are likely to sense their worse condition, but the dichotomy between tenants and owner-occupiers is not perhaps clear enough to validate the 'underclass' notion completely. We wish, however, to take the analysis further, for the social divisions already noted also relate to health conditions which we have observed in the four localities.

Social Conditions and Aspects of Health

As if to pile insult on injury, studies of the health of mining areas show them to be subject to illness and ill-health with much higher prevalence than is the case regionally

17

or nationally. In the Pontefract Health District, which includes our research area, and drawing on data from the Yorkshire Regional Health Authority for the years 1984–86, the standardized mortality ratio was 197 for men and 167 for women, and for heart disease 115 for men and 130 for women (UK = 100). Taking deaths from chronic bronchitis and emphysema alone, the ratios in the Wakefield and Pontefract Health Districts are twice the average for the Yorkshire Region. For these two diseases, the standardized mortality ratio is 54 in Harrogate, 103 in Leeds East, and 210 in Pontefract. Contrary to the situation in Harrogate and Leeds East, the rates are higher for men than for women in the Pontefract District.

Earlier evidence drawn from a large study undertaken in the 1960s in South Wales showed that 'chronic bronchitis is two or three times more common among coal miners than among non-miners living in the same district' (Lowe, 1969). There is some debate about how far this is a consequence of environmental, occupational and personal activities and conditions, and in what relative proportions. In our 1987 survey, in partnership with the Chest Consultant at Pontefract General Infirmary, we collected data within households on respondents' experience of respiratory symptoms, using Medical Research Council validated questions. We asked both respondents and their partners about the incidence of coughing, phlegm, breathlessness and wheezing, and then about smoking, industrial experience and forms of heating used in the household. Two symptoms are crucial indicators of potentially chronic chest diseases. These are coughing frequently on most days for as much as three months in the year, an indicator which we have labelled COF3M, and shortage of breath experienced when undertaking various forms of activity, which we have labelled SBREATH.[2] (Table 2.3 shows the reported incidence of these symptoms in the four localities.)

Table 2.3 COF3M and SBREATH by locality and sex, 1987

Percentages		Localities				
		Loc. 1	Loc. 2	Loc. 3	Loc. 4	All locs
With COF3M	Men	6	31	14	15	16
	Women	12	11	10	3	9
	All	9	20	12	9	12
With SBREATH	Men	6	18	18	12	13
	Women	17	38	36	21	27
	All	11	28	25	16	20

The immediately obvious fact is that rates tend to be higher in the localities which have a higher proportion of mining households. There are also differences between the men and the women, so that with the exception of Locality One, men have much higher experience of COF3M and women of SBREATH. Overall the prevalence ratios are reversed. Men are about twice as likely to experience COF3M and women about twice as likely to experience SBREATH. (These points are illustrated in Figures 2.1 and 2.2.)

Figure 2.1 COF3M by locality: men and women

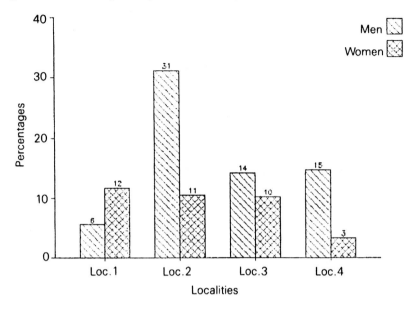

Figure 2.2 SBREATH by locality: men and women

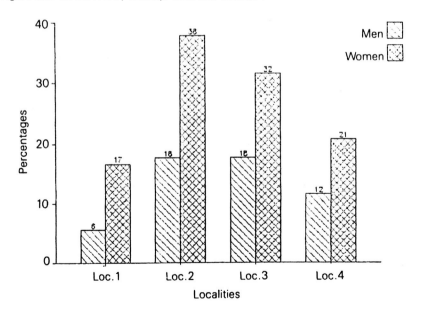

As we have noted above, there are debates about how far the extent of respiratoty disease is a consequence of environmental, occupational and personal activities and conditions. We will therefore attempt to examine these different possibilities as systematically as our data will allow. The smallness of our sample means that we are examining the reported incidence of thirty-four cases of COF3M among two hundred and seventy-one men and women for whom we have complete data, and fifty-five cases of SBREATH among two hundred and seventy men and women. When these are divided for analysis into more than three or four categories, the percentage variations begin to lose reliability, and when we wish to examine the interrelationship between a number of independent variables, again we quickly run into similar problems. Our analysis for this reason has to be seen as preliminary rather than exhaustive. The main value, however, is to be able to bring to bear a wider variety of variables than has been possible in previous researches.

We would assume that the environmental, occupational and personal can not in any real sense be separated from each other as factors in explaining the cause of respiratory symptoms. Sociological analysis has always pointed to the importance of recognizing the interaction of factors in a social context of institutions and processes. Our variables are no more than indicators of the complex which makes up that social context. We have already noted that in drawing samples of respondents from four different localities, we have found variations in the prevalence of the respiratory symptoms. There is therefore a likelihood that while the whole of our research area has high levels of respiratory disease there are crucial variations of activities and conditions within the area which should be explored. Already in summarizing the socio-economic conditions, we have pointed to crucial variations between mining and non-mining households, tenants and owner-occupiers, and household income groups. We know too that variations occur according to sex and age group. Different forms of household heating, particularly the difference between use of open fires and other means, could also be significant, since they would be likely to create smoke within the household. Tobacco smoking is known to be related to respiratory symptoms. Increasing concern about air pollution and respiratory symptoms leads us to see whether there were variations, such as smokeless zones, which could explain the locality variations.

Smoke and Air Pollution

Through communication with the Health, Environment and Recreation Department of Wakefield Metropolitan District Council we have been given access to their data concerning smoke control areas and the monitoring of smoke and sulphur dioxide in the atmosphere. Though there is a programme for extending smoke control throughout the District, which may indeed be accelerated in the near future, only one locality

(Three) is in a smoke control area. As can be seen from Figures 2.1 and 2.2. above, it does not have the lowest incidence of respiratory symptoms. Locality One contains one of the monitoring sites, which has registered above average levels of smoke and sulphur dioxide in the atmosphere, and yet for men it has significantly lower respiratory symptoms and those for women are not significantly different. In discussion with the Principal Environmental Health Officer, it was however admitted that a much more detailed study would be required before coming to any conclusion on any links between atmosphere pollution and respiratory diseases. The areas where smoke control has not yet been established do experience rather high levels of pollution particularly on peak days, and this is likely to be related to the incidence of symptoms.

Age

Our samples of respondents were drawn from adults of what for this area is euphemistically called working age, that is between school leaving age and 65 years. Most were over 21 years, but two localities had an older age structure (Two and Four) than the others. (Table 2.4 shows the distribution of over 40s.)

Table 2.4 Older age groups by locality and sex, 1987

	Locality				
Percentage of	Loc. 1	Loc. 2	Loc. 3	Loc. 4	All
Men					
Aged 41–50	24	24	23	39	27
Over 50 yrs	21	21	20	23	24
Women					
Aged 41–50	27	43	18	47	34
Over 50 yrs	17	17	18	9	15

The apparent discrepancy between the age structure of men and women in Locality Two is removed when it is known that the proportion of men there between 35 and 40 is almost twice that in the other three localities. The relationship between age and the two respiratory symptoms varies somewhat for men and women. (The position over the whole sample is as shown in Table 2.5.)

For the symptom COF3M the differences by age group are statistically significant for both men and women, though the relation with age is different. For men the incidence of the symptom appears greatest for those in their forties, after which it falls. For women there is a linear relationship, the incidence increasing directly with age. Exactly the same pattern occurs for the other symptom. This time only the differences

Table 2.5 Respiratory symptoms by age and sex

	Age		
Percentages	Under 41	41–50 yrs	Over 50
With COF3M			
Men	10.00	33.33	12.00
Women	4.11	13.04	22.22
With SBREATH			
Men	2.82	27.27	24.00
Women	20.27	32.61	44.44

among men reach statistical significance beyond the 95 per cent confidence level. At least this difference between men and women suggests that for men the symptoms are related to industrial effects, given that many men are now taking early retirement at about 50 years of age, especially in the mining industry. Clearly as far as locality differences are concerned we would expect that those localities with an older age structure would experience a higher incidence of the symptoms, but as Figures 2.1 and 2.2. show, this is not borne out entirely. Locality Two has the highest occurrence of the symptoms generally, and has an older age structure, but in Locality Four which also has a more elderly population, the incidence of symptoms is generally much lower. Thus other factors have to be explored, and the relationship to occupation has been shown to be significant in other studies.

Involvement in the Mining Industry

In these localities the distinction between involvement in the mining industry and others is the only one which allows any meaningful categorization, for our sampling has not yielded any other large grouping involved in another occupation. We would expect that the effects of being in the mining industry would vary according to the specification of the job, for example surface or underground, and to location in one seam rather than another, as Lowe showed (1969). Unfortunately again our samples are too small to measure such effects, and we crudely divide our sample into those with experience of mining and those without. Since we collected data by households it is also useful to show whether there are gender differences in and between mining and non-mining households. (Table 2.6 summarizes the differences and Figure 2.3 displays the information graphically.)

We are faced with an anomaly: while for both symptoms overall respondents in mining households show a higher incidence, women in mining households have a much lower experience of COF3M. The men in mining households have a higher occurrence of both symptoms, but the difference is only significant for COF3M. This suggests that industrial experience, especially for men in coal mining, is related to the prevalence of the respiratory symptoms.

Table 2.6 Respiratory symptoms in mining and non-mining households

Percentages	EMH	NMH
With COF3M		
Men	24.53	10.67
Women	6.00	11.63
All	15.53	11.18
With SBREATH		
Men	18.18	9.33
Women	29.41	26.74
All	23.58	18.63

Note: EMH = ever mining household;
NMH = never mining household.

Figure 2.3 COF3M and SBREATH by households: mining and non-mining

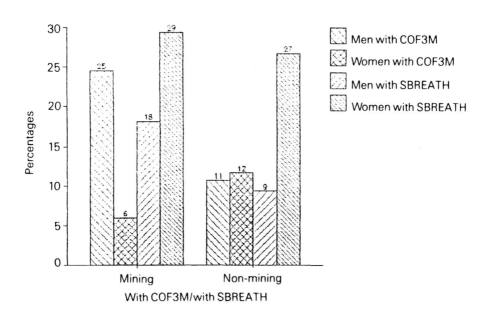

Use of Open Fires

It was thought that open fires, more common in mining households than non-mining households, might also be related to the respiratory symptoms, but certainly in the case of COF3M this looks to be unlikely given its lower incidence among women in mining households. Mining households have usually had concessionary coal for home heating, though financial allowances have also been available in some cases instead of coal. Mining households registered more open fires than non-mining households in our sample, though the differences of 47 per cent to 37 per cent are not statistically significant. There was little difference between localities, with the exception of the more affluent one, Locality One, where 32 per cent of the sample households had open fires, compared with 44 per cent in each of the others. (Table 2.7 shows the relation between the use of open fires and the occurrence of the respiratory symptoms among men and women.)

Table 2.7 Respiratory symptoms and the use of open fires .

Percentages	Yes	No
With COF3M		
Men	25.00	11.39
Women	5.66	11.63
All	14.85	11.52
With SBREATH		
Men	16.67	11.39
Women	19.23	33.33
All	18.00	22.70

The difference between men in households with and without open fires in the incidence of COF3M are significant, but other differences are not statistically significant. It is very clear, however, that the experience of men and women is quite contradictory, as far as the use of open fires is concerned, and therefore we can rule out the open fire as being an invariable indicator of potential respiratory disease.

House Tenure and the Incidence of Respiratory Symptoms

In a summary of research into respiratory diseases (Townsend *et al.*, Eds, 1988) it is noted that age, and an unhealthy working environment, as well as open fires may be significant factors. It is further suggested that housing differences are associated with variations in their prevalence. We have already noted how this distinction seems to indicate important differences in socio-economic conditions in our localities. (Table 2.8 and Figure 2.4 reveal this with regard to the two respiratory symptoms.)

The differences between tenants and owner-occupiers are in each case in the same direction and generally significant statistically or close to being so at the 95 per cent level. This seems to indicate that generally disadvantaged living conditions, in terms of high rates of unemployment and low incomes, relate strongly to the occurrence of these respiratory symptoms. It is not household income alone, however, which is the

Table 2.8 Respiratory symptoms by house tenure and sex

Percentages	Tenants	Owner-occupiers
With COF3M		
Men	29.03	12.12
Women	15.38	6.86
All	21.43	9.45
With SBREATH		
Men	20.00	11.00
Women	41.03	22.22
All	31.88	16.58

Figure 2.4 COF3M and SBREATH by tenure: all respondents

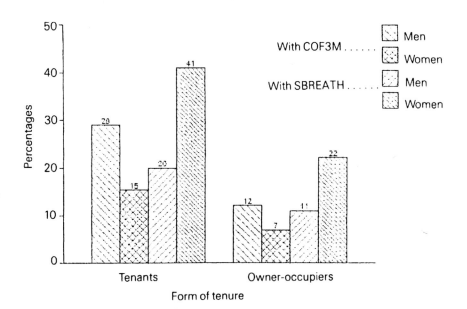

causal factor, since the relation between income and the respiratory symptoms is not linear, that is there is no clear inverse relation between the symptoms and level of income. (Table 2.9 shows this.) As Figure 2.5 shows, for all respondents, irrespective of sex, there is a curvilinear relation between income group and the respiratory symptoms, with the poorest having the highest incidence, while middle income groups have less, but with a rise again in the highest income category. This, however, hides the variation between men and women. The same U-curve occurs for both

Table 2.9 Respiratory symptoms and monthly household income

Percentages	Up to £400	£401–850	£851–1300	Over £1300	All
With COF3M					
Men	25.93	15.56	9.09	18.75	16.53
Women	9.68	14.00	6.06	.00	9.16
All	17.24	14.74	7.58	9.09	12.70
With SBREATH					
Men	18.52	12.50	6.06	18.75	12.90
Women	35.48	26.00	27.27	17.65	27.48
All	27.59	19.39	16.67	18.18	20.39

Figure 2.5 COF3M and SBREATH by monthly income

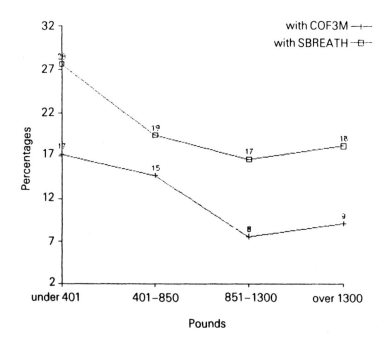

symptoms in men, whereas for women the relation between income and the symptom varies according to the symptom. None of the associations is statistically significant, however.

So far, then, amongst the variables we have considered, for men the highest incidence of both COF3M and SBREATH is among those in their forties. Being a tenant of a house is the next. Among women the symptoms are also associated most with age, but this time with those over 50 years old, and secondly, with being in a tenant household. Living in Locality Two and having low income are also indicative of high rates of incidence.

Tobacco Smoking and the Respiratory Symptoms

Previous research has also shown that tobacco smoking is strongly related to respiratory symptoms, and in Lowe's paper (1969) it is argued that smoking is more significant than industrial working conditions. In the 1987 survey we asked respondents whether they were regular smokers up to at least a month ago, and whether they had ever smoked. From their responses we have created an index of smoking by dividing the sample into smokers, ex-smokers and non-smokers. Tables 2.10 to 2.13 indicate the relation between smoking and the other factors which we have found strongly linked to the respiratory symptoms. Differences between localities do not reach the 95 per cent level of statistical significance, but the variations between them are clear for both men and women. Generally, rates of smoking are higher than in England and Wales. Comparison with Table 2.3 shows that the relation between high levels of smoking and of respiratory symptoms by localities is not consistent. Among men there are significant age related differences in smoking, and the age group with the highest level of respiratory symptoms is also the highest for smoking. The differences between age

Table 2.10 Smoking by localities

Percentages	Loc. 1	Loc. 2	Loc. 3	Loc. 4	All locs	Eng. & Wales[1]
Men						
Smokers	38.89	58.06	42.86	62.96	49.61	36
Ex-smokers	27.78	12.90	22.86	22.22	21.71	30
Non-smokers	33.33	29.03	34.29	14.81	28.68	34
Women						
Smokers	24.24	52.78	38.46	34.48	37.96	32
Ex-smokers	27.27	11.11	15.38	31.03	20.44	17
Non-smokers	48.48	36.11	46.15	34.48	41.61	51

Note 1. Taken from OPCS, 1986.

groups among women are not significant, but smoking does increase with age, which compares with the incidence of COF3M and SBREATH among women. Smoking rates are lower among women than among men, except in the over fifties category (see Table 2.5). The differences in smoking between mining and non-mining households both for men and women are significant beyond the 99 per cent probability level. As

Table 2.11 Smoking by age and sex

Percentages	Age groups		
	Under 41	41–50 yrs	Over 50
Men			
Smokers	45.71	66.67	36.00
Ex-smokers	17.14	18.18	40.00
Non-smokers	37.14	15.15	24.00
Women			
Smokers	32.88	43.48	44.44
Ex-smokers	19.18	23.91	16.67
Non-smokers	47.95	32.61	38.89

Table 2.12 Smoking and mining/non-mining households

Percentages	Mining h'hld	Non-mining h'hld
Men		
Smokers	64.15	39.47
Ex-smokers	24.53	19.74
Non-smokers	11.32	40.79
Women		
Smokers	60.00	25.58
Ex-smokers	16.00	22.09
Non-smokers	24.00	52.33

Table 2.13 Smoking by household tenure

Percentages	Tenants	Owner-occupiers
Men		
Smokers	64.52	44.90
Ex-smokers	16.13	23.47
Non-smokers	19.35	31.63
Women		
Smokers	44.74	35.35
Ex-smokers	21.05	20.20
Non-smokers	34.21	44.44

we have noted there are differences between the occurrence of respiratory symptoms, but they are not in the same direction entirely, nor as significant (see Table 2.6). The differences in Table 2.13 are clear, with tenants smoking more than owner-occupiers, but the differences are not statistically significant at the 95 per cent level. The evidence does not entirely suggest that tobacco smoking is necessarily the strongest correlate of respiratory symptoms. (In Table 2.14 and Figure 2.6, we show our findings that among ex-smokers the occurrence of symptoms is lowest.)

Table 2.14 Smoking and respiratory symptoms

Percentages	with COF3M	SBREATH
Men		
Smokers	28.57	21.88
Ex-smokers	3.57	7.14
Non-smokers	5.41	2.86
Women		
Smokers	13.46	34.62
Ex-smokers	3.57	22.22
Non-smokers	8.77	25.00
All		
Smokers	21.74	27.59
Ex-smokers	3.57	14.55
Non-smokers	7.45	16.48

Figure 2.6 COF3M and SBREATH by smoking

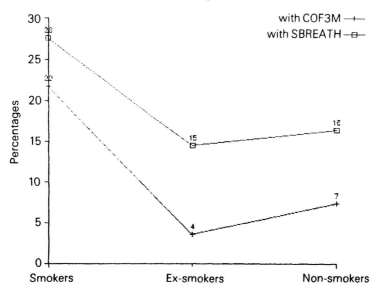

The relationship between smoking and the respiratory symptoms for all respondents irrespective of sex is shown in Table 2.14 and Figure 2.6, as a curvilinear distribution. The finding that the prevalence of COF3M and SBREATH is least among ex-smokers may indicate that as far as these symptoms are concerned their reduction may be associated with giving up smoking. Giving up smoking requires motivation and determination, and these are aspects of personality as well as of culture and society, about which we have no data. It is interesting to speculate that they too may have some relation to the incidence of respiratory symptoms. The differences between men and women, however, are noteworthy. We have already seen that COF3M rates are higher among men than women, and vice versa for SBREATH. What is interesting when we control for smoking, is that among men there are distinct differences in the incidence of the symptoms which are statistically significant beyond the 98 per cent confidence level. This is not true for women and they are likely to have the symptoms irrespective of smoking.

Thus, though smoking is a crucial variable among men, it does not explain it all. Smoking is a part of the culture of our society about which there is much current debate, but as with the other variables which we have considered, it is part of a way of life and not separable from these others when we are attempting to explain the incidence of aspects of health, such as the respiratory symptoms. The prevalence of respiratory symptoms is related to the culture of our localities and not simply to one or two predisposing conditions.

In addition, what we concluded earlier about the significance of age, being a tenant, having low income and living in Locality Two is not negated when we control for smoking.

Table 2.15 Respiratory symptoms by income group and smoking

Percentages	Monthly household income groups (pounds)				
	Under 401	401–850	851–1300	Over 1300	All
With COF3M					
Smokers	26.92	23.64	9.09	27.27	20.80
Ex-smokers	.00	.00	9.52	.00	3.64
Non-smokers	13.04	6.25	3.85	.00	6.19
With SBREATH					
Smokers	40.91	25.49	23.08	18.18	27.27
Ex-smokers	7.69	33.33	10.53	12.50	15.38
Non-smokers	26.09	6.90	14.29	21.43	16.09

We have indicated above that with the relative smallness of our samples, as soon as we begin to expand the number of categories and cells in an attempt to produce a more complex analysis, it is difficult to estimate the significance of the differences observed, since there are a number of empty cells and others with less than five respondents in them. The distribution in Table 2.15 for COF3M, however, comes close to being significant at the 95 per cent probability level. The differences for SBREATH are not significant. In general we can conclude that when we control for smoking, there is still an association between income levels and respiratory symptoms, which suggests that they are more likely to occur in poorer households. Nevertheless, there is also an increase in the symptoms in the highest income group, which we noted in Table 2.9, though this is generally not to levels above the rate for all respondents, except in the case of smokers with COF3M. Affluent smokers display a prevalence of COF3M which is over twice the rate for all respondents and as high as that of the smokers in the poorest income group.

When we control for smoking in relation to age and sex, the combined effects of smoking and age on men are further clarified, though there is some unreliability based on small numbers in some of the cells (Table 2.16). The highest occurrence of both respiratory symptoms among males is found among smokers in their forties, with rates three times the average for men. Similarly among women the highest incidence of both symptoms tends to be among the over-forties group, with rates approaching twice the average for women. The differences between smokers, ex-smokers and non-smokers appear not to be as great among women as among men. Nevertheless, the combined effects of smoking and ageing seem to be very important for men and women, in predicting the likelihood of respiratory symptoms. However, we have to explore the social conditions of those with the symptoms and house tenure suggests itself as perhaps the most crucial, as Table 2.17 shows.

We have already seen that the prevalence of both COF3M and SBREATH among tenants, both men and women, is about twice the average rate for men and women, and significantly higher than among owner-occupiers. When we control for

Table 2.16 Respiratory symptoms by sex, age and smoking

	Men			Women		
Percentages	Under 41	41–50 yrs	Over 50	Under 41	41–50 yrs	Over 50
With COF3M						
Smokers	15.63	50.00	22.22	8.33	20.00	12.50
Ex-smokers	8.33	(.00)	.00	.00	.00	(33.33)
Non-smokers	3.85	(.00)	(16.67)	2.86	13.33	(28.57)
With SBREATH						
Smokers	6.25	40.91	33.33	25.00	40.00	50.00
Ex-smokers	.00	(.00)	20.00	7.69	36.36	(33.33)
Non-smokers	.00	(.00)	(20.00)	22.86	21.43	(42.86)

Note: Percentages in brackets are based on cells containing less than eight respondents.

31

Table 2.17 Respiratory symptoms by smoking, tenure and sex

	Men		Women	
Percentages	Tenants	Owner-occupiers	Tenants	Owner-occupiers
With COF3M				
Smokers	42.11	22.73	29.41	5.71
Ex-smokers	(.00)	4.35	.00	5.00
Non-smokers	(16.67)	3.23	7.69	9.09
With SBREATH				
Smokers	25.00	20.45	52.94	25.71
Ex-smokers	(20.00)	4.35	37.50	15.79
Non-smokers	(.00)	3.23	30.77	23.26

Note: Percentages in brackets are based on cells containing less than eight respondents.

smoking, certain divergences from that situation are shown (Table 2.17). Among men, though smoking is the crucial determinant of high rates of incidence for both symptoms, clearly also tenants have higher rates than owner-occupiers. Among male ex-smokers and non-smokers there are too few tenants to give any reliable indication of difference, but what there is suggests that male tenants do still have a higher likelihood of displaying the respiratory symptoms. Among women, as we have seen before, smoking is not as crucial a discriminator as it is among men. Generally, though not entirely in the case of COF3M, female tenants experience higher rates of the symptoms than owner-occupiers. Where this is the case, the rates are either above or well above the general rate for women.

Table 2.18 Respiratory symptoms by smoking, mining/non-mining households and sex

	Men		Women	
Percentages	EMH	NMH	EMH	NMH
With COF3M				
Smokers	35.29	20.69	6.67	22.73
Ex-smokers	7.69	.00	.00	5.26
Non-smokers	.00	6.45	8.33	8.89
With SBREATH				
Smokers	23.53	20.69	33.33	34.78
Ex-smokers	15.38	.00	37.50	16.67
Non-smokers	.00	3.45	18.18	26.67

Note: EMH = ever mining household;
NMH = never mining household.

Returning finally to the question of smoking and industrial involvement, we can show clearly (Table 2.18) that the likelihood of men with experience of the coal mining industry having respiratory symptoms is greater than that of other men.

Among smokers, men from the mining industry are nearly twice as likely as other men to have COF3M, and they are also likely to have higher rates of SBREATH. Thus our data would seem at least to question Lowe's conclusion (1969) that smoking is more significant than industrial experience in explaining respiratory disease, though clearly he had the advantage of much larger samples of male respondents. The differences between men and women are also very noticeable, and this seems to reinforce the view that the industrial experience of men in mining is a more crucial indicator of respiratory symptoms than smoking, notwithstanding that the combined effect of that experience and smoking also discriminates among the males in mining households. As we have shown, however, neither smoking nor involvement in the mining industry are the whole story if we are to understand why there should be such high rates of respiratory disease in the localities we have studied.

Conclusion

Our starting point is this paper has been the question of high mortality rates related to respiratory diseases in the Health District which includes the four mining localities in our research area. Those localities vary in terms of relative affluence, age structure, house tenure, employment opportunities for men and women and, particularly, in the numbers of men employed in the mining industry. Locality One is slightly better than the average income for England and Wales, but the other localities are below the national average. Locality Two is the poorest, and is also the locality with the highest proportion of mining households, an older age structure, highest levels of male unemployment and largest proportion of tenant householders. We have assumed that consonant with other studies of aspects of health, there is a strong relation between relative affluence and good health (Townsend *et al.*, 1988) and that a major contributory factor to the high rates of respiratory infection is the socio-economic and cultural condition of the mining localities.

We have examined the incidence of symptoms of respiratory disease through interviews in about 200 households. This paper reports on findings from over 170 households for which we have complete data, which includes a number of socio-economic and cultural variables. From earlier research on chronic bronchitis among coal miners, it was asserted that tobacco smoking was more crucial than the experience of the industry in explaining the incidence of the disease (Lowe, 1969) and we have collected information on smoking. We have also noted current concern with smoke and sulphur dioxide pollution in the atmosphere, and examined data provided for us by the Environmental Health Office of the local authority.

We have given indications of the relation between all these conditions and two symptoms of chronic respiratory disease, coughing frequently for at least three months in the year (COF3M) and shortage of breath experienced when being active (SBREATH). Over 12 (12.55) per cent of all our respondents displayed COF3M and 20.37 per cent, SBREATH. The latter is a rather less stringent indicator of likely respiratory disorder, since there were not enough cases of more serious breathlessness to use in the analysis. The incidence of COF3M was greater among men (16.53 per cent) than among women (9.16 per cent), whereas SBREATH occurred more in women (27.5 per cent) than among men (12.9 per cent). Both COF3M and SBREATH are recognized by the Medical Research Council as being crucial indicators of respiratory disease, and the distribution of COF3M conforms with the variation which is noted in Yorkshire Regional Health Statistics, that is, the higher incidence of respiratory disease among men than among women.

In terms of the possible explanations for the high rates of respiratory disease in the research area, we have no clear indication of the strength of the effect of air pollution. High rates of pollution occur on peak days in the area, and measures to increase smoke control are not yet complete, so that we must assume some relation exists, but await the results of further research to make any valid statements about that. It is clear that involvement in the mining industry is a related factor, with 24.53 per cent of men in mining households experiencing COF3M compared with 10.67 per cent of other men. When we control for tobacco smoking, it is clear that the incidence of COF3M is higher among smokers than ex-smokers or non-smokers, but the significant difference between men in mining households and other men remains (35.29 per cent among miners who smoke regularly compared with 20.69 per cent among other male smokers). The crucial significance of involvement in the mining industry is further evidenced when we note that COF3M among women smokers is lower among those in mining households (6.67 per cent) than those in non-mining households (22.73 per cent).

The differences between men and women are quite large generally, but we have not been able to assess the effect of different kinds of industrial experience (as for instance in textiles or garment making) on women, since there are no large groups of women with particular kinds of experience within the sample to make valid comparisons possible. Respiratory symptoms do generally increase in incidence for men and women with age, and it is clear that house tenure, which summarizes the effect of a number of social and cultural variables, affects men and women similarly. Tenants experience virtually twice the rates of both COF3M and SBREATH observable in the four localities. This may not confirm evidence of 'polarization' or the formation of an 'underclass', but it certainly seems to be further confirmation of the significance of what Rex and Moore (1969) termed 'housing class', in the determination of lifestyle and position in the social structure.

Finally, we note the significance of living in particular localities. Those in which the mining industry has played a salient role as far as the labour market and the local economy is concerned have been centres of particular kinds of social disadvantage. Locality Two seems to be particularly 'cross'd with adversity', and is the locality which experiences the highest rates of respiratory symptoms. The locality is, among the four that we researched, the one that most nearly fits the character of a traditional mining community. The economic, social and cultural aspects of its environment predispose its inhabitants towards the highest rates of respiratory disease. The collapse of the mining industry in the area will, however, be a doubtful blessing, for although it may remove some of the causes of ill health, without the reconstruction of the local economy, it will merely allow other predisposing agents to assume greater significance.

Further research will be necessary to assess the real significance of these findings, since our samples have been rather small. More data is being collected by using objective tests of respiratory function from respondents who have indicated their willingness to take part, and this will help to provide a further basis of a more stringent kind for estimating the context for respiratory diseases. It would be useful to have more detailed information on air pollution, since clearly there is more to be discovered about the relation of that to the other predisposing factors of these diseases. Nevertheless, there are pointers here to the fact that public policies with the aim of raising the levels of life-expectation and standards of living would be a sign not only of caring, but also of social justice.

Notes

1. The research on which this chapter is based was supported by grant G1325005 from the Economic and Social Research Council and from the Pontefract General Infirmary Chest Unit Research Fund.
2. The indicators COF3M and SBREATH were constructed out of answers to questions which progressively indicated more serious respiratory conditions. COF3M is based in the answers to the final question in the series on coughing. It is a crucial part of the Medical Research Council definition of chronic bronchitis. SBREATH is based on the answers to the first in the series of four questions on breathlessness. Only a small number of respondents gave affirmative answers to the later questions.

Table 2.19 Frequency of responses to SBREATH questions by sex

	Frequency	Percentage	Percentage Males	Percentage Females
SBREATH 1	68	21.18	12.90	27.50
SBREATH 2	20	6.23	5.38	7.97
SBREATH 3	10	3.11	3.08	3.52
SBREATH 4	9	2.80	2.79	2.81
Total Respondents = 321				

As shown in Table 2.19, the disparity between male and female experience of shortage of breath disappears as the seriousness of the symptom increases. This is unlike the coughing symptom where the disparity increases slightly with the seriousness of the symptom, and where the incidence among men is always higher than that among women. Our use of SBREATH1 in the analysis provides an indicator which is certainly not as stringent as COF3M but is generally indicative of a somewhat different aspect of respiratory problems. Nevertheless, as with COF3M, SBREATH, at any level, seems to be more common among the relatively disadvantaged respondents, and the general findings for SBREATH1 are indicative of those for the other more stringent levels, as far as we can judge. For example SBREATH2 is experienced by 14.49 per cent of tenants compared with 4.02 per cent of owner-occupiers.

Chapter 3

Opening the 'Black Box': Inequalities in Women's Health

Sara Arber

The Black Report on Inequalities in Health (DHSS, 1980) is ten years old, but inequalities in women's health remains largely uncharted territory. This chapter argues, first, that existing work has been constrained by the mould of male-dominated class analyses. Inequalities in women's health may be better understood outside the straitjacket of class by using indicators which more sensitively measure women's structural position. Second, the dominance of structural/materialist explanations of inequalities in women's health has blinded researchers to the ways in which women's roles intersect and amplify structural inequalities. A fuller understanding of women's health requires analysis of women's marital, parental and employment roles within a structural context. Third, there has been a failure to distinguish inequalities in health *status* (long-term health or chronic illness) from inequalities in health *state* (short-term or acute illness).

After reviewing studies on inequalities in women's health published since the Black Report, the *Health Divide* concluded:

all in all, these studies raise more questions than answers and the whole field is ripe for further research (p. 245).

... research is only just beginning to unravel the complexities of inequality in health for women (Townsend, Davidson and Whitehead, 1988, p. 255)

This chapter seeks to unravel some of this complexity by addressing six conceptual issues which have been neglected in analyses of women's health. A consideration of these issues helps both in understanding women's health, and in shedding light on more general explanations of inequalities in health. Building on these conceptual distinctions, models are formulated to explain the pattern of inequalities in women's health. Data from the 1985 and 1986 General Household Survey are used to illustrate components of these models.

Individual-based versus Household-based Measures of Class

A distinction which is often not explicitly recognized in studies of women's health is that class measures relate to two conceptually distinct explanations of inequalities in health. First, the material circumstances of the individual's household influence an individual's health, and second, the nature of the individual's paid employment may have a direct influence on health. For men, these two aspects of material position work in concert to increase inequalities in health, since a man's occupation is assumed both to be a primary determinant of his material circumstances, and to have a direct bearing on his health.

For a married woman there may be some direct effect of her own paid employment on her health, but the major effect of material conditions is likely to be better captured by a household-based measure. A man's occupational class can be used as a surrogate for *both* the material conditions extant in the household (a household-level variable) *and* the direct effects of the nature of paid employment on his health (an individual-level variable). For women, it is necessary to theorize and measure the effects of a woman's material circumstances (household variables) *separately* from any effects of her own employment status and the nature of her own occupation (individual-level variables).

However, the assumption that a man's occupational class measures both these types of material effects may have been appropriate in the 1950s, when few married women were in employment, but is less valid today. For the two-thirds of married men with working wives, it is likely that their wife's labour market position will influence the material circumstances of the household. A married man's health would be expected to be better if his wife is a teacher than if he is married to a cleaner.

Male-dominated Measures of Class

It is hardly new to argue that existing occupational class schema were devised from, and for use with, men's occupations (Arber, Dale and Gilbert, 1986; Abbott and Sapsford, 1987). Class schema provide better discrimination between men's than women's occupations, and criteria such as skill level may be less relevant for women's jobs (Coyle, 1982; Armstrong, 1982; Thompson, 1983). For example, a high proportion of women are employed in personal service work and as shop assistants, but in the Registrar General's social classes the former are grouped with semi-skilled manual work — Class IV — and the latter with clerical and secretarial work as 'Routine non-manual' work — Class IIIN (OPCS, 1980). These two occupations have been shown to be relatively interchangeable in terms of job mobility between them (Gilbert, 1986), but in the Registrar General's classes they are on either side of the conventional manual/non-manual divide.

If the meaning of working in particular occupational classes differs for men and women, one would not expect the same pattern of relationships between health and occupational class for both sexes. The gender segregated nature of occupations means that, for example, women employed in male-dominated occupations, such as working as 'employers or managers', may be in a more contradictory and stressful work situation, than men in comparable occupations. Women in semi-professional occupations may experience their work in a different way, and be accorded different status, from men working in female-dominated jobs such as nursing and teaching. There is no necessary reason to expect a similar relationship for men and women between occupational class and health. The fact that a weaker relationship or a different relationship has been found for women than for men, should not be seen as an aberration. For example, Moser and Goldblatt (1985) found that the 'skill' distinctions between manual occupations embodied in the RG social classes do not discriminate between women's mortality in the same way as for men, and that 'the main anomaly is the low relative mortality of women in Social Class V' (p. 24). Such an interpretation reflects the male-bias in class schema and analyses. Analyses which present smaller class differences for women are in danger of interpreting this as evidence of less health inequality among women than men, rather than the occupational inadequacy of the tools being used to measure women's class and material position.

Relationships between class and health for women should be considered in their own right rather than always held up to and compared with the male standard. Occupational class analyses should use classifications which more adequately reflect meaningful distinctions between women's occupation. However, if the primary concern is to understand how material circumstances influence women's health it may be more appropriate to leave the strait-jacket of class, and more directly measure women's material circumstances.

Measuring Material Circumstances

The method of measuring a woman's material circumstances needs to open the 'black box' of the family. Can a woman's material circumstances be captured by her husband's occupation? This practice is still used in analyses of health published in the General Household Survey annual reports (OPCS, 1988a). It is supported by Goldthorpe (1983, 1984), but strongly criticized by Stanworth (1984), Allen (1982) and others.

Within an occupational class framework for measuring women's material circumstances, analysts can consider four alternatives:

1   Using a woman's own current (or last) occupation to measure her class (irrespective of her marital status and position in the labour market). This has been characterized as an *'individualistic approach'* (Arber, 1989).

2   Using husband's class for married women, and for other women class based on their own current or last occupation. This approach has been characterized as the *'conventional view'* (Goldthorpe, 1983).

3   Measuring class based on the occupation of the 'occupational dominant' member of the household, as suggested by Erickson (1984) — the *'dominance approach'*.

4   Using some kind of combined measure of class, such as those proposed by Britten and Heath (1983), and Roberts and Barker (1986) — a *'combined class approach'*.

These occupation-based solutions all have difficulties incorporating non-employment. How valid is it simply to use last occupation for those not currently in paid work? This solution is adopted in virtually all analyses of men's health, but may be inappropriate for women, who have not been in paid work for many years, and may be less appropriate for men when there is large-scale unemployment (Arber, 1987). It begs the question of whether occupational class measures should incorporate within them an indicator of labour force participation.

Occupational class, however measured, cannot be used as a universal measure for women living in various types of households. Therefore, there may be advantages in using other measures which are universal, simple to collect and easy to apply to *all* households irrespective of their composition or age structure. These criteria are fulfilled by consumption (or asset-based) measures, such as housing tenure and car ownership (Fox and Goldblatt, 1982; Townsend, Phillimore and Beattie, 1988). However, it is a moot point whether their advantages of simplicity and universality outweigh any disadvantages of their conceptual interpretation and the direction of causality.

An alternative measure of material circumstances is current income. This needs to be standardized to take into account differences in household structure, for example, by using measures such as Relative Net Resources (RNR), which assesses household income in relation to the current Supplementary Benefit levels for households of varying composition (Dale, 1987). However, few datasets contain sufficient information to derive RNR, and there is more often missing data on income questions than on most other potential indicators of material circumstances. A simple surrogate measure of household income is the extent of the household's reliance on state benefits, e.g. a proportionate measure varying from under 10 per cent of income derived from state benefits through to heavy reliance (over 50 per cent) and to total dependence (100 per cent).

Like occupational class measures, consumption and income measures may also be gender-biased. More men than women are car owners and drivers (Dale, 1986) and women may lack access to the 'family' car. Income-based measures usually assume equal sharing of income within families; an assumption which has been questioned in recent work (Pahl, 1989). Measures of household and family income may be poor predictors of women's health because they render women's poverty invisible (Glendinning and Millar, 1987).

Single versus Multiple Roles

Occupational class has dominated analyses of men's health, but role analysis has been the predominant framework used for analyzing women's health. With the development of large-scale unemployment a large literature has developed on unemployment and health; however, there have been few studies which have linked an occupational class analysis to unemployment. A previous article (Arber, 1987) showed that class differences and ill health were greater among the non-employed than among the employed. There has been even less concern for the ways in which men's marital and parental roles influence their health; the recent work of Popay and Jones (1988) on the influence of the fatherhood role on men's health is an exception.

Work on women's health has been dominated, particularly in American literature, by analyses of the marital role and mental health. Gove and his colleagues have demonstrated how marriage is detrimental to women's health (Gove, 1978; Gove and Hughes, 1979; Gove, 1984). Other researchers have analyzed the parental role as providing health benefits by counteracting the monotony and isolation of the housewife role (Nathanson, 1975). Paid employment has been considered as an additional role within this conceptual framework, some arguing that paid employment has beneficial health consequences because of role accumulation (Nathanson, 1980; Verbrugge, 1983) and others that paid employment, in addition to the parental and marital role, has detrimental health consequences because of role overload and role strain (Stellman, 1977). The problem with these 'role based' analyses is that they have failed to analyze the effects of roles within the structural context of women's lives. It is essential to consider *both* women's roles *and* the material circumstances within which those roles are enacted. The same roles of motherhood and lack of paid employment are likely to have very different health consequences for a woman in a high-rise flat (whose husband is unemployed), and a woman married to a professional living in a large house with her own car.

Thus, previous analyses of inequalities in men's health have been partial by excluding any consideration of men's marital and parental roles, and analyses of women's health need to integrate the insights from role analyses within a structural framework, which measures both a woman's own class position and her material circumstances.

Roles and Health Selection

The Black Report found little evidence that poor health selects people out of higher classes resulting in their 'drift' down the class structure (DHSS, 1980). Since 1980 there has been no new evidence to support *intra*-generational health selection down the class structure (Townsend, Davidson and Whitehead, 1988). Empirical studies have indicated that there may be some health selection *inter*-generationally. Wadsworth (1986) demonstrates that children in the 1946 birth cohort who suffered serious ill health during childhood are less likely to achieve educationally and occupationally, but this effect is relatively small and was found to a greater extent for boys than for girls. In the 1958 cohort study, those who had been upwardly mobile by age 23 were on the whole healthier than those who had been downwardly mobile (Fogelman, Fox and Power, 1989).

The lack of evidence that health selection is responsible for social class inequalities contrasts with debates on the association between unemployment and poor mental or physical health (Warr, 1985; Stern, 1983; Fox , Goldblatt, Jones, 1985). A substantial proportion of this association is assumed to be due to health selection — men with poor health are more likely to lose their jobs, and less likely to obtain another job once unemployed. It is therefore surprising that the literature on women's health and their paid employment has argued for the opposite direction of causality — focusing on the way in which employment improves women's health through 'role accumulation' (Nathanson, 1980; Verbrugge, 1983). For women it is paramount to consider seriously the direction of influence, since, as shown later, there are marked differences between the health of women in paid employment, 'housewives' and 'unemployed' women (Waldron, 1980; Warr and Parry, 1982). There has been a parallel lack of attention given to the direction of causality of the association between domestic roles (marital and parental status) and poor health (Verbrugge, 1979).

Health Status and Health State

A final problem in many analyses of inequalities in women's health has been a failure to distinguish adequately various measures of health, and to theorize how they relate to material circumstances and women's domestic and employment roles. The key distinction is between indicators of temporary health state — 'Am I ill today?' — which represent the present state of health of the individual, and indicators of longer term health status — 'Am I a basically healthy or unhealthy person?' — which provides a more general characteristic (Blaxter, 1985). Health *state* refers to current health and is similar to acute illness, whereas health *status* is a longer-term concept, measuring the person's 'stock' of health. This chapter will illustrate the importance of making this distinction by using two health measures in the General Household Survey.

The chapter suggests that health *status* has an important effect on whether women occupy different roles, and in turn women's roles have a major impact on their health *state*. However, these relationships can only be fully understood within a structural framework of women's material position.

Data Source and Measures

The research data in this chapter are drawn from the General Household Survey (GHS), providing a nationally representative sample of adults aged 20 to 59 living in private households. Data from 1985 and 1986 were combined to provide a larger sample for analysis. A response rate of 82 per cent and 84 per cent was obtained in these two years respectively (OPCS, 1988a, 1989). A measure of health status — limiting long-standing illness (LLI) — and a measure of health state — restricted activity due to illness in the previous 14 days — are used.

1. *Limiting long-standing illness (LLI)*. The General Household Survey asks 'Have you any long-standing illness, disability or infirmity?' If the answer is 'Yes', there is a follow-up question on whether it limits their activities in any way (OPCS, 1988a). This measure represents the consequence of health *status* for what the individual perceives as his or her 'normal' activities. It represents a self-assessment of the effect of any chronic ill health on daily life.

2. *Restricted activity*. The proportion of women who reported restricted activity days due to illness in the previous two weeks is a measure of health *state*, based on the individual's perception of whether symptoms have altered their 'normal' activities over this time period.

To understand inequalities in health among women it is essential to distinguish these two concepts of health and understand how they interrelate. Health status is strongly associated with age, but the association for health state is much weaker. Table 3.1 shows that a higher proportion of older women report both limiting and non-limiting long-standing illnesses. Only 9 per cent of women in their twenties compared with 27 per cent of women in their fifties report a limiting long-standing illness. The following analyses are restricted to *limiting* long-standing illness.

Since age is closely related to health status, it is essential to remove any effects of age when analyzing relationships between women's attributes and their health status. For example, previously married women are on average older than single women, therefore to compare the health of previously married and single women it is necessary to remove the effects of age. Analyses of mortality usually remove the effects of age by calculating Standardized Mortality Ratios (SMRs), which compare the mortality of

Table 3.1 Measures of ill health by age for women, age 20–59

	20–29	30–39	40–49	50–59	Total
Long-standing illness					
–limits activities	9	12	18	27	16
–non-limiting	10	11	14	17	13
–no long-standing illness	80	77	68	56	71
	100%	100%	100%	100%	100%
N =	(3707)	(3864)	(2919)	(2793)	(13283)
Restriction of activity due to illness					
–any in last 2 weeks	12.2%	12.9%	13.2%	16.0%	13.4%
–4 or more days in last 2 weeks	7.4%	8.1%	8.7%	12.3%	8.9%
N =	(3713)	(3872)	(2930)	(2799)	(13314)

Source: General Household Survey, 1985–86 (own analyses). Figure have been rounded.

different groups of women with a standard of 100, which represents the mortality of all women. In this chapter, the same procedure is used to analyze limiting long-standing illness. Differences in age structure between groups of women are removed using the indirect method of standardization to calculate Standardized Limiting Long-standing Illness (SLLI) Ratios, using ten-year age bands.

Health state is less associated with age: 12 per cent of women under 40 report illness which restricted their activity in the previous two weeks, which increased to 16 per cent of women over 50. When the proportion of women reporting more serious illness — restricted activity which lasted four or more days — is examined, the age trend becomes clearer, varying from 7 per cent for women in their twenties to over 12 per cent for women in their fifties. Since different factors influence health status and health state, the following discussion proposes separate models for understanding each measure of health.

Factors Influencing Women's Health Status

To help understand inequalities in women's health it is essential to have a clear model of the relationships between relevant variables. Figure 3.1 presents a simple model of the key factors associated with poor health status (limiting long-standing illness). In some cases the direction of influence is not clear, so double-headed arrows are used. An important research issue is to clarify the predominant direction of influence in different social contexts.

Figure 3.1 Key variables associated with health status

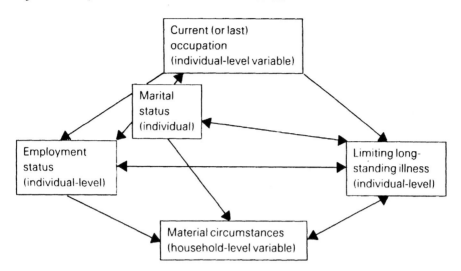

My concern is to provide a better understanding of various components of the model, which could serve as building blocks for inclusion in multivariate analyses (see Arber, under submission). This simple model excludes a consideration of lifestyle variables, such as smoking, drinking, or any cultural or attitudinal variables. It involves only two roles — marital status and employment status (parental status is excluded); and two structural variables — the individual's own occupation and the material circumstances of the individual's household. The association of each of these four variables with limiting long-standing illness (LLI) will be discussed in turn.

Own Occupational Class

Occupational class is associated with health status, both because of direct effects of occupation (an individual-level variable) and because an individual's occupational class is related to the material/structural circumstances of the household. For women the latter effect is expected to be weaker than for men. The influence of an individual's own occupational class should be treated as conceptually distinct from the influence of material circumstances of the household, but empirically this may not be possible.

For women classified by an 'individualistic approach' (using their own current or last occupation) there is a class gradient from 7 per cent of women in higher professional occupations to 23 per cent of unskilled manual women reporting a limiting long-standing illness (Table 3.2). The gradient is curved with poorer health status reported by women 'employers and managers' (14 per cent) than by women in other

Table 3.2 Percentage reporting limiting long-standing illness by socio-economic group – (a) women – own occupation, (b) women – conventional approach *, i.e. husband's occupation if married, (c) men – own occupation. (Ages 20–59)

| | Socio-economic group | | | | | | | |
| | Non-manual | | | | Manual | | | All |
	1	2	3a	3b	4	5	6	
(a) Women								
– Own occupation (current or last)	6.6%	14.3%	11.6%	13.8%	19.5%	18.7%	22.6%	15.7%
N =	(137)	(929)	(1785)	(4838)	(1050)	(3265)	(806)	(12810)
(b) Women								
– Conventional Approach *	9.6%	12.9%	12.1%	14.6%	17.0%	20.2%	26.8%	15.8%
N =	(803)	(2457)	(1135)	(1936)	(3992)	(1981)	(426)	(12730)
(c) Men								
– Own occupation	9.0%	11.2%	12.2%	12.9%	15.9%	18.8%	24.0%	14.6%
N =	(899)	(2476)	(912)	(1161)	(4713)	(1709)	(500)	(12370)

Socio-economic group
1   Higher Professional
2   Employers and Managers
3a Lower Professional
3b Supervisory and Junior Non-manual

4   Skilled Manual and Own Account
5   Semi-skilled Manual and Personal Service
6   Unskilled Manual

* Women with husbands are classified by their husband's occupation, women of other marital statuses are attributed their own (current or last) occupational class.

Source: General Household Survey, 1985–86 (own analyses)

non-manual occupations. The gradient for men is linear, varying from 9 per cent for higher professionals to 24 per cent for unskilled manual workers. However, because of differences in age structure between classes a clearer comparison can be gauged from the standardized ratios in Figure 3.2 and Table 3.3.

Figure 3.2 Standardized limiting long-standing illness ratios by socio-economic group: (a) women – own class; (b) women – conventional approach, (c) men – own class

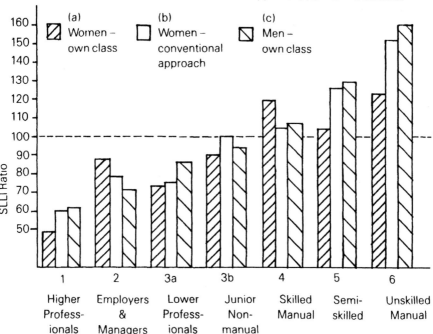

[*]All women
Source: General Household Survey (1985–86 (own analyses)

The class gradient is stronger for men than for women classified by their own occupation, and for men is linear but is curved for women. The standardized gradient for men (Figure 3.2) is very similar to the social class mortality gradient in the last UK Decennial Supplement (OPCS, 1986). Unskilled men have a very disadvantaged health status, reporting 60 per cent more limiting long-standing illness than the national average. Women who are 'employers and managers' have a poorer health status than most other non-manual women and than men in the same class. This illustrates the way in which the same class has different effects for men and women. The 'individualistic approach' shows small differences in health status among women in the three manual classes. This is partly because of the way in which women's domestic roles

Table 3.3 Standardized limiting long-standing illness ratios by socio-economic group – (a) women – own occupation, (b) women – conventional approach *, i.e. husband's occupation if married, (c) men – own occupation. (Ages 20–59). (NB. This table gives the actual numbers on which figure 3.2 is based)

| | Socio-economic group | | | | | | | |
| | Non-manual | | | | Manual | | | All |
	1	2	3a	3b	4	5	6	
(a) *Women* –Own occupation (current or last)	48+	88	73	90	119	114	123	99
(b) *Women* –Conventional Approach*	60	78	75	100	105	126	152	99
(c) *Men* –Own occupation	61	71	86	94	107	129	160	99

Socio-economic group

1	Higher Professional	4	Skilled Manual and Own Account
2	Employers and Managers	5	Semi-skilled Manual and Personal
3a	Lower Professional		Service
3b	Supervisory and Junior Non-manual	6	Unskilled Manual

+ Expected frequency 10 < 20

* Women with husbands are classified by their husband's occupation, women of other marital statuses are attributed their own (current or last) occupational class.

Standardized using age groups 20–29, 30–39, 40–49 and 50–59.

Source: General Household Survey, 1985–86 (own analyses)

constrain their labour force participation; for example, many married women re-enter lower status, frequently part-time jobs, after childbearing (Martin and Roberts, 1984; Arber, 1987). In addition, there are smaller distinctions of skill level and remuneration between women in different manual classes than is the case for men (Arber, Dale and Gilbert, 1986). Thus, women's manual occupations have different meanings in terms of relative standing compared with the class distinctions conventionally drawn between men's occupations. However, when considering women's health it is clear that the manual/non-manual divide is a particularly important distinction.

Wider class inequalities in health status are found for men than women probably because a man's own occupational class is a better indicator of the household's material circumstances than is the case for women. Women's health status measured by the 'conventional approach' (classifying married women by their husband's occupation and other women by their own current or last occupation) shows a pattern which is linear, and only slightly weaker than for men. If researchers are interested in 'explaining variance' in women's health status, then the 'conventional approach' may be preferred over an 'individualistic approach'. However, using the 'conventional approach' is conceptually complex because it combines two gender-differentiated occupational structures. Married women are assigned to the male occupational structure, which is skewed to the higher reaches of both non-manual and manual segments of the labour market. Never married and previously married women are categorized by their own occupation and therefore assigned disproportionately to the lower reaches of the class structure. In the 'conventional approach' a woman's marital role is the sole criterion for deciding which gender-segregated class structure to use, yet as shown in the next section, marital status itself is associated with health status.

Marital Roles

Married women have better health status than single women, and previously married women have the poorest health status. Married women are 9 per cent less likely, and previously married women are 47 per cent more likely, to report a limiting long-standing illness than all women (see Table 3.4 under 'All'). The direction of influence between marital status and poor health is not entirely clear, poor health status may be a disadvantageous factor in the marriage and remarriage markets.

Table 3.4 Standardized limiting long-standing illness ratios by socio-economic group and marital status for women (Ages 20–59)

| | \multicolumn{7}{c}{Socio-economic group} | |
| | \multicolumn{4}{c}{Non-manual} | \multicolumn{3}{c}{Manual} | All |
	1	2	3a	3b	4	5	6	
Married women:								
–husband's SEG	61	75	72	93	101	110	131	91
–own SEG	47 +	81	71	85	107	103	108	91
Single women	94		87	80		138		103
Previously married women	104 +	72	135	164 +	175	173	147	

Socio-economic group
1   Higher Professional
2   Employers and Managers
3a   Lower Professional
3b   Supervisory and Junior Non-manual
4   Skilled Manual and Own Account
5   Semi-skilled Manual and Personal Service
6   Unskilled Manual

+ Expected frequency $10 < 20$

Source: General Household Survey, 1985–86 (own analyses)

The association between own class and health status varies markedly according to a woman's marital status. For single and previously married women, the major health disadvantage is experienced by women in manual occupations. Single women employed in non-manual occupations have nearly as good health status as equivalent married women. For married women, occupational class has less effect on health status than for other women. A comparison of the class gradient using a woman's own occupation and using her husband's class reveals a somewhat stronger influence for husband's class (Table 3.4).

The occupational class of single women reflects both the direct effects of occupation and the effects of materal circumstances in the same way as for men. Previously married women have a particularly poor health status. They are more likely to live in poor material circumstances, because their earnings are often insufficient as a 'family wage', and because of the inadequate level of state benefits on which previously married women with children frequently rely (Glendinning and Millar, 1987). Thus, material factors may be the crucial determinant of whether particular roles for women have disadvantageous health consequences.

Employment Status

Most studies of class inequalities in health, including the Black Report, classify people who are not currently employed by their last occupation. This is problematic because

Table 3.5 Percentage of women reporting limiting long-standing illness by employment status

Age	Full-time	Part-time	Unemployed	Housewives	Other non-employed*
20–29	7%	11%	11%	8%	24%
(N =)	(1762)	(505)	(302)	(958)	(180)
30–39	11%	10%	14%	12%	53%
(N =)	(1049)	(1283)	(171)	(1273)	(88)
40–49	14%	14%	22%	24%	73%
(N =)	(936)	(1139)	(91)	(158)	(95)
50–59	15%	17%	44%	31%	64%
(N =)	(735)	(798)	(80)	(836)	(344)
All	11%	13%	17%	17%	54%
SLLI Ratio	74	77	128	110	501
N =	(4482)	(3725)	(644)	(3725)	(707)

*Other 'non-employed' includes the early retired, long-term sick or disabled, and full-time students.

Source: General Household Survey, 1985–86 (own analyses)

the non-employed are more likely to be in poor health and are concentrated in lower occupational classes (Arber, 1987). Unlike the literature on unemployment and men's health, the literature on women's health and their paid employment has focused mainly on whether employment *improves* women's health through 'role accumulation' (Nathanson, 1980; Verbrugge, 1983; Marcus, Seeman and Telesky, 1983).

There is little difference in the health status of women who work part-time and those who work full-time (Table 3.5). Unemployed women and housewives at each age above 30 report more limiting long-standing illness than employed women. Their health disadvantages increases with age. Unemployed women report poorer health status than housewives at all ages except 40–49. The poor health of unemployed women in their fifties is particularly marked. The pattern of associations suggests that the predominant direction of influence is from poor health status to reduced participation in the labour market. Poor health is likely to affect whether a woman re-enters paid employment after childbearing, and women may be particularly likely to leave employment because of ill health.

To make headway in understanding differentials in women's health status, it is necessary to analyze simultaneously marital roles, employment status and the woman's social class. Table 3.6 provides this analysis, with class coded as non-manual or manual. Among married women, the best health status is reported by those working full-time in non-manual jobs (SLLI-60), and the worst by unemployed women previously working in manual jobs, 31 per cent more than the average reporting limiting long-

Table 3.6 Standardized limiting long-standing illness ratios by employment status *, marital status and whether non-manual or manual class, women aged 20–59

	Full-time	Part-time	Unemployed	Housewives
Married				
–Non-manual	60	70	87	104
–Manual	86	73	117	131
Previously married				
–Non-manual	80	94	167	
–Manual	95	101	201	
Single				
–Non-manual		74	72 +	
–Manual		109	123 +	

+ Expected frequency 10 < 20

* Other 'non-employed' (the early retired, long-term sick or disabled, and full-time students) are excluded from this table.

Source: General Household Survey, 1985–86 (own analyses)

standing illness. Women working part-time in manual jobs have better health than those working full-time. In all other cases manual women report poorer health than non-manual. The variation in health status for previously married women is particularly great; for example, women who are working full-time in non-manual occupations have a 20 per cent below average chance of poor health status, but previously married women who are unemployed or housewives and previously had a manual job are more than twice as likely to report poor health status than the average. For single women, the small numbers in some categories make it impossible for detailed analysis, but it appears that the major distinction is between the relatively good health status of never-married women in non-manual occupations and the poorer health of those in manual jobs.

The above discussion has shown that to understand women's health status it is important to analyze simultaneously occupational class, marital roles and employment status. An analysis restricted to only one or two of these variables can lead to misleading conclusions about the extent and nature of inequalities in women's health. The usual practice of simply using occupational class as the basis for analyzing inequalities in men's health is inadequate for women. It is therefore no surprise that contradictory findings have emerged from the research literature which has been cast in this unidimensional class framework. It is essential to consider the interactions between marital roles, participation in paid employment and occupational class. Groups of women who are disadvantaged on all these factors experience particularly poor health status.

Material Circumstances

The crux of much sociological debate on inequalities in health is to demonstrate that disadvantaged material circumstances are the major determinant of poor health status. The Black Report concentrated on social class as a way of measuring the disadvantages of structural position. More recently there has been some change of emphasis from a concentration on class, to an emphasis on participation in the labour market and to using various alternative measures of the structural position of households. Housing tenure and car ownership have been used by Fox and his colleagues at City University (Fox and Goldblatt, 1982; Moser and Goldblatt, 1985; Moser, Pugh and Goldblatt, 1988a, 1988b; Fogelman, Fox and Power, 1989). Townsend, Phillimore and Beattie (1988) constructed a deprivation index which included housing tenure and car ownership, together with a measure of unemployment and overcrowding. They argue that car ownership is the best available surrogate measure of current income. Their deprivation index explained more of the variance in an index measuring the health of wards in the North of England, than was explained by occupational class.

Because of recent changes in the labour market position of men and women, it is essential to address the complexity of measuring the structural position of households. Figure 3.3 illustrates, for married couple households, the various types of factors likely to be associated with material circumstances. Six variables measure the impact of the husband's and wife's labour market contribution to the household's material position. Housing tenure, housing conditions and car ownership reflect the material circumstances of the household, and can be seen as 'outcome' measures. They can be used as surrogate measures of material conditions. Dependence on state benefits is a direct measure of the degree of financial deprivation of households.

In the late 1980s, it is more complex to measure the 'inputs' into material circumstances (the six variables at the top of Figure 3.3), than in the past when a single variable — husband's occupational class — was adequate. In contemporary households different variables will be more or less important depending on work patterns within the household. The alternative of using 'asset-based' measures — 'outcome' variables — may be attractive because of their simplicity and universality. They are easier to collect than occupational class and more likely to be collected reliably. All households can be characterized by these measures irrespective of their household composition or the labour market position of their members. For women, these advantages may be particularly significant because of the complexities of class-based analyses outlined earlier.

The present chapter aims to point to the complexity of measuring material circumstances and women's health status, rather than presenting detailed empirical analyses, which can be found elsewhere (Arber, 1989; Arber, under submission). The discussion so far suggests that structural factors have a profound impact on women's

Figure 3.3 Key factors influencing material circumstances (assuming a married couple household)

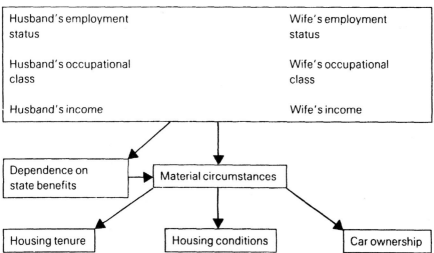

health status, but health status also influences women's roles, particularly whether they are in paid employment and marital status.

Factors Influencing Women's Health State

The factors which influence women's health *state* (restriction of activity due to illness) are likely to differ from those influencing health *status*. Any model of such factors must include an understanding of the effect of health status on health state. Table 3.7 shows that about a third of women with a limiting long-standing illness report restriction of activity due to illness in the previous two weeks. There is a surprising lack of difference by age. Indeed older women without limiting long-standing illness report the lowest levels of restricted activity.

Table 3.7 Percentage of women reporting restricted activity by long-standing illness and age

	20–29	30–39	40–49	50–59	Total
Long-standing illness					
–limits activities	30%	33%	31%	38%	34%
(N =)	(334)	(476)	(532)	(758)	(2100)
–non-limiting illness	14%	14%	13%	11%	13%
(N =)	(391)	(427)	(406)	(464)	(1688)
–no long-standing illness	10%	10%	8%	7%	9%
(N =)	(2974)	(2951)	(1974)	(1568)	(9467)
Total	12%	13%	13%	16%	13%
	(3713)	(3872)	(2930)	(2799)	(13314)

Source: General Household Survey, 1985–86 (own analyses)

Figure 3.4 provides an outline model of the key structural and role-related factors associated with health state. The combination of women's employment, parental and marital roles interact with a woman's structural position to influence health state. Women in disadvantaged material circumstances are less likely to be able to cope with the stresses of fulfilling parental, domestic and full-time employment roles than women in more 'privileged' circumstances. The extent to which partners contribute to the domestic division of labour will influence a woman's ability to manage the demands of a number of roles, and the likelihood of role overload and poor health state.

This model is presented as illustrative of the range of factors which need to be taken into consideration to provide an adequate understanding of women's health state. Part of this model was examined in an earlier study (Arber, Gilbert and Dale, 1985), which found adverse health consequences of full-time work for women with

Figure 3.4 Key factors associated with health state among women (restricted activity due to illness)

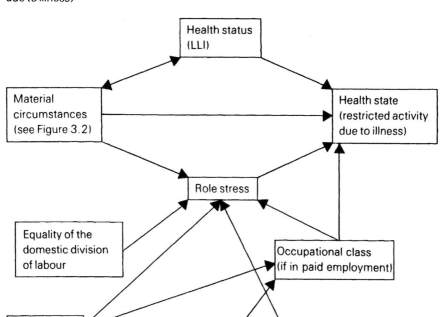

children who were employed in lower non-manual or manual occupations. Equivalent women with professional and managerial jobs did not have a poorer health state. It was argued that their greater financial resources could be used to ease some of the burdens of housework and childcare, so reducing role strain and fatigue. In addition, women working full-time in professional and managerial ocupations are more likely to have flexible hours and more control over their work, making it easier to fit in with the demands of children, compared with women in jobs which have less autonomy and more rigid work schedules. A key factor which might mediate this relationship is the degree of equality of the domestic division of labour; yet there is little sign of fundamental changes in traditional gender roles in the home.

The pattern of associations in Figure 3.4 may serve to increase inequality of both health status and material resources between families. Women already in a disadvantaged structural position who work full-time are more likely to suffer adverse health consequences, both because of the nature of their work and because the level of remuneration from their work is insufficient to buy additional supportive services.

Women with a poor health status are less likely to be in paid employment, but whether their lack of paid employment adversely affects the material circumstances of the woman's household will depend on the class and labour market position of their partner, and for women without a partner will depend on the adequacy of state benefits. Thus, the relationship between health and women's roles cannot be divorced from their material position.

Conclusion

This chapter has attempted to redress some of the imbalance in previous research on inequalities in women's health. Six conceptual issues were discussed, which have been neglected in previous research: the need to separate analyses of a woman's own occupational class from analyses of her material circumstances, the inadequacy of male-dominated measures of occupational class, the complexity of measuring women's material circumstances, the need to consider both a woman's domestic roles and her structural position, a questioning of the direction of causation between role occupancy and health status, and the conceptual distinction between measures of health status and measures of health state.

Conceptual frameworks were proposed which take seriously the relationships between marital, parental and employment roles and consider how they influence women's health within a structural context. It is concluded that structural factors have a profound impact on women's health status, but that health status also influences women's roles, especially whether they are in paid employment. Inequalities in health state are associated with the fulfilment of certain combinations of parental, marital and employment roles in 'disadvantaged' as opposed to 'privileged' material circumstances.

Acknowledgments

I would like to thank the Office of Population Censuses and Surveys for permission to use the General Household Survey, and the ESRC Data Archive, University of Essex, for supplying the data. I am grateful to Jay Ginn for assistance in extracting the GHS data files and to Gill Jones for her comments on an earlier version of this paper.

Chapter 4

Distance Decay and Information Deprivation: Health Implications for People in Rural Isolation

George G. Giarchi

Introduction

Deprivation is frequently associated with the lives of inner city dwellers in old densely packed terraced housing built in the last century, or with the residents in high-rise city slums and concrete council houses. However, deprivation is not determined by spatial location *per se*, be it the countryside or urbanscape. As every major study of poverty has demonstrated, deprivation can be as serious a problem in the rural setting as it is in the worst inner city neighbourhood. None the less, rural deprivation tends to be overlooked. As shown by the studies of Bradley and Lowe (1984), there is an urban bias in the social sciences. Brogden (1984) has also referred to the development of indicators of social malaise produced by such an urban bias. At the same time Walker (1978), Pacione (1984) and Gilder (1984), amongst other recent writers, have demonstrated that a romanticized view of rural life still survives. That view is best described by Pahl (1970) as the 'village of the mind'.

In substantive socio-economic terms the deprivation of both the urban and the rural setting are the effects of the same structural dysfunctions, as aptly demonstrated by Townsend's 1968 classic study of poverty. There is a danger, however, that politically urban issues can completely overshadow rural problems and attract more attention than the miserable lot of people who are out of sight and mind in remote rural areas, especially the elderly. There is also a real danger amongst academics of throwing out the rural issues with the rural dichotomy. Having agreed that there is no real dichotomy between the rural and the urban, there can be a tendency to discard the very real qualitative differences between the two settings. Anthropologists such as Cohen (1982) and Strathern (1982) have reminded the researchers of this danger. Social science is not confined to a discussion solely of the substantive; the qualitative differences must also be explored.

On the basis of empirical studies rural deprivation affects the standards of health of many people in the countrysides of the UK particularly the most vulnerable dependent populations, such as younger children and older adults at the lower end of the social scale. The explanation of why they are so deprived is based upon several factors.

Rural Deprivation and Health

The pursuit of health in the countryside is adversely affected by:

1 poor rural housing provisions;
2 insufficient health and medical resources;
3 peripheral skeletal welfare and social service facilities;
4 difficulties of access due to distance decay;
5 information deprivation related to health service provisions;
6 local reluctance and sometimes resistance to utlilize 'outsider' resources and facilities when they require crossing cultural boundaries to obtain them.

These major rural deprivations also exist in urban areas, but they are either overlooked in the urban-biased welfare studies, or not regarded as qualitatively different.

Before checking these deprivations and the negative effects upon the pursuit of health, the concept of 'rural deprivation' needs to be clarified. 'Rural deprivation' is described by Phillips and Williams (1984, p. 220) as:

> an absence, or in a rural context unavailability because of distance, of goods and services, but it can also relate to a 'lack' of well-being. This could be caused by an uneven distribution or unavailibility of 'impure' public goods such as health care, education and welfare services, but also by a lack of choice, say, for rural dwellers to obtain good housing at a fair price, to enjoy cultural and recreational activities and to have access to the range of jobs, services and information available to urban residents.

Herbert and Thomas (1982), and Marx (1867) would view deprivation, wherever it is to be found, as stemming from class conflicts brought about by an unequal distribution of power and the maintenance of class disparities. It is this very process which creates deprivation at the peripheral margins of society, so that Toffler (1980), in a world wide analysis, regards the emergence of sub economics as reactive consequences of centralized urban economics. He observes that the majority of the world's poor reside in the rural areas. Also the rural deprivation, referred to and described by Phillips and Williams above, tends to be less visible. This is so for two reasons: one sociological and the other geographic. Firstly, according to Wrong (1963), the invisibility of poverty is associated with the absence of class distinctions. In rural areas the 'class situation' is less obtrusive phenomenonologically than in the urban areas. Secondly, a distinctive dimension is the likelihood of greater physical isolation, which leads Dillman and Tremblay (1977, p. 121) to state that in general rural areas experience more deprivation than the urban, and 'the more rural the area the greater this discrepancy'. In addition, Rikkinen (1968), Butler and Fuguitt (1970) and the Association of County Councils (1979), have presented empirical data to support the view that small settlement size and remoteness bring their own associated problems. A *contextual* sociology cannot afford to lose sight of spatial dimensions and their socio-economic implications.

The relevance of the above observations will be clarified when considering the six major aspects of 'rural' negatively affecting the pursuit of health.

The Pursuit of Health in the Countryside is Adversely Affected by Bad Housing

McLaughlin (1983, p. 7) quotes a national survey in 1981, which revealed that 6.7 per cent of all houses in rural areas of England were unfit. This was 0.2 per cent more than in urban areas. He then draws attention to a South Shropshire rural study of the early eighties, where one house in ten lacked one or more basic amenities. The houses which are 'unfit' are damp, poorly lit, badly ventilated or lack healthy sanitation: clothes are rotten with mildew. The adverse effects on health particularly for the elderly need hardly to be stressed. Larkin (1978, p. 40) conducted studies in Dorset which provided 'practical evidence that the poor who are badly housed in rural areas often suffer greater hardships than their urban fellow workers'. He based this upon his visits to cramped 'rural slums' in thirteen different centres where the housing deprivation had lasted for decades. His other studies of Derwentside, New Forest and Tonbridge and Malling demonstrated that the rural dwellings were in greater housing 'stress areas' than the worst in Manchester, Salford, Birmingham and Hammersmith. Psychological stress accompanies rural slum conditions as also urban counterparts, but the isolation factor in the rural situation adds to the stress involved. Giarchi (1988) came across rural dwellings without water or lighting in East Cornwall and some without running water. His Cornish study showed that approximately 29 per cent of households with dependent children and 10 per cent of the others shared bathrooms and toilets. In addition 56 per cent of households with children and 54 per cent of those with elderly people relied upon fireplaces for heating, often in one room. The elderly usually slept upstairs so that the danger of hypothermia was greatly increased.

Country areas have always lacked the higher proportion of rented accommodation and of council houses in urban areas. The escalation in the past ten years of second home ownership and the sale of council houses have exacerbated the already disproportionate number of homeless people in rural areas. McLaughlin (1983,

p. 9) points to the frustration and stress experienced by first-time buyers, often young parents. Keeping down the rural rates, protecting agricultural land, or the property value of those already securely housed are suggested explanations for the housing deprivation. Dumping 'problem' people in caravan sites has already been cited by Larkin (1978). This persists in many rural areas.

Also country areas have increasingly been populated by in-migrant elderly people. The Eurosocial Report no. 16 (1985), referring to this, observed: 'The village has become an asylum where the elderly are dumped to die slowly.' When one partner dies, the remaining partner is usually the woman, who often does not drive; which will be referred to below when considering transport problems. When the in-migrants have few poor relationships and no local contacts, particularly when they are in remote areas, there can be an adverse affect on health (Cassel, 1976; Henderson, 1974, 1977, 1980 and Duncan-Jones, 1981).

The Pursuit of Health in the Countryside is Adversely Affected by Insufficient Health and Medical Resources

Leschinsky's (1977) nationwide survey of rural health services indicates that centralization of health provision is a major reason for health disparities in rural areas. The emphasis in recent years has been upon bringing services closer to the population, but health policies of so many authorities have been to create services farther from the rural people. Joseph and Bantock (1983) indicate empirically that rural people are at a lasting disadvantage relative to city folk in terms of health services. Inevitably, major hospitals are in the larger cities. Almost all the elderly in Giarchi's 1988 Cornish study complained in their interviews about the distance from the rural areas into Plymouth both for treatment and to visit hospitalized relatives. There were also about 5 per cent of 415 randomly rural interviewees in East Caradon, who were not registered with any GP. They explained that if they were dying or very ill, the GP would never get there in time. Like most countryfolk they had little choice but to be fatalistic.

Alternative medicine appears to flourish in Cornish areas (Giarchi, 1988). Was this because services were not readily available? In the previous three years, 62.3 per cent of the elderly had not been to their dentists, and 73.7 per cent had not been to a chiropodist. A local social worker remarked to Giarchi (1988) that 'older people in the urban areas are just as reluctant to see either their dentist, chiropodist or optician, but when they do have to see them, it's a whole day's effort and the costs of getting to them are usually greater. Rural folk exaggerate distance; the urban folk minimize it.' Health centres are increasingly located in urban centres. And ironically those in the greatest need of their facilities are the least able to have access to them, particularly frail, elderly people in the peripheral isolated rural areas. Hart (1971) and Stacey (1977) refer to the 'inverse care law', in which those who suffer more ill health are less likely to be assisted. In Cornwall, according to McLaughlin (1983, p. 22), 19 per cent of doctors' surgeries have recently been closed, and 14 per cent in rural Devon.

Harvey (1973) referred to 'territorial social justice' as a way of assessing the distribution of income, wealth, shelter and health care in 'spatial terms'. McLaughlin (1985) suggests that the focus of rural attention should be upon *the deprived*: 'It is people who are deprived, not places *per se.*' Where health is concerned on the basis of equity, people should have access to the same treatment when ill, or the same preventative measures in accordance with the principles of equal rights. But health provision is impure (Cox and Reynolds, 1974) because people are unevenly located and services are not uniformly available. The resultant disparities, however, as shall later be shown, are not determined by geography, but by socio-economic and political forces in urban centres where rural needs are not prioritized.

The Pursuit of Health in the Countryside is Adversely Affected by Peripheral Skeletal Welfare and Social Service Facilities

The definitions of a rural area usually includes a reference to a low public service infrastructure (Stockford, 1978). Service delivery statistics over the years have shown that expenditure on services *per capita* is generally lower in rural areas. In addition, the referral rate to the Social Services in rural areas is lower *per capita* than in the urban areas, on the basis of studies in the 1970s (Bath SSD, 1970; Norfolk SSD Research Team, 1976; Standing Conference of Rural Community Councils, 1978) and in the 1980s (e.g. Giarchi, 1988). Occupational therapists, the Home Help service and meals on wheels enable older people to remain healthy or prevent deterioration setting in. So also do the Day Care Centres, which provide stimulation and respite for carers. However, the rural continuum of community care is stretched to the extreme in remote areas and often cannot stretch far enough to reach the more isolated residents.

Giarchi (1988) has shown how the Cornwall Social Service policy has had to decentralize, get rid of 'cathedral sites' and create strong local ties, but social work catalysts are sparse in the rural areas. The 'network density' discussed by Willmott (1987) has been weakened in many of the villages where 'community of attachment' (as defined by Willmott, 1986) is affected by the incomers, dividing territorial interest and blurring the local sense of identity. 'Going local' is difficult to achieve when there are weak friendship ties and a loss of kinship networks. In urban areas, these lacks can be counterbalanced by the greater concentration of collaborative formal services establishing 'neighbourhoodism'. The necessary requisite is the 'collaborative' effort. Abrams (1980) made the point that formal neighbourhood care may not exist with informal neighbourliness. When the latter is lacking, as in Cornish rural areas, the former cannot adequately fill the gap locally because the resources cannot be stretched sufficiently to reach the many villages, hamlets and lone dwellings, due to the lack of funds. It takes countryside workers hours, and sometimes most of the day, to reach people in need.

Harper (1986) makes the point with regard to older people that 'kin relationships of the elderly are dependent on the current spatial proximity of kin'. When the in-migrant elderly have no local kin, as in Giarchi's (1988) study, the majority of the elderly face psychological isolation. In that study, 61.3 per cent of the elderly lived outside the town; 60 per cent of them were not Cornish: more than half of them were migrants without local kin. They were easy prey for depression with nobody close by to turn to.

Often great confusion for both the client and the social worker exists over the location of DSS offices in rural areas. For example, in Giarchi's (1988) study of the Liskeard area, three DSS offices served the area: one in Launceston, miles away to the north; one in St Austell; and the third in Devonport, Plymouth. There was no DSS office in the market town of Liskeard. A small DSS unit was open for limited periods in the town, but it could not provide payments. At times, even the DSS officers were confused over the boundaries. Moreover, people in rural areas whose giros, due on a Friday, do not in fact arrive, have greater difficulty in contacting social workers to obtain a holding payment to carry them over the weekend than people in urban areas. Also, people in the rural area of Caradon who had difficulties over their payments were often told to hire taxis, hitch-hike or get a lift to DHSS offices miles away — because of infrequent buses. (Transport problems will be dealt with later.)

In rural areas voluntary agencies are legion. For example, with regard to the voluntary organizations which work alongside the personal social services and the welfare agencies, there are at least 200 serving Cornwall (the Cornwall Rural Community Council, 1985). However, Giarchi discovered that addresses of agencies, circulated locally or deposited in the library, were over ten years out of date. Voluntary agencies fulfil a social function but also an information giving role. However, in the Cornish study Giarchi shows how 53.9 per cent of randomly selected rural people will not turn to a voluntary agency in a crisis. People often explained that knowing whom to turn to was the problem; finding out where they were was a greater one.

The Pursuit of Health is Adversely Affected by Difficulties of Access due to 'Distance Decay'

Discussions concerning rural problems in social geographic terms stress the spatial difficulty of access affecting the consumers of care and in turn the spatial difficulties of access affecting the providers of care in their attempts to reach rural clients. 'Distance decay' requires some sociological explanation. The discussion in sociological terms emphasizes that social processes determine the spatial and temporal context. Just as Pahl (1970) stated that it is an error to look to the city for an understanding of the city, so too rural topography does not explain why 'distance decay' exists. The latter is socially constructed by the criteria of central planners who decide upon the location of hospitals, schools, social services and GP surgeries, etc., 'in a reward distributing-system', in which space is a significant component. So said Pahl (1975, p. 10) with reference to the city, when he related the urban process to that of society. The rural must also be seen in the same societal context. Substantively, the same spatial determinants work in rural areas as in the urban. Castells (1976, p.70) regards space as the 'real object' within the process of consumption, which brings one to consider the economic structure. Space is rateable and value laden; morphologies reflect the shape of justice and equity. The distance between the consumers and the producers' facilities, whether public or private, is determined by urban entrepreneurs and planners. Rural landscapes in the urban-scape of the UK can only be understood in socio-economic terms within the context of consumption.

Dunleavy (1979) refers to collective consumption of public housing, transport, education and health provision, which are determined not only by social attitudes but also by economic, political and ideological forces. These forces determine where facilities and markets are located. In addition, social stratification helps to explain why most people live where they do: as consumers in the pursuit of well-being, they struggle to purchase scarce resources such as health facilities and service agencies. Economies of scale and market policies largely determine the range of choices facing the planners and builders, and availability of goods and location of shops; and these in turn determine what is or is not available locally.

To some extent all the six rural factors affecting the pursuit of health are consumption variables. Each is provided and maintained within a reward-distributing system; each is affected by social space. When there is an imbalance between spacial provision and areal demand, between equity of access and locational need, socio-economic deprivation occurs. When these imbalances occur, 'distance decay' sets in and further compounds rural deprivation.

'Distance decay' has been transferred from agrarian economics in which activity decreases with the increasing distance from the city (von Thunen, 1826). Harvey (1970) makes the distinction between those who focus primarily upon *physical* space/distance, and those who focus primarily upon *social* space/distance: the former presupposes a 'geographic imagination' and the latter a 'sociological imagination'; but as Harvey states, these orientations are not exclusive; in fact they are complementary. Harvey asks the social scientists to harmonize thinking about space. The externality is an outward sign of ideologies (internalities). The underdevelopment that accompanies rural deprivation can be plotted spatially from the urban centres outwards, as communication road systems to and from the cities wind through distant villages without transport and essential local facilities: but it is the economy, the urban ideology, and market centrist policies, which create the distance between consumers and services, because of which socio-economic environments simply decay. Also, the managers of 'capital' distance themselves from the rural environs, and in a sense create the 'periphery', in which rural people are beyond the economic landscape and are marginal to urban planning and objectives. Saunders (1981) also discusses the economics of space, citing Pahl's emphasis upon the inherent inequality of space. Although Saunders was discussing *urban* sociology, his statement that a pattern of social distribution is superimposed upon an underlying spatial logic (Saunders, 1981, p. 117) can also be applied to space in the rural setting, because the logic of rural economy is ideologically peripheral to the urban logic.

The factor of remoteness needs also to be considered. It has been customary in community studies simply to refer to 'rural people' in remote areas and statistically to lump lone dwellers, residents in hamlets and villages together. What is meant by 'remote' is not always defined. However, if the researcher explores the difficulties faced by people in terms of whether they live in a lone dwelling, hamlet, village or market town, the findings become more meaningful. Living at a distance from resources raises questions of whether transport is available, affordable, and whether the resources are locationally accessible. The state of the roads to the remoter dwellings creates hazards not replicated in urban settings. Reaching these residents in crises is particularly constrained by temporal and spatial factors. For example, in Giarchi's (1988) Caradon study lone elderly dwellers in houses standing alone, at least half a mile radius from the nearest house, without a phone or car, were more at risk, especially when living in impassable country lanes. In contrast neighbours were more available as potential helpers/contacts in the hamlets; and more again in the village. This is not to say that people, even in the most densely populated settlements, are always better cared for, or have more more visitors or coverage than people in more isolated dwellings. The point to make is that help for the latter was usually less available, and reaching them in an emergency was often more problematic. For example, seven persons interviewed at random lived in lone dwellings without a car, where houses were more than three miles radius from the nearest dwellings. Four of these persons were from the lowest socio-economic groups (SEGs). Ten (17.2 per cent) of the 58 interviewees in the sample without phones lived in either hamlets or lone dwellings. A social worker remarked: 'Keeping an eye on the elderly in these situations is much more difficult than on loners in an urban social work patch'.

When householders are also from lower SEGs, the remoteness is usually more acute. For example, in Giarchi's (1988) sample there were twenty-seven lower SEG residents living in lone dwellings. In each of these cases access to the doctor, community nurses and the chiropodist was significantly exacerbated and more costly because of 'distance decay', particularly in the case of lone dwellers. Distance per se is not the problem, but the 'trip frustration' (Coles, 1978, pp. 78–80) is; and for those at the lower end of the SEGs the frustration is accompanied by unacceptable costs. The rural households generally do have a disproportionate number of cars, but it is a situation described as 'forced car ownership' (see Coles 1978, p. 82).

Haynes and Bentham (1982), in a study of GP services in remote villages of East Anglia, show that the nearer the surgery is to the householders the higher rate of consultation. Moreover, groups which have a higher need for health care, such as manual worker households and the elderly, made considerably less use of hospital outpatient facilities. It also appears that GPs in remoter rural areas (in the East Anglia study) are less likely to refer the manual worker household and elderly to an outpatient clinic than GPs in rural areas which are more accessible. This study confirms that of Walmsley (1978), whose investigations show that in rural New South Wales the chances of admission lessen the farther the patient lives from hospital. Giarchi (1988) discovered in East Cornwall that the farther the households are from the hospitals, the less people visit sick relatives or friends, especially in the case of older persons. Herbert and Thomas (1982), with regard to the usage of the health service, show that the lowest social classes or ethnic minorities are more disadvantaged (described as 'disadvantaged consumers': see Joseph and Phillips, 1984, p. 138), because when faced with distance decay they constitute 'the transport poor' (Wibberley, 1978; Phillips and Williams, 1984).

Distance from health services is also a concern for many in cities, but there is a significant difference — the urban providers of services are more able to reach the urban consumers of goods or care. Consumers in rural areas are more inaccessible. It is a two-way situation. Most studies tend to consider accessibility from the point of view only of the consumers. Ambulance teams, post office workers, GPs, district nurses, newspaper deliverers, etc., know only too well what difficulties there are in reaching rural households. Their experience contrasts with that of their counterparts in urban areas, especially in snowdrifts, or on the icy winter roads. Abstract thinking may make the point that substantively life is the same in the urban and rural setting, but empirical studies (not always 'mindless') and people's everyday experience substantiate the thesis that experientially the 'life-world' in the rural area contrasts sharply with that in the urban area in qualitative terms.

The Pursuit of Health in the Countryside is Adversely Affected by 'Information Deprivation'

'Information deprivation' (Giarchi, 1988) is the lack of essential information. Brogden (1978, 1984) presents empirical data, showing that access to information is lacking in many isolated areas with low population density. Also, the National Consumer Council (NCC, 1977) refers to advise and information as the 'fourth right of citizenship'. The NCC in its report *The Right to Know* (1978), as well as Brogden, emphasize that advice and information are vital because of the difficulty people frequently encounter in understanding the complex clauses in the social security benefit schemes. Many gaps in information exist in remote rural areas because of communication difficulties associated with 'distance decay' and cultural barriers related to 'vernacular values' (to be discussed). They also exist in terms of communication problems in urban areas, but in rural areas the potential pool of informants and information centres is considerably less than that of denser scapes, where the communication of information is subsidized more by the statutory services than in the less populated rural areas. The accelerated process of concentrated services brings with it more centralized urban information services, where there are more hoardings, more leaflets and advice workers. Once again a rural blight sets in, creating diseconomies and so many problems for so many isolated, under-informed and under-claiming rural people.

Information sets out to extend people's 'life chances'. However, public services disseminate it unevenly. It is mediated by the class system and enables 'better off' people to have access to services and resources. The dissemination maintains the infrastructure in urban and rural terms, which create spatial injustices, affecting daily living — in other words information is a 'capital' commodity. The lack of essential information constitutes 'information deprivation'; which should surely be one of the indices of deprivation. Without it, particularly in remoter rural areas, people are often cut off from essential living; and these people are mainly from the lowest SEGs. Giarchi (1988) discovered in his interviews with 415 randomly selected people in East Cornwall that lower SEGs are less likely to know of the local CAB or of community services (see Tables 4.1 and 4.2).

Table 4.1 The respondents who did not know about the local community services

	Major sub-groups in:		Did not know about community services:		Percentage who did not know:	
	Bottom SEGs	Upper SEGs	Bottom SEGs	Upper SEGs	Bottom SEGs	Upper SEGs
Employed	33	110	30	73	90.9	51.0
Unemployed	17	0	15	0	88.2	00.0
Retired	17	105	14	70	82.4	66.6
Full-time houseworkers with dependent children	29	97	24	62	82.8	63.9
Totals	96	312	83	205	86.4	65.7

With regard to the advice and legal services, in 1983 the National Council for Voluntary Organisations (NCVO) and NACAB estimated that over 4 million people lived more than five miles from advice centres in rural areas in the UK. *CAB News* (1985) stressed how for many rural people long distance calls were the only means of obtaining specialist advice. However, 58 (13.9 per cent) out of 415 rural householders in Giarchi's (1988) sample had no phone.

Table 4.2 The socio-economic status of the residents who knew where there was a CAB in Liskeard and those who did not know

The SEGs	The 301 who did know		The 114 who did not know		Totals
Top	111	(94.1%)	7	(5.9%)	118 (100.0%)
Middle	150	(74.6%)	51	(25.4%)	201 (100.0%)
Bottom	40	(41.7%)	56	(58.3%)	96 (100.0%)

The Pursuit of Health in the Countryside is Adversely Affected by Local Reluctance and Sometimes Resistance to Utilize 'Outsider' Resources and Facilities When they Require Crossing Cultural Boundaries to Obtain them.

'Vernacular values' were introduced into the social sciences by Illich (1981). The 'people's vernacular', which is the colloquial language, is homespun and informally taught. It is the language of the native literature and brings together the raw material of daily life and the standard local form. It conveys 'local' meaning, imparting street-wise ideas. Illich (1981, p. 24) states that the vernacular was 'used in Rome to designate any value that was homebred . . . derived from the commons that a person could protect and defend'. Illich's 'vernacular values' are incorporated into this rural study because his conceptualization brings together the homespun rural values, localism and peripheral culture. Geertz (1975) would refer to this localized process as the local 'web of significance'. As is shown by Giarchi (1988) when discussing the Liskeard area in East Cornwall, the incoming migrants across the Tamar are viewed as a threat by the local Cornish. The concern motivates them to stress their Cornishness: 'the consciousness and valuing of difference — the awareness of commitment and of belonging to a culture — is a ubiquitous feature of peripheral communities' (Cohen, 1982, p. 6).

Thomas (1976), Phillips (1981), Giggs (1983) and Joseph and Phillips (1984), to mention only a few, have demonstrated that services are used on the basis of values rather than simply distance. 'Being Cornish', for example, creates normative assumptions — vernacular values going back to the days of St Piran — which involve being born in Cornwall, living there, being cared for there, eventually dying there and being buried there. Young and Mills (1980) refer to the actors' 'assumptive world' in which the people welcome arrangements and policies which fit into and confirm their existing values. Giarchi (1988) describes how Cornish mothers have always complained that the children born in hospital are delivered in Plymouth and so registered Devonian! Cornish ambulance persons refer to mothers who beg the drivers on their way to the maternity hospital to stop on the 'Kernow' side of the Tamar, so that they can deliver their child on Cornish soil. Worse still, the Cornish of Caradon are cremated in Plymouth. One Cornishman said to the researcher, 'Many Cornish in

Table 4.3 *The preference for treatment in Cornwall and elsewhere by the Cornish-born respondents*

Social characteristics	Origin: born in Cornwall	Preferences for hospitals located in:						
		Liskeard	Elsewhere in Cornwall	Totals	Plymouth	Elsewhere outside Cornwall	Totals
Employed	59	30	9	39	17	3	20
Unemployed	5	3	2	5	0	0	0
Retired	44	36	8	44	0	0	0
Carers of dependent children	45	25	7	32	7	6	13
Carers of aged with special needs	5	4	0	4	0	1	1
Totals	158	98	26	124	24	10	34
	(100%)	(62.0%)	(16.5%)	(78.5%)	(15.2%)	(6.3%)	(21.5%)

these parts are born in and cremated in Plymouth. You could say, in between we're Cornish because we're so damn angry about it.' The nearest crematorium and maternity hospital dictate where Caradon children are registered and where final mourning takes place; getting across the river for many of the Cornish people is a cultural dirge. Some Cornish declare their cultural difference by daubing the Celtic word 'Kernow' on the concrete portals of the Tamar bridge to remind the tourists (the 'Emmets' — a summer insect that comes out and infests the area) that the Tamar is a cultural divide. It is also a health-care divide.

When the interviewees were asked by Giarchi (1988) where they would prefer to be hospitalized, the majority preferred Plymouth, but when the origin was taken into consideration, it was significant that most of the Cornish folk preferred to be hospitalized elsewhere, as shown in Table 4.3. Guptill (1975), Schultz (1975), Knox (1978), Joseph and Bantock (1982) and Joseph and Phillips (1984) develop the 'gravity model' — the economic pull of market centres upon surrounding areas; but there is another 'pull' — of the cultural hinterland which either blocks that process or turns it into a 'drag' extending the social and psychological distance between the peripheral rural environs and health provision within the economic urban centre.

Conclusion

Whatever the merits of living in the countryside, in terms of its more peaceful environs, its greener setting and retreat from the rat race of urbanized areas, people in the countryside have their problems. These are related to: housing; the provision of health/medical services and welfare/social services; accessibility; information deprivation and sometimes local reluctance to utilize the 'outsider' resources when the locals have to cross cultural boundaries to reach them.

This study has shown that the major problems related to these factors are aggravated by remoteness, constraints associated with normative rural assumptions, and lack of information concerning access to health services and 'what's on offer'. The interrelationship between 'distance decay', 'vernacular values' and 'information deprivation' create peculiar problems and painful implications for people residing in rural areas which are qualitatively different from those facing the deprived residents within urban centres. Planners ought to target the lone dwellers and the residents in hamlets, especially if they are to cater for the rural peripheries.

Chapter 5

'We're Home Helps because we Care': The Experience of Home Helps Caring for Elderly People

Lorna Warren

Introduction

A number of studies exist which are concerned with the *what* and the *how* of home care (cf. Hunt (assisted by Fox), 1970; Hedley and Norman, 1982; Dexter and Harbert, 1983; Clarke, 1984); few exist which have explored questions of *why*. In my investigation of a branch of local services — domiciliary care for elderly people — in Salford, I looked at the perceptions that home helps and old people have of their relationship with one another. Specifically, I wanted to know why home helps care in the way they do and why old people feel as they do about using that care. In the following chapter I concentrate on the experiences of home helps. With gender as a central focusing point, I attempt to elucidate what 'being a home help' means. Clare Ungerson (1987) has shown that the basis on which individuals become informal carers is both material and ideological. This division of motivations applies similarly to the formal carer, though, as Ungerson confirms, the dichotomy is rather crude, each set of factors being mediated by the other. I look first at the material foundation to the motivation to become a home help: the economic climate, household resources and the life-cycle position of women in Salford. Their family role is an important consideration in the employment of home helps who are largely drawn from a population of otherwise unqualified working-class women. The domiciliary services are based on a model of informal care which derives from ordinary social life. I therefore go on to explore the extent to which women justify their reasons for becoming home helps in terms of this model. An important theme in both discussions is the testing of the 'vocational' character of home help as one of the caring jobs fulfilled by women. Finally, I attempt to show how these different interests and perspectives influence the anticipation of a role as a home help. In the second part of the chapter I examine the process of caring: that is, I look at what home helps actually have to do in terms of non-personal and personal tasks, how they feel about doing those things, and how they feel about the elderly people for whom they care. Here I use Parker's terms 'tending' and 'caring' to show how the distinction between caring for and caring about appertains to the work of home helps (Parker, 1981). Home help is a kind of domestic labour: it involves the work of looking after those who cannot do certain things for themselves — cleaning, washing, shopping, preparing food. But home care cannot be understood objectively and abstractly in terms of these activities alone. As it became clear very early on in the course of each interview, their work has a personal significance for home helps to which they felt it important to draw my attention. Below, I make the distinction between the two transactions in order to tease out their finer details but, at the same time, I have tried to show how women fitted them together to construct models and rationales of their caring relationships.

Reasons for Becoming a Home Help

Over a sixteen month period, from November 1983 to February 1985, I observed home helps at work in the homes of elderly people and in the setting of the local patch offices. I also conducted group interviews in each of these ten patches involving a total of fifty-four home helps. With the exception of four women, all had case loads composed entirely of old people. Nevertheless, contrary to my expectations — influenced by the findings of other researchers (cf. Marks, 1975) — home helps did not explain why they had joined the service in vocational terms. They spoke of wanting to help or meet people but it tended to be in very general terms:

I wanted to do something worthwhile for a change.

Because I like working with people mainly.

Of the fifty-four home helps interviewed, only five pointed to the desire to work with elderly people as a specific reason for taking the job. Of these, two alone felt encouraged by their own experiences of caring for elderly relatives. Instead, home helps put much more stress on the material necessity of paid employment as reason for taking up their posts. One woman became a home help because she wanted to care but, in her words, 'couldn't afford to do it voluntarily'. 'Well, we need the bloody money, don't we?', was the laughingly given if rather blunt answer I received on another occasion.

The harsh economic climate in Salford, where unemployment was above the national and county average, had clearly affected the circumstances of a number of home helps. Several reported looking for posts within the social services following redundancy from jobs in factories and small businesses (mainly within the manufacturing industry) which had closed or cut back their workforce. Not all women in this situation had necessarily looked for a job as a home help:

> I got made redundant and I tried for a care assistant but that was taken, and I tried this. Well I knew somebody on it and they were all right and, let's face it welfare is the only place where there's any jobs, so I thought well . . .

A handful of home helps indicated that they were single parents and that their wage was the only source of income from employment. One woman, who described herself as the family breadwinner, had a husband who was physically handicapped and unable to work. She also cared for and supported five children. At the other extreme, another woman was widowed and lived alone, her children having married and left home. A few women claimed to have moved to jobs in the home help service to increase their earnings. For example, one woman, who had previously worked as a school cleaner, said she found the money very useful in meeting the growing demands of her two teenage children for clothes, records, and 'spends' (pocket money).

I was still left with the question of why women had applied for posts as home helps as opposed to seeking other forms of paid employment. The chief reason, it soon became clear, lay in the convenient working hours which could be arranged to fit in with family responsibilities. Of those interviewed, 87 per cent worked part time, in the mornings only (although all were obliged to take their turn to provide weekend cover for very dependent elderly people). More than 50 per cent of women actually listed flexible hours as the major reason for joining the service. Fifteen specifically stated that they had sought part-time hours to fit in with caring for infant and school-age children. One home help looked after her disabled son, another two were caring for their elderly fathers. A number of women explained their attraction with respect to their previous employment: for example, three women had taken on shift-work but subsequently found that unsociable hours meant that they spent little time with their families. In every case, the interviewee praised the advantage of handy hours, though the convenience of working locally was mentioned by others. The majority of women saw their 'primary' roles as housewives and mothers. Becoming a home help first and foremost meant the (better) fulfilment of these private roles. At a time when women's commitment to their families was often at its highest, the job of home help was a means to meet material demands — to pay essential bills in low-income or single-parent families, and to purchase so-called 'family luxuries' such as children's clothes and other goods and services which higher-income families take for granted. At the same time its flexible nature ensured that women were still free to carry out the practical activities involved in caring for kin. It should be noted that it is not quite so easy to separate out economic and ideological factors as this statement suggests. That is, some women might have stressed the importance of caring for their children themselves because childcare facilities were inadequate and they could not afford to pay childminders to look after their children for them. A final reason was a lack or absence of formal qualifications. Interviewees did not go into detailed explanations for this lack. It was my judgment that most came from the sort of working-class background where little importance was placed on education for girls whose future was expected to be dominated by their roles as housewives and mothers. While the majority had been previously employed, it was in a limited range of jobs, typically in the public service sector or in factories, shops or offices (see below). Home help work not only offered flexible hours but it also demanded no formal training.

Skills and Experience

Given that their reasons for becoming home helps were largely to do with caring for their own family rather than for elderly people, compounded by a lack of qualifications, I was interested to know just how these factors influenced interviewees in the anticipation and construction of their roles. What were the implications for the skills and experiences which home helps possessed, and how did this experience — or lack of it — shape the background assumptions and common-sense knowledge, as well as the subjective meanings, which women brought to the role of home help? A handful of women said they had looked after old people and they acknowledged the part this experience had played as regards their work. For example, being witness to her father's gradual decline into a state of mental confusion — in the four years before becoming a home help, and in the seven years since — had enabled one woman to develop a successful and exclusive role caring for and supporting confused elderly people. However, perhaps in part because so few women had found themselves in the position of caring for an elderly person prior to becoming home helps, the experience was not considered to be crucial to the construction of a workable role. Indeed, just as much weight was given to caring for a disabled son. A small number of home helps had found themselves in the position of caring for elderly kin since joining the home help service. However, while interviewees were not uninterested in the reciprocal influence of this new development on the role of home help, its significance tended to be subsumed under the immediate concern of how to fit in caring for an elderly dependent with the demands of work and home.

Neither did knowledge of the home help service prove to be a key factor in the process of becoming a home help. None of the interviewees said they had made use of the domiciliary services, either directly for themselves or as a source of support in caring for elderly relatives, prior to becoming home helps for the first time. Only two women had applied for their posts without any knowledge of what was involved in home help work, however. A significant proportion of women had learned of the job through informal contact with other home helps. In a small number of cases these home helps were friends, neighbours and relatives. One woman, Maureen, had followed her mother into the service (they sat side-by-side in the interview). More commonly, women learnt of the job from casual acquaintances:

> I used to speak to a home help in Kwik Save. I thought she didn't work. I brought it up, you know, I said, 'Don't you work?' She said, 'Oh *yes*'. I said, 'Well, I often see you in here'. She said, 'Yes, I'm on the home help.' And I thought, 'Ooh, I'd like to do that, you know, get about, see different people.'

Others knew far less about the job and set about applying for a post in an even more casual manner. Indeed, three women joined the service after failing to secure preferred jobs elsewhere — all had applied for positions as auxiliary nurses, two in local hospitals, the third in a day care centre. They took the job of home help instead since the skills required were perceived to be similar.

In sum, while the majority of interviewees had possessed an idea of what was involved in domiciliary care, the extent of their knowledge varied quite considerably. Almost without exception, women obtained information from secondary sources. Few, it seemed, had a grasp of the finer details of the job. One organizer commented on her surprise at the number of applicants she 'weeded out' because of 'their negative attitude towards old people'. What most women drew on in the anticipation of their roles were, in fact, knowledge, skills and experience, the sources of which lay in their positions as housewives and mothers and, where relevant, former positions held in the labour market. Quite a high percentage of women had, at one time, been employed in other posts within the public services sector as hospital domestics, nursing auxiliaries and assistants, cooks and dinner ladies, nursery-nurse assistants, and welfare assistants and supervisors. Others had worked as waitresses or as cleaners in schools, offices or pubs. Domestic and general nursing skills, in particular, were felt to lend themselves well to home help work. Those interviewees who had not worked in the public services sector had commonly held jobs in factories (for example, as machinists, assembly line workers or weavers) and shops (typically as shop assistants) or in other semi- and un-skilled posts (including clerical jobs and jobs as postwomen, basket-weavers and hand-weavers). While all referred to general, common-sense knowledge of cleaning and caring activities, this latter group of home helps, without the formal experience of the first, placed more stress on domestic and tending skills acquired informally, both to secure jobs and to anticipate guidelines for their work. In the words of one home help:

> When I filled in the application form it's got on: 'What experience have you had?' and I just put 'Housewife for how many years'.

There existed, then, a crude division amongst women based on the *sources* of experience available to them from which to secure and anticipate, and, by implication, to construct their roles. However, cross-cutting this was another division based on the *types* of experience from which they drew. In this case, what mattered more was the point it time at which women joined the service. The average period for which interviewees had been working as home helps was seven years, though this varied from twenty-three years at one extreme to three months at the other. Independent of length of service, all interviewees realized the importance to the job of home help of non-personal care activities — cleaning, washing and shopping. It tended to be amongst more recent recruits to the service, however, that tasks of personal care — helping clients to wash and dress themselves, for example — were given relatively equal weight. This was due to the growing shift in policy and practice from institutional care to care in the community. It should be stressed, however, that these divisions were not deep or of a major significance to interviewees. Overall, first-hand knowledge of caring for an *elderly* person — either formally or informally — was limited. Most women anticipated the job of home help to be organized as a female task. Interviews with organizers suggested that the process of recruitment did little to challenge this perspective. Evidence for this emerged in the comments which organizers made about the qualities they looked for in home helps. One organizer described women as being suitable to the jobs because they were 'traditionally more domesticated'. The qualities most frequently stressed were general social traits of flexibility and reliability, sympathy and compassion, and common sense rather than formal skills or educational qualifications. On the whole, therefore, the home help service encouraged the recruitment of 'dependent housewives and mothers with the attributes of good womanhood' (Bond, 1980). A desire to care for the elderly played a secondary role to these features. As I was to find out, this had consequences for home helps which studies had rarely acknowledged. In the second part of this chapter I consider some of those consequences.

The Process of Caring

Having discussed their reasons for becoming home helps and the experiences they drew on to secure and anticipate their roles, interviewees were very quick to indicate the extent to which the job did not match with their initial expectations both with respect to the activities they found themselves called to do and in the way they felt towards the elderly people whom they visited. In terms of light housework and tasks such as shopping, most women found their assumptions about the job to be correct. What struck many (independently of length of service or orientation to cleaning or caring) was the degree of squalor encountered in some (in the words of one home help) 'choice' homes and the subsequent amount of heavy housework demanded of them. A number who had entered the service more recently expressed surprise at the proportion of time devoted to cleaning work. Conversely, other home helps had not expected to do more personal tasks such as managing people's finances or emptying commodes.

Some noted how the service had changed, again commonly involving them in personal care or 'nursing' duties. A significant proportion said that they were preparing food for an increasing number of old people unable to prepare themselves even simple snacks. None of the interviewees reported being unable to fulfil these unexpected demands, rather women were simply unprepared for them.

What, then, were the various activities constituting the work of home helps? Departmental descriptions of duties were very basic. Written policy defined activities very looseley as 'all the *usual* [my emphasis] household duties' and talked of achieving a 'good standard of cleanliness'. Guidelines appeared to distinguish between 'general care' — which translated very widely as the maintenance of users' welfare or 'well-being' — and 'domestic duties' — part and parcel of general care, which involved washing, shopping, cooking and cleaning. In addition to tasks which contravene rules of health and safety at work — high dusting, for example — duties forbidden to home helps included arrears of washing, cleaning unoccupied rooms and outside windows and other outdoor activities on the house and garden not conceived of as part of what is an essentially female home help model. Policy also forbade home helps to do 'nursing duties', though exactly what nursing duties encompassed was not specified.

Such loosely-worded policy allowed the service to be flexible and provision to be varied slightly to suit individual elderly people. On the other hand, I recognized that this housewifery model of care could potentially place a heavy burden on women since tasks lacked clearly defined limits, rules and standards for performance and they carried alone the responsibility for (often very) vulnerable elderly people. In general, home

Table 5.1 A classification of home help care

---

i *Domestic Care:* 'housework'/'domestic chores'/'just what you'd do in your own home'.

  e.g. vacuuming, sweeping and mopping floors, dusting, wiping down tables/work surfaces, etc., washing windows (inside), dishes and laundry (hand and machine), ironing, fires.

  Also, 'heavy'/'dirty' housework.

  e.g. emptying commodes.

ii *Errand Care:* tasks performed outside elderly people's homes.

  e.g. shopping, launderette, pensions/prescriptions, bills, doctor/library, etc.

iii *Personal Care:* 'personal'/'private'/'intimate' tasks relating directly to elderly people themselves.

  e.g. help with dressing/undressing, washing and bathing, using the commode/toilet. Includes cooking.

iv *Emotional Care:* 'stroking' (Bernard, 1971).

  e.g. *Being* concerned/friendly/sympathetic.

    Being an advisor/confidant/friend.

---

helps themselves appeared to distinguish between four different areas of care — domestic, errand, personal and emotional — summarized in Table 5.1.

Of course, it is important to remember that what home helps do at work depends on the needs of the elderly people they visit. Interviewees grouped elderly people into categories based on duration of visits and nature of disability or circumstances. All users of the service were known as 'clients' (I choose, instead, the term 'user' in an attempt to avoid the negative connotations of passivity, for example, suggested by the labels 'recipient', 'case' and 'client'). Depending on duration of visits, elderly people were divided into two groups: 'short-term' and 'regular' clients. Short-term clients were typically people who had been discharged from hospital and/or who were terminally ill. Regular clients — or simply 'regulars' — were those old people visited consistently over a sustained period of time such that they became a regular part of home helps' timetables. Timetables were composed in large part of 'regulars' (the number of old people's households called at each week averaged at five to six, and most households were visited twice weekly). Perhaps partly for this reason, interviewees further distinguished amongst elderly people on the basis of disability or circumstances. Old people were classed as 'routine', 'handicapped/disabled', 'confused' or 'dirty cases' (see Table 5.2).

These were some of the criteria for organizing home help work. I stress that the classifications are my own: women did not necessarily use such cut and dried labels especially to describe elderly individuals many of whom fit into a number of types. (For fuller discussion of categories see Warren, 1988.) The categorizations were useful for apprehending the activities encompassed by the job, but they were not sufficient to understand the complexities of women's roles. Home help is one of the 'human service industries' (Stevenson, 1976). David Soloman has described service roles as those

Table 5.2 A classification of elderly users of home help

i *Routine Clients*
   Composed of mainly 'regular', frail elderly people requiring non-personal type care (chiefly vacuuming and dusting).

ii *Handicapped/Disabled Clients*
   Includes more severely disabled: e.g. amputees, sufferers of strokes, etc. More likely to require help of personal kind: e.g. getting in and out of bed, dressing, preparing food, etc.

iii *Confused Clients*
   Confused/senile clients usually requiring mix of domestic, errand and personal care.

iv *Dirty Clients/Dirty Homes*
   Elderly people maintaining low standards of personal hygiene or living in dirty/dilapidated homes. Usually confused or mentally handicapped people requiring 'heavy housework'.

whose outstanding characteristic is the face-to-face relationship between the person who performs the occupational role and the client to whom the service is given (Soloman, 1968). I realized that I had to set aside the tasks of home helps and the disabilities and handicaps of users and concentrate on the negotiations and transactions to begin to comprehend their real significance (I use the concepts in an interactionistic sense) between women and elderly people.

Perhaps not surprisingly, I found interviewees' relationships with users to be individually (though usually covertly) negotiable. At the same time, however, they were obviously operating within limits which were socially determined. It was clear that transactions were very different from those which might take place between, for example, a cleaner and her employer, or a nurse and her patients. These are based respectively on public service and medical models of care. Instead, interviewees constructed models and rationales of their caring relationships based on the ideology of the good housewife and caring relative. The ideology of housewifery 'places a premium upon making do and mending, upon coping and budgeting, and upon managing within the resources available' (Bond, 1980, p. 24), while that of the caring (female) relative places a premium on the handling of personal care tasks which are 'intimately connected with the bodily expressions of ... values of privacy, autonomy and adulthood' (Twigg, 1986, p. 15). These models were used to explain why interviewees found themselves involved with clients to a degree they had not anticipated, and in a way which meant they shouldered large burdens of responsibility without public acknowledgment. How and why interviewees used these models I explore below. But first, I examine evidence of involvement.

Just as home helps found themselves doing tasks which they had not anticipated would be part of their work, so they felt responsibility for old people in ways, or to an extent, they had not expected. In general, women were not prepared for what they described as their 'involvement' with elderly people. As noted above, their primary reasons for joining the service were to do with family commitments, especially in the case of women with young children. It was not surprising, therefore that rules governing involvement in their work were particularly important to interviewees: in the words of one home help, 'Flesh and blood come first.' Indeed, the feelings of many women as new recruits were encapsulated by the adage 'Remember, it's only a job'. Nevertheless, despite warnings from others, interviewees did become involved or attached. Even amongst those who had worked with elderly people in previous jobs there were interviewees who were unprepared for the intensity of their involvement with users. One woman who had worked on a geriatric ward of the local hospital claimed:

> I knew I'd get involved — you always had your favourites on the wing — but I didn't realize I'd worry so much about them, them being alone and that.

From my earliest contact with interviewees, I was impressed by this sense of involvement. But it was not enough simply to note its unexpected nature. I wanted to know what exactly home helps meant by the term: in what way were they involved and why? Interviewees, in fact, offered evidence of involvement chiefly through descriptions of what I have chosen to call their 'unofficial activities'.

Unofficial activities comprised two types of jobs: those done outside what is agreed verbally between home helps and their organizers following the organizer's assessment of an elderly person, and which women referred to as 'favours'; and those done which contravene official policy. Favours comprise both tasks which old people were able to do for themselves — such as hand-washing or ironing odd items of laundry, doing light dusting, or preparing snacks — and those considered generally unnecessary but of importance to individuals — for example, one home help reported polishing the toilet seat for an elderly woman. More commonly, favours constituted things done outside working hours in home helps' time. Women washed laundry or mended clothes at their own homes, or they ran additional errands to the doctor's surgery, the chemist or to the shops. The doing of favours increased markedly at Christmas when many baked special 'fancies' — mince pies and cakes — for elderly people or chose presents (often from shops outside the locality) on their behalf. Home helps not only extended the length of but also paid extra or 'personal' visits to old people living alone or who had been admitted to hospital.

Although it was possible to describe most of the activities which contravened official policy similarly as examples of 'doing favours', interviewees were aware in this case that they were actually breaking written rules by performing the tasks. Yet, in many instances, activities were performed so regularly that they were felt to be an institutionalized part of the home help role. This was certainly the case with respect to tasks like changing light bulbs and hanging curtains, while windows, walls and ceilings were frequently washed more often than was stipulated. Women routinely bathed elderly people and most had, at one time in their career, performed 'nursing duties' such as dispensing medicines, changing bandages, giving shaves and cutting toenails. Home helps also accepted food from old people, or they 'neglected' domestic activities, considering it more beneficial for a user to sit and talk instead. Less common examples of rule-breaking included light gardening, unblocking sinks and decorating (in a couple of cases, women's husbands had helped to hang wallpaper). A number of rule-breaking activities were forbidden because of their inherent risks. Above and beyond this, home helps were not officially encouraged to do extra work for elderly people since this created false expectations of the service. My findings were by no means exceptional, however (cf. Hunt, 1970; Egington, 1983).

What, then, were the reasons for this involvement and the form which it took?

Caring for Elderly People: a Question of Relationships

It would be easy to suppose that the explanation for home helps seeing themselves as surrogate relatives was the fact that they visited elderly people without family and living alone. This undoubtedly played a part in home helps' involvement: for example, three women said that in the past they had taken home clients at Christmas who otherwise would have been on their own. Nevertheless, while the majority of old people using home help live in isolation (in Hunt's study (1970) roughly 90 per cent of the men and 80 per cent of women receiving home help were non-married and lived alone) the greater proportion of elderly people for whom home helps care have close relatives alive (according to Hunt (1970) the figure is 90 per cent). It was just as possible for home helps to become involved with old people who had family as with people who did not.

Instead, the reason why home helps constructed models of care which placed them in the role of caring relatives, lay chiefly in the nature of care and in the setting in which care was given. Personal care tasks, as indicated by the above definition, are those tasks that an adult would normally do for him or herself without assistance. They are characterized by such things as touching, nakedness, and contact with excreta. Drawing on the work of Mauss, Douglas and Elias, amongst others, Julia Twigg has shown how these tasks are intimately connected with the bodily expressions of values of privacy, autonomy and adulthood. For this reason, personal care is so often conceived of as a nursing activity, despite the fact that the skills required are not in any way medical. The medical model offers a means to negotiate these boundaries through the restructuring of the social body into the medical body.

The problem which home helps and elderly people alike faced was how to renegotiate these rules of intimacy without the aid of a medical model and the concomitant symbols of technical language, starched uniforms and rules and explanations of hygiene. Their solution was to fall back on to personal relationships, on 'particularistic rather than role-specific aspects' (Twigg, 1986, p. 17). The favoured model seemed to be that of the caring relative:

> Well, we treat them with a mum attitude, and they look at you as their daughter.

Elderly people clearly played a role in this process.

> Like one old lady, every week I get an apple and an orange, and at first I kept thinking, 'Where the hell are these coming from?' They were just in my bag ... Anyway, I found out who was putting them in, and she said, 'You didn't leave them in? ... they're for you', and I felt myself fill up because I thought, 'Hell', it meant like your mum used to when you were little: 'Now that's your apple and your orange for school'. And she's a lovely lady.

On the one level, the user's actions reminded the interviewee of things done for her by her mother when she was a child. On another, the action of gift-giving, and the notion of reciprocity central to it, suggested a process of renegotiation, particularly since reciprocity is usually taken to be a key principle in kin relations.

Gender was, of course, particularly significant in this context, since the skills regarded as necessary to carry out personal tasks are imbued with sex-role stereotyping. As Ungerson has pointed out, women have a virtual monopoly in dealing with taboo aspects of tending such as the management of human excreta and tasks involving touching and nakedness which, when carried out by men, appear to threaten rules of incest. For this reason, home helps became involved with elderly people who had family, it usually being the case, here, that relatives were sons who drew the line at personal care:

> I have an old lady, 92, who had a club foot, she's had cancer. She has to be put to bed and everything now . . . and her son said to me last Monday, 'They can do what they like to her, they can put her in a home, but I'm buggered if I'm coming in to undress my mother at night, that's not my job'.

Some women drew the line for them, while on other occasions, old people themselves preferred to turn to home helps rather than ask sons (etc.) for help with personal care.

But how did home helps rationalize their involvement with old people not requiring such intimate personal care? Again, reasons were rooted in the nature of tasks performed by interviewees. Anthropologists have long recognized that in all societies the preparation and serving of food and drink have symbolic significance and may act as indicators of social relations (cf. Douglas and Nicod, 1974). Hilary Graham argues that often the provision of healthy, nutritious, filling meals lies at the heart of women's family caring role (Graham, 1984). Amongst those home helps who were responsible for ensuring that elderly people received 'proper' meals, it was not surprising, then, that they conceived of their role in familial terms. What mattered here was not so much the absence of models for public, social production but the strength of the pre-existing informal ones. The fact that these tasks were performed in elderly people's own homes was, of course, central to their interpretation. Twigg notes how intimate personal care tasks are fully nursing tasks when performed in the classically defining locus of the hospital. This, she argues, is not just a product of dependency, but relates to the ways in which hospitals are total environments. Total environments deny the existence of boundaries of autonomy, privacy and adulthood. (This also helps to explain why personal care is much less of an issue with Part III homes than within the home help service.) In turn, the preparation and serving of food are service activities when carried out in restaurants, or office or school canteens, since they operate independently of local structuring and its pressures (Mars and Nicod, 1984). The resources and power which reside in the territorial autonomy of the first environment, and the anonymity which characterizes the second were absent in the setting of old people's own homes.

This, in part, explains why few interviewees saw themselves as nurses and cooks-cum-waitresses (with the concomitant detachment). Why then did they give themselves the label of caring relative? The majority of interviewees and elderly people were working-class people. According to Graham Allan (1979), amongst working-class people, the home remains largely the preserve of kin. Non-kin are rarely entertained in this social setting. Home helps, as non-kin, were threatening these 'rules of relevance', in particular because of their intimate knowledge of elderly people's rooms. One way to negotiate the subsequent sense of dissonance felt by both parties, was to conceive of each other as kin. Thus, in some cases, home helps who were carrying out domestic tasks alone described themselves and were described using kin terms. Their perspective and understanding of the ways in which elderly people's households functioned was quite different from that of the professional, whose focus is likely to be highly concentrated. Home helps saw elderly people in unguarded moments and had knowledge of how they managed their lives (Dexter and Harbert, 1983, p. 35). Their relationship was more akin to that usually shared by primary kin, especially when conversation was relaxed and reciprocal, embracing home helps' own lives. Finally, at all levels of care existed moral qualities which echoed qualities characterizing relationships between kin or 'true friends' (Allan, 1979, p. 160). These were qualities of trust and loyalty. Home helps were sources of comfort and support in situations of personal crises. It was this sense of friendship which was used to justify home helps taking elderly people into their own homes.

Caring for the Whole Person: a Question of Time and Responsibility

As I stressed before, relationships with old people were individually negotiable. Not all women saw themselves as caring relatives, and of those who did, it was not necessarily with respect to every elderly person whom they visited: involvement was explained not just in terms of this model. Women also spoke of their role at work as being allied to that of a 'good housewife'. In this context, they highlighted other features inherent to the wider setting of the local authority: chiefly, resources and responsibility.

Many recent studies have pointed out that increasingly the 'jam' of home help provision is being spread more thinly. Demands for domestic help alone outstrip resources. Interviewees placed a very marked emphasis on the lack of time they had to perform tasks:

> I've got one tomorrow where I'm doing his shopping, all his shopping for the weekend, *and* I've got to go back and do some work for him. Then he

want his curtains sorting out . . . so you haven't enough time in two hours to do it, particularly when it gets to the end of the week and the shops are busy. You can go in Tesco and be at the bacon counter ten to fifteen minutes or even longer, well all that time's taken up . . . and then they ask you if you've been to Blackpool for the day.

Ungerson has described one of the aspects of caring as 'time available at short notice and in flexible lumps' (Ungerson, 1983, p. 64). Cleaning tasks were more or less routine and consumed relatively little time. In addition to errand tasks, it was the cooking and the 'being with' (Graham, 1984, p. 150) activities which consumed most in terms of time and, for that matter, energy.

Yet within the context of bounded time, interviewees felt themselves to be given a great deal of responsibility — in terms of both charring and caring — for often very vulnerable old people:

There used to be an old lady living in the flats and I used to get her pension, leave it with her. As soon as I'd gone out the door, she'd take the book out, rip it in half, take the money and throw it out of the window.

Women stressed the fact that they often cared alone. In some instances, they were the sole source of human contact for old people. In other cases, interviewees felt families wanted to off-load responsibilities on to their shoulder. A number spoke of filling the role of neighbours. Whatever the reason, home helps carried a heavy responsibility for the well-being of old people with little time in which to fulfil their caring duties. It was in terms of these factors — singly or in combination — that women explained their unofficial activities. For example, some indicated practical exigences. Most suffered a shortage of time, though insufficiency of other resources also led them to break rules: home helps commonly stood on chairs to clean windows when step-ladders were unavailable. For other interviewees, involvement arose from a sense of moral obligation, whether it be to listen or to lend a hand. More often than not, interviewees rationalized their actions in terms of a mixture of the two:

I don't like saying no. Especially when it's somebody elderly, you know they're stuck, and you know they'll worry, you know they're lonely. *You* haven't got the time but you're not going to say no.

Quite often women did things such as bathing elderly people or cutting their toenails because there was no one else available. With responsibility came feelings of worry, guilt and concern.

Organizers did not operate a general policy of rotating staff since, as interviewees explained, this was believed to worsen problems caused by shortages of time: ascertaining even the most basic needs of elderly people may be a time-consuming process. But, inevitably, this served to increase women's involvement with elderly people and vice versa. Home helps felt a responsibility to persist with visits to users, even when they were recognized as being 'dirty', 'awkward' or 'difficult' people.

The whole situation was exacerbated by the fact that the boundaries of tasks remained largely ill-defined. Women certainly enjoy autonomy at work: within very broad limits, what, where and when tasks were to be done was left to their discretion and choice. But as Oakley (1974) has pointed out, ideas about the kind of activity housework is may differ quite significantly between individuals (and over time). Hilary Graham writes that 'caring is experienced as an unspecific and unspecifiable kind of labour, the contours of which shift constantly'. Since it aims 'to make cohesive what is often fragmentary and disintegrating', it is only visible when it is not done (Graham, 1983, p. 26). In other words, women felt under pressure to prove that caring was being done. But while duties were not codified or spelt out, it was very difficult for home helps to judge where to draw the line, and, even where it was drawn, it appeared easy to cross. Indeed, by organizers' own admissions, they 'turned a blind eye' to most unofficial activities and even privately condoned them, rationalizing and justifying them as evidence of women's caring nature.

Conclusion

The general climate of anti-institutionalization in the fifties and the growth of support for community care policies coupled with the dramatic projected increase in the number of very elderly people in the foreseeable future have drawn the issue of the care of old people to the attention of social scientists. However, lines of investigation have been narrow. Social policy, with its concern for the collective organization of welfare provision, has tended to concentrate at a more macro level on the activities of the formal bureaucratic social services (Qureshi and Walker, 1986, p. 109). Individual researchers have examined what caring means and entails. Hilary Graham (1983) believes that caring involves two dimensions, identity and activity. But she points out that our understanding of the concept of care has been limited by the actions of social scientists who have carefully dismantled these two interlocking transactions to reconstruct them separately within the disciplinary domains of psychology and social policy. Both perspectives, she argues, offer a reified picture of caring either as a means by which a specific feminine identity is achieved, or as an example of exploitation in the sexual division of labour in patriarchal capitalist society. An anthropological approach to the topic can help to provide a conceptual framework (as sought by Graham) in which the two elements of care can be fitted together in an everyday subjective experience of caring. Providing answers to the questions of how and why people live as they do is the driving force of modern social anthropology, and Roger Ballard (1983) and Judith Okely (1983) both show the relevance (as well as the difficulties) of the anthropological perspective in illuminating, in particular, the interests of subgroups usually lost in generalizations. Thus we can see that caring, in a formal context, is not simply a 'vocational concern', but must be understood in terms of a complex interplay of material and ideological factors.

Here I have explained home helps' relationship to work in terms of their responsibilities within the family. I do not wish to suggest, however, that women lacked commitment to their jobs. In her study, Sharpe found that a suitable job, especially with 'friendly and flexible' conditions, was of such importance to working mothers that employers often received more hard work and loyalty than the work and pay deserved (Sharpe, 1984, p. 57). Interviewees expressed a comparable conscientiousness. But it was clear, too, that the nature of work and related job experiences were important for women. Indeed, they defended their status vehemently against suggestions that they were simply 'skivvies', 'dogsbodies', 'chars', 'cleaners' or 'menials', especially when they were so regarded and treated by members of elderly people's families whom interviewees saw as their equals (Morrow, 1983). Reid and Wormald (1982, p. 127) have caricatured women's work by the list of the 'ten deadly Cs': catering, cleaning, clerking, cashiering, counter-minding, clothes-making, clothes-washing, coiffure, child-minding and care of the sick. These are jobs which, they argue, involve the direct servicing of people's immediate needs. But, while home helps were involved in human service work, it was not typical of most 'people work'. It involved care of a personal nature which took place outside the total institution, in the setting of elderly people's own homes. Women used a language and ideology to articulate the public domain which was taken directly from the private domain since, in this instance, activities clearly straddled both. They saw themselves as doing work *for* as well as *to* old people, they *cared* as well as *tended*.

The paradox for home helps lay in the fact that their roles at home and at work were so closely related. The first qualified women to undertake the second. The second was constructed in terms of the first. Since they performed these roles simultaneously, women felt locked into a double bind: if they were devalued and found wanting as home helps then they themselves, as 'natural' housewives and carers, were found wanting. (This was a problem pointed out by Fiona Poland (1986) in relation to mothers working as childminders, but it appears to me to apply equally to housewives and mothers working as home helps.) Indeed, describing the intense pressures of the service for a home help and the huge burdens which she takes on, Meg Bond concluded: 'To admit that she cannot meet all these demands with the resources available to her would strike at her good womanhood — at the very qualities for which the staff of the service are selected' (Bond, 1980, p. 24). So what were the consequences for interviewees who were essentially performing 'women's work in a women's world' (Bond, 1980, p. 13) characterized by self-sacrifice and a sense of altruism (Dalley, 1988, p. 15)? Hilary Graham has argued that services which substitute for informal carers are not seen as 'care' since they are believed to lack the qualities of commitment and affection which transform caring-work into a life-work, a job into a duty. Payment underplays the symbolic bonds that hold the caring relationship together (Graham, 1983, p. 19). This was certainly true for some home helps: as I have stressed, by no means did all women conceive themselves as caring relatives. At the other extreme, there were those who saw their obligations to elderly people as having a moral quality which was over and above that demanded by the job.

Whatever the nature and degree of involvement or obligation experienced towards elderly people, what was certain was that many home helps did not believe pay to reflect their responsibility (despite a recent upgrading of status to a level commensurate with that of care assistant, plus the concomitant pay rise). But, as Marilyn Porter has noted, women's self-sacrifice for the pay packet is often ignored or assumed as part of her 'nature' (Porter, 1983, p. 113). This is not to suggest that women did not enjoy or gain a sense of satisfaction from their work. Several thought their jobs particularly worthwhile when elderly people confided their problems to them. One interviewee felt she had become a lot more patient and tolerant as a result of looking after elderly people. Another derived much pleasure from doing favours for people, especially when her actions had measurable pay-offs: she cited the example of a 'psychiatric case' whose disturbed behaviour had lessened considerably since she had begun to bake home-made cakes and pies for her. Few, however, felt able to treat the job as a nine-to-five — or eight-to-one, as was more likely to be the case. If they did not take work, then they took worries away with them. In some cases, worries followed them: that is, a number of women reported being bothered by elderly people phoning or even calling on them at home, although organizers advised them not to give out their addresses or telephone numbers. In this situation, it was possible for women's families to resent their involvement. Work was described as both physically and emotionally very tiring. In particular, women emphasized the emotional toll it took. They spoke of the 'double burden of worry' of caring simultaneously for confused elderly people and their own families. Inevitably home helps faced the death of elderly people, which could be an emotionally stressful experience. Finally, women spoke of feeling manipulated and exploited, though they were surprisingly few in number. This may be because, as Rossi has pointed out, people are often less willing to express ambivalent or negative feelings about roles which feel 'obligatory' than about roles which feel 'optional' (quoted by Fay Fransella and Kay Frost, 1977, p. 107). Of those who did talk in these terms, most reported being taken advantage of by elderly people rather than their employers (perhaps because, in many ways, they saw organizers as being equally involved with elderly people as they were). This is not to suggest that women felt themselves powerless to resist pressure: they cited instances when they had refused to administer medication or to given weekend or evening cover to elderly people. But the majority appeared to shoulder the blame for manipulation themselves:

We do these things because we care . . . We're home helps because we care.

Chapter 6

Hooked? Media Responses to Tranquillizer Dependence

Michael Bury and Jonathan Gabe

Introduction

While the study of social problems has been a major concern for American sociologists throughout this century, it has received relatively little attention in Britain. Indeed Manning (1985, 1987) is one of the few British sociologists to have recently considered the benefits of analyzing issues which are of current public concern from a social problem standpoint. In an earlier paper (Gabe and Bury, 1988) we argued that the current debate about benzodiazepine tranquillizers like Ativan and Valium could usefully be analyzed in terms of a social problem perspective which emphasizes its developmental nature. As Blumer (1971) and Spector and Kitsuse (1977) amongst others have argued, there is value in trying to identify the various stages in the history of a social problem, starting with its emergence and ending with its resolution. One of the merits of this approach is that it highlights the dynamic nature of this history. Moreover, as developed by Blumer and Spector and Kitsuse, the movement between stages is seen as contingent and hence as highly problematic.

One of the key features of our approach has been to recognize the need to try and develop more fully a detailed analysis of the role of the media in legitimating claims about the social problem status of a phenomenon and mobilizing public opinion about it. As far as tranquillizer dependence is concerned we have already started to map out the media's involvement in its development as a social problem. This has involved paying particular attention to the way in which it has become a vehicle for the claims-making activities of particular professional and lay groups (Gabe and Bury, 1988). However, as Burns (1977) has argued, the media do more than simply reflect social forces. They bring their own influence to bear and this does not necessarily coincide with the aims of claims-makers. What we wish to do in this paper, therefore, is to develop a more fine grained analysis of the media, particularly televison, and the way in

87

which they have legitimated, shaped and amplified concern about tranquillizers as a social problem. Furthermore, it is only by means of such an analysis that it will be possible to explore the potential variability of television's effect on various publics.

Analyzing Media Products

In a recent article on sociological approaches to mass communications, Thompson (1988) has outlined a framework for analyzing and interpreting media products involving critical and interpretive methodologies. This framework requires that media products be seen in terms of the *external* context of social and historical forces and their influences, and the *internal* factors and processes of programme making. In turn, these influence the appropriation and creation of meanings by programme makers and their audiences. There are three dimensions to Thompson's framework which we intend to follow in this paper.

First, there is the question of the *production and diffusion* of programmes. This refers in part to the historical and institutional contexts within which programmes are made, and in part to the technical problems which different programme formats present.

Second, there is the *construction* of media messages. This requires that attention be given to the meaningful character of media products and the way in which television narratives and myths are created. This interpretive exercise confronts the variable nature of meanings and their attachment to specific social contexts. As Thompson (1988, p. 375) says, this involves a variety of techniques of content and symbolic analysis.

Third, there is a set of questions concerned with the *reception and appropriation* of televison programmes. Here, the focus is on the effects of media products and the nature of audience responses. In attempting to analyze such responses we move away from internal mechanisms and procedures of television production and creation, towards a more critical appraisal of how meanings may or may not be acted upon or incorporated into people's lives.

Before going on to apply this approach to television coverage of tranquillizer dependence we identify three types of programme format which have shaped media products in this area. These formats are important in helping us consider the extent to which the media's treatment of tranquillizer dependence is heterogeneous or monolithic in form.

Formats and Programmes

The first format we wish to consider is that of the *magazine*. This format mixes together purely entertainment items with either 'once off' or running reports on campaigns and issues. Short filmed sequences are mixed together with studio presentations, often with a live audience. The example we wish to discuss here is the popular BBC television programme *That's Life* which covered the issue on at least four occasions between 1983 and 1985.

Our second format is that of *current affairs*. This format covers filmed reports and studio discussions. Unlike the magazine format, current affairs programmes usually focus on a single issue, though they may well draw on expert opinion or case material. Perhaps the distinction here is between reportage and journalism, in that the producers and presenters working within the current affairs format have a more 'heavy weight', journalistic view of their task. The example of this format is the BBC Two programme *Brass Tacks* which dealt with the drug Ativan in October 1987.

We have called the third and final format the *exposé*. This format comprises a film report with a clearly identifiable reporter and a sharply drawn issue usually identifying a culprit. Elements of the other formats are present but the main aim is exposure and advocacy rather than providing information or debate. This avowed advocacy approach leads to foot-in-the-door interviewing rather than 'balanced' reporting or studio discussion. The example we have been examining here is that of *The Cook Report*, which tackled the subject of tranquillizers, again Ativan, in its weekly Tuesday night slot on the main ITV channel in May 1988.

It is our contention that the three formats outlined above both enable and constrain the production and construction of television programmes, and may have wider implications for studying their effects. Whilst formats clearly overlap in practice, establishing their basic characteristics underlines some important features of media coverage. We now go on to analyze television's treatment of tranquillizer dependence through the use of Thompson's three analytic categories.

The Production and Diffusion of Programmes

In his essay on mass communications, Thompson (1988) points to two kinds of context within which television programmes are made. First is what might be called the socio-historical context which comprises the changing economic, cultural and political environment within which programmes are made. Second is the institutional context comprising the organizations, procedures and technologies of television production. This involves attending to the conventions and routines of production dictated, for example, by working within particular formats of the sort we have outlined here. We would like to follow the distinction with respect to the production of television coverage of tranquillizer dependence.

The social context. At the 'socio-historical' level there are at least three 'conditions of possibility' which have influenced the decisions to make programmes about tranquillizers. The first of these must surely be the rise of health as a cultural domain. Far from being regarded as a 'given' of social life, only to be regarded as a problem when it fails, it is now regarded by journalists, broadcasters, and indeed sociologists alike, as a major part of the social and cultural order. In part, of course, this stems from the growth of health care expenditure, and thus the growth of the political significance of health. The development of contemporary discourses on health also relates to other important cultural motifs, notably those of the body and the mind. This can be seen in the widespread production and diffusion of materials on food, dieting and physical and mental health in all its forms.

Increasing activity surrounding health raises the second major issue we want to highlight, namely that of consumerism. Until the 1970s it was widely assumed that health could not properly be treated as a commodity (Stacey, 1976), but this view has come under increasing pressure in recent years. Health is now widely and publicly discussed in these terms. In a consumer society concerned with success and failure in the exercise of control and the sophisticated management of the body and interpersonal behaviour (Crawford, 1984; Featherstone, 1987), these tensions invest concepts of health with a wide range of meanings. The problem of tranquillizer dependence exemplifies many of the issues of health and consumerism. On the one hand, anti-anxiety drugs are prescribed by figures of authority (doctors) as legitimate treatment for ill health. On the other hand, the consumption of these drugs suggest an inability to cope with life's difficulties; a reliance on 'chemical comforters' (Helman, 1981). Thus tranquillizers may turn from being a source of help to a source of illness itself, and those providing them from benefactors to malefactors. If, as Fiske (1987) amongst others maintains, television is a key means of working through socially ambiguous problems, we can understand why such attention has been given to these drugs.

The third related general feature of the changing social and cultural context surrounding health concerns the role of the law. As health has taken on a wider range of meanings, and as the authority of doctors and scientists has been partially displaced, the possibility of the law playing a greater role in medical matters has grown (Ham *et al.*, 1988). What were once matters of internal regulation by the medical profession are now frequently potential litigation issues, as the massive rise in doctors' defence insurance testifies (Rosenthal, 1987). In the case of tranquillizer dependence this has meant that individual patients, self-help and mental health groups have all turned to the possibility of suing either GPs, manufacturers or indeed state agencies for causing dependence. At the time of writing, cases in Britain have yet to appear in court, though we are aware that at least two groups of lawyers are preparing such cases. The rise of groups of specialized lawyers in health extends the range of 'consumer law', just as 'health culture' itself extends consumerism. We see the law playing an increasingly critical role in the fate of social problems and thus in the way in which television tackles them. Certainly in the programmes under review the question of legal as well as moral responsibility, especially that of doctors and pharmaceutical manufacturers, was tackled on more than one occasion.

To summarize, we have argued that the 'external' context of changing conceptions of health, consumerism and the role of the legal profession are critical in understanding why television has showed so much interest in tranquillizer dependence. The perceived widespread taking of these drugs throws into relief a range of socially ambiguous problems concerned with responsibility for personal conduct, the ability to cope with life's pressures, and reliance on quasi-legitimate sources of support. Television is drawn to the topic as one of heightened popular concern, and in turn rehearses and amplifies many of its features.

The institutional context. The second context focuses on how programmes are shaped within specific media organizations with specific technologies. In order to demonstrate this we would like to concentrate on two main features of tranquillizer dependence programmes and their formats which facilitate and circumscribe the production process. First, we comment on the technological devices, procedures and resources used by the programmes in their relationships with viewers or in our case, patients. Second, we consider the problems and possibilities of using expert advice and argument. According to Thompson (1988, p. 364), one of the main difficulties facing the production of programmes concerns the 'instituted break' between the worlds of producers and viewers. The 'indeterminacy' of mass communications arises, in part, because programmes are produced in the absence of direct and continuous monitoring of audience response. However, Thompson also goes on to suggest that television producers employ a variety of means to reduce this indeterminacy, though many of these are used on an 'occasional' basis. We think that this is significant and indeed would go further and say that such devices are now at the centre of production processes in television and not simply employed to close the gap between producers and consumers.

In the first place devices which have traditionally been used to monitor programme reception have been developed in new ways to enable the expansion of production possibilities. For example, letters from viewers are used in deciding whether to cover a particular issue and in the production of programmes themselves. This is particularly important for the magazine format. *That's Life* decided to continue coverage of the tranquillizer issue on the basis of the letters it received and used these to provide case histories for subsequent programmes. Similarly, telephone links with audiences have been developed in order to aid production, as well as to allow feedback. This is especially the case where programme formats involve the serialization of an issue. Both the magazine and current affairs programmes, *That's Life* and *Brass Tacks*, used telephone calls to underline themes that were developing and to introduce new elements to the story. Programmes have also commissioned surveys of viewers' attitudes and public opinion through a number of different channels, including polling agencies and self-help groups. These have been adopted in the production processes used by the magazine format of *That's Life* and to a lesser extent in the exposé format of *The Cook Report*. In this way programmes have been able to give an air of authority to their views, in the sense that survey material conveys an objectivity to the evidence being presented.

However, new forms of contact with audiences constrain as well as facilitate production in that the interests of producers (to entertain and inform) may well differ from those of participating viewers (to express an opinion or advance a cause). For example, magazine programmes such as *That's Life* cannot allow viewers to overshadow the presenter and her reporters, for it is they that keep the jaunty pace of the magazine going. To dwell too long on one individual's story, however heart-rending, may upset the tenor of the whole show. This production problem is even more sharply defined in the exposé format where patient involvement may be greater but where the presenter is central to the story being told. Much of the success of the programme turns on the effective resolution of this tension.

In the current affairs example there is ostensibly more room for equal participation between studio discussants (with the presenter acting more as a chairperson), in line with the format's aim of facilitating a balanced debate. But even here production problems arise in trying to ensure that dominant individuals, those practised in television techniques (one participant on *Brass Tacks*, from a mental health group, had 'flash cards' ready to hold up to the camera) or those with 'idiosyncratic' views do not disrupt the balance. Video and editing can, of course, provide a measure of control to producers, but they still have to work within the constraints of a discussion format.

The *second* set of interactions we wish to mention are those between television and experts. In the present context two key features of these interactions will be considered: who count as experts for programme makers and how much influence should they have in the production of programmes? Here again the formats we have outlined present different answers.

As far as the question 'Who is the expert?' is concerned, it is clear that only a restricted number of individuals appear in most instances. The main example of this in the case of tranquillizers is Professor Malcolm Lader, a psycho-pharmacologist from the Institute of Psychiatry, University of London. Lader, who has established an international reputation for his opposition to benzodiazepines, especially Ativan, in fact appears in part of each of the programmes under discussion here. Having been involved in one programme it is clear that other producers have come to hear of his name, or made a note of it for their own future reference. Insofar as his message fits in with the programmes' general stance against tranquillizers and because it is issued by a senior member of the medical profession, his use is almost assured on each occasion. Indeed, it becomes difficult not to use such an established part of the package.

Each format, however, produces different interactions. In the magazine format expert opinion plays a minor part, alongside a variety of other voices. Magazine programme makers cannot afford to allow it to become too dominant, partly because of the 'consumer' emphasis and partly because expert opinion is itself being questioned more readily but in different ways. Makers of exposé programmes use expert opinion to help them establish their case, which may be 'sensational' in character. In *The Cook Report* Lader's call for Ativan to be withdrawn from the market was used as part of the programme's attack on the company responsible for its manufacture. In addition they used interviews with two lawyers to bolster their case. In the current affairs format expertise is used to create a sense of 'balance' between competing interests. Whilst Lader had appeared in the first *Brass Tacks* programme he was not invited to the second on the grounds that his well known views might dominate the proceedings. Several general practitioners were therefore invited in order to be given 'the right of reply' and the chairman of the Committee on the Safety of Medicines was interviewed separately to introduce the studio debate. From this it is clear that the programme was keen to provide a forum for professional as well as 'consumer' views and to ensure that well known critics such as Lader were not the only ones to be heard.

In summary, the production and diffusion of programmes is influenced by a number of complex 'external' and 'internal' factors. Producers become aware that a matter of public concern is 'on the public agenda' and then consider how this might be treated by their programme's format. If it fits with the overall aims and style of the programme, it becomes a candidate for inclusion. Once adopted in this way the programme makers set in motion their standard routines and procedures. In this way television both reflects and organizes the shape of social problems. This becomes even more clear when we turn to the way in which producers and presenters create or construct meanings in the making of the programmes.

The Construction of Media Messages

In turning from problems of production to those of construction, we are concerned with two types of question. First we want to examine the imagery employed and created by the programmes and second we want to analyze the structures of 'narrative' and 'myth' in television. The purpose of this stage in our analysis is to provide a bridge between the worlds of producers and consumers. How and why television programmes 'work' (or not) depends crucially on the way in which meanings are constructed and manipulated by those involved. In this section of the paper we focus on some of the ingredients at work in the content of tranquillizer programmes, and how they vary depending on format. This discussion will then lead into the final part of our paper which is concerned with the assimilation of and response to television by its audience(s).

Imagery. Two sets of images dominate television coverage of tranquillizer dependence. First there are those of the people at the centre of the story, including patients, particularly women who are in distress, and the manufacturers and doctors who are held responsible or give expert opinion to the programme makers. Second, there are images of the drugs themselves and their alleged addictive effects. As far as patients are concerned, each programme presented a clear and largely similar image of their social characteristics. In the main the patients were young middle-aged individuals, largely, though not exclusively female. Other kinds of tranquillizer users that may be found in the community, especially older people or those using them on a more limited or intermittent basis, were excluded. By portraying 'ordinary' people, who seemed to have relatively minor reasons for starting to take tranquillizers, the emphasis of the programmes on the dangers of the drugs themselves could be heightened. Thus *Brass Tacks* viewers were informed that 'hundreds of thousands take it (Ativan) and many become addicted to it'. The construction of this image of 'the distressed patient', however, varied from format to format. So, for example, *That's Life* presented patients in line with its magazine framework, in a similar fashion to the way it presented other consumer issues. The main image which is then developed is of women being taken over by the drugs, experiencing startling results of withdrawal and being caught in a spiral of dependence. This image of dependence has come to dominate the media construction of the problem, and clearly has the potential to play on the fears of many viewers, not just those taking tranquillizers. However, in the magazine format, the portrayal of dependence and withdrawal is limited to brief glimpses of patients in items interwoven with others. This is less true with programme formats which concentrate on one topic at a time.

A more unconstrained image of patient dependence was provided in *The Cook Report's* programme. Here, the dramatic and emotional potential of television imagery was given fuller range. In line with the exposé format this programme wished to go much further than simply providing evidence for consumers. Thus it focused on the story of one patient in particular, Ada, who was seen undergoing withdrawal in front of the cameras, in the presence of the presenter. She was shown in a state of extreme distress, as a result of withdrawal, underlined by the number of hours she had been without Ativan logged in on the bottom of the screen. Roger Cook's commentary, and presence in Ada's home to witness the event, underscored her distress. In one sequence Ada, who by this time was in a state of near panic, said she could not leave the house. Cook then put this to the test by opening her door to the garden and inviting her to step outside. Ada backed off in fear and apprehension. Finally, she was seen in a clinic as an in-patient undergoing an attempt at a planned and supervised withdrawal programme.

In between *That's Life's* imagery and *The Cook Report's* stands that of *Brass Tacks*. The current affairs format employed here combines elements of both filmed interview and reportage which fashions images that will help sustain a more 'measured' argument. Thus, whilst the opening sequence of *Brass Tacks* showed a male patient drawing up a syringe of blue liquid (an Ativan solution as it turns out) ready for his first 'fix' of the day, strong images of withdrawal were not in evidence. Moreover, patients were interviewed more fully and often in a more positive light, for example in their attempts to pursue normal life. The filmed report and the studio discussion of *Brass Tacks* showed patients as suffering, but also as capable of rational discussion of the issues involved. Several were invited to participate in the studio debate, alongside doctors and other experts. Unlike Ada, who when asked what she would like to do to the chairman of the company producing Ativan, replied 'I'd get a bleeding gun and shoot him', patients on *Brass Tacks* were asked to present themselves in more measured terms. In other words, though patients throughout these programmes were portrayed as largely passive victims of tranquillizer prescribing, the programmes necessarily constructed several different versions of the image, serving different programme messages.

Similarly, variations can be seen in the way in which the drugs were portrayed. By themselves, tranquillizers are innocuous in appearance. Wrapped in silver foil or stored in medicine bottles, they are like many preparations that are part of our everyday lives. But when presented as dangerous drugs they can appear frightening and fearful, just as white powder appears harmless until we are told that it is heroin or cocaine. In television, two ways have been employed to create a dramatic effect with tranquillizers. First, tranquillizers have been portrayed as drugs of 'addiction'. Each programme we have considered here opened with a sequence that either described, or showed, an individual patient 'hooked' on these drugs. On the *Brass Tacks* programme the opening sequence already mentioned, in which a man drew up his fix, was followed by pictures of packets of tablets which were then repeated throughout the programme. Second, the television pictures of the drugs themselves have enhanced the image of them as dangerous and frightening, especially in *The Cook Report*. Whilst the other formats were prepared to rely largely on descriptions of the drugs provided by the patients, *The Cook Report* created graphic representations in order to ram home its message. The drugs were shown being manufactured in large quantities, emerging from the factory production line in their thousand, or showering down from the top of the screen in a colourful cascade. As the programme unfolded this latter image was repeated no less than seven times, reinforcing the image of a massive quantity of the drugs that are made and consumed, and conveying the idea that we are almost drowning in them. Ada's hoard of tranquillizers was also used in Roger Cook's confrontation with her general practitioner.

In summary, television coverage has employed a variety of images in its portrayal of tranquillizer dependence, including vulnerable, disturbed or 'out of control' women. The dominant image here is of people from ordinary backgrounds, with a range of 'naturally occurring' problems, being overtaken by tranquillizer dependence. The main messages of the programmes, of inadequate care by general practitioners and possible negligence by drug companies, is thus constructed. It is reinforced by images of the wide availability and manufacture of the drugs themselves. However, this message takes on different meanings, depending on the formats the programmes employ. The tendency toward sensationalizing tranquillizer dependence was present in all programmes, but, inevitably perhaps, was most marked in *The Cook Report*. We shall return to the implications of these differences in the last section of this paper. They suggest that media coverage is less uniform than is often supposed, despite similarities in approach.

Narrative. In many ways, television might be thought to be heavily dependent on images, given that it is 'ephemeral, episodic, specific, concrete and dramatic in mode' (Fiske, 1987). Yet the sociological analysis of television has also drawn upon the concept of narrative in order to analyze the 'textuality' of television products. This approach to 'reading television' relies on anthropological insights into the structures of narrative as fundamental to human cultures, and on the related concepts of reality and myth, encoded and revealed by narratives. Approaching television programmes as forms of narrative requires identifying what we might call 'first order' and 'second order' levels of meaning. The first concerns the narrative of the 'real' nature of the problem in hand, in our case the emergence of tranquillizer dependence, its putative widespread or increasing occurrence, and its deleterious consequences for those affected. To this end estimates of dependence, surveys, expert views and patient experiences are all used to create a realistic narrative which establishes tranquillizers as a cause for concern. The 'second order' level of meaning creates varieties of 'deeper' emotional and symbolic forms of story telling. The oppositions involved in the narratives can be shown as follows:

> suffering : exploitation
> innocence : responsibility
> victim : culprit
> good : evil
> hero : villain

When we look at the narrative of tranquillizer dependence at a realistic level, each programme we have considered here tells a somewhat different story. In *That's Life* tranquillizers are made to fit in with its overall portrayal of 'consumer' problems. Patients' own stories are retold in the same way as those of other consumers. Such stories usually involve an 'innocent' (in retrospect possibly gullible) request for goods or services, the machinations of corrupt or incompetent providers and the promise (sometimes hoped for) of a resolution in favour of the consumer.

In *The Cook Report* this kind of story is given particularly dramatic treatment, as we have noted with the patient Ada's withdrawal episode. Here, the story of tranquillizer dependence is not simply an example or extension of the pitfalls of a consumer culture. Forces of good (patient) and evil (doctors, drug companies) are invoked which lay the foundations, and legitimize the 'denouement' of the confrontation scene, between Cook and the chairman of Wyeth. The need for such a highly dramatic scene is central to the investigatory format, whereas in consumer programmes it is more muted, interwoven as it must be with other lighter stories.

In contrast, the current affairs format of *Brass Tacks*, though it uses bold imagery and patients' stories, fashions a more 'realistic' narrative in the sense that it attempts to provide a basis for public debate. Debate, especially live studio discussion, cannot afford to generate too hot and emotional a climate. Usually the presenter/chairperson of such a debate has to tread a line between encouraging participants to put forward strong views and keeping them in check. Not only that, but the stronger the 'realism' the stronger the necessity to draw heavily on expert opinion about the objective nature of the problem in hand. In the case of tranquillizers *Brass Tacks* had to balance the stories of patients with the views and 'lines' of doctors, 'informed' public opinion in the shape of representatives of self help groups, and the official statements of representatives of regulatory bodies. The emerging 'narrative' is thus 'heavier' in tone.

As we have said, the 'second order' level of meaning in television rehearses and constructs components of a deeper form of narrative. In referring to these deeper structures the influence of Levi-Strauss (1978) and Barthes (1972) is noticeable in sociological writings. Silverstone (1988), for example, has employed a narrative framework based on notions of myth and symbol in analyzing science and its representation on television. More broadly, Fiske (1987, p. 148) has argued for this kind of analysis in approaching a wide range of television products, given that these have 'simple repeated structures' not unlike the conventions of folk tales. With respect to tranquillizer dependence three kinds of 'representation' can be mentioned at this level, drawing on the 'oppositions' laid out earlier in this section. First, we discuss suffering and responsibility; second, representations of good and evil; and third confrontation and conflict with which, we contend, television is frequently concerned. Though we think differences in format are important at this level, considerations of space restrict us to sketching out the general themes that might be explored in a more detailed analysis.

As will be clear by now, tranquillizer dependence involves considering suffering and responsibility. Mental health, and especially anxiety and depression, touches the lives of millions of people in contemporary societies. The apparent widespread availability of anti-anxiety and antidepressant drugs testifies to this fact. Yet contemporary cultures remain persistently ambiguous in their attitudes towards mental health, and drug taking. On the one hand increased 'tolerance' of diversity and difference is evident, yet so too is the need for increasing levels of social and psychological 'competence' in the management of everyday life (Hirst and Woolley, 1982). Drug taking, even that which is officially sanctioned by doctors, remains an ambivalent reality for many users (Gabe and Lipchitz-Phillips, 1984; Gabe and Thorogood, 1986b). In these circumstances the public recognition of tranquillizer dependence offers possible explanations, or 'working narratives', through which individuals may express and explore intractable personal problems. Whilst tranquillizer dependence, at the 'real' level, concerns the alleged effects of the drugs, irrespective of the mental state of the user, the programmes under review create a story which goes further than this and displace responsibility for the taking of the drugs on to doctors and drug companies. The latter are particularly culpable in the sense that they profit from the weaknesses of patients. Viewers of such programmes can identify with or distance themselves from, the problems and stories patients disclose to the cameras, and even ask themselves whether they would be prepared to do the same. Tranquillizer users are likely to be particularly 'engaged' in the programmes and may be reassured to see sources of responsibility identified in a public way. But non-users may also rehearse the moral issues of responsibility and react to the deeper issues of suffering which the programmes show. As we have seen, the exposé format is particularly concerned to identify powerful figures as culprits and thus patients as victims.

This takes us to the second and related issue, namely that of good and evil. At this point the programmes rehearse the moral order in a fuller form. Tranquillizer dependence offers a fruitful opportunity for evoking such meanings. Drug companies in particular have had a long-standing role in contemporary society as being potential symbols of evil, especially when drugs are shown to be damaging. High levels of profitability have fed into this picture, giving the impression that the companies trade off suffering and illness and remain cold and indifferent, not to say defensive, when challenged. Roger Cook's attacks on the companies in particular resonated with a deeply held view of good and evil. Cook appears as the embodiment of the fight of good against evil, in more or less dramatic ways. Such sentiments revolve around the third issue of confrontation and conflict. At this level television provides a ritualized and frequent 'working through' of social conflict. Following Elias (1978), we might say that contemporary social relations are premised on the suppression or avoidance of confrontation. Calls for consumers and now patients to be more active and demanding cut across deep structures of collectively held sentiments which seek to limit confrontation. Television, however, can rehearse and even enact such difficulties on behalf of viewers. In the case of tranquillizer dependence each of the programmes involved gave expression to the conflicts inherent in the problem of dependence, and again projected these firmly on to doctors and manufacturers. Cook's dramatic confrontation with two general practitioners and then the Chairman of Wyeth took this part of the narrative to its furthest point. Cook has in fact become famous for a series of confrontations, as has Esther Rantzen, though in line with her 'lighter' treatment of such topics this has been limited. Cook, on the other hand, has turned it into an art form. Like a postmodern knight we see him taking on the forces of evil on behalf of the innocent. As a media hero he strikes fear (we hope) into the hearts of the guilty and brings feelings of satisfaction to the wronged. As Fiske puts it: 'the hero thus has excessive meaning, extraordinary semiotic powers' (1987; p. 133).

In summary, the construction of meaning by television involves at least two aspects of narrative. The first of these, the 'realistic' narrative, presents a picture of the world that 'imposes coherence and resolution upon a world that has neither' (Fiske, 1987; p. 130). The story must unfold in a natural way, present causal connections and be sufficient unto itself. In each of the programmes reviewed here, tranquillizer dependence was portrayed as being caused by doctors overprescribing and companies willfully imposing potentially dangerous drugs on the public, without due regard for their side effects. The sequence of events from first receiving a prescription for a tranquillizer through to the reality of withdrawal symptoms appears as a series of self evident steps. In this way programmes in their different ways could quickly and effectively construct the meaning of dependence as a 'reality'. But the story goes beyond this level to construct a moral tale in which suffering and responsibility can be worked through. On the basis of these narratives tranquillizer dependence on television takes on elements a modern myth. The construction of its meaning moves between realist and symbolic levels, not so much to resolve the issues but to focus on them and allow the audience to work through them. Quite how these audiences' responses take shape is the focus of the next and final section of the paper.

Reception and Appropriation

In this section we want to consider the 'effects' of the media products we have been describing and analyzing. As Fejes (1984) notes, a critical media studies has tended to ignore this issue, preferring instead to concentrate on the control, production and content of media messages. Yet questions about the reception and appropriation of media content need to be addressed in order to demonstrate the significance of identifying the range of meanings found in such content. Focusing on 'effects' does not mean, however, that we accept unproblematically the traditional stimulus-response model of human behaviour and media impact. On the contrary, as we argued earlier, we see individual viewers as active interpreters of media messages, responding to what they see and hear within particular social contexts (Thompson, 1988). Moreover, we do not see individuals as the sole unit of analysis for assessing the impact of programmes. The responsiveness of institutions to media content also needs to be considered. In what follows we sketch out the 'effects' of the media products we have been considering at both an individual and institutional level, before turning finally to assess their cultural and ideological impact. Our analysis at this stage is only suggestive pending further, more systematic research in this area. However it does identify certain important differences in the apparent impact of the programmes which would seem to justify the analytic approach we have adopted.

The response of viewers. Most research into media 'effects' starts with the size of audience viewing figures. Although such data tell us little about how particular programmes are received they provide an important base line for comparison. In the case of the tranquillizer programmes *That's Life* was seen by the largest audience, averaging about 10 million for each of the four programmes which featured tranquillizers. *The Cook Report* was seen by 6 million viewers while *Brass Tacks* recorded a figure of about 2.5 million for each of its two programmes.

More interesting are the data about the number of phone calls and letters received by the programme makers as these give some idea of the extent to which viewers had reacted to the content transmitted. According to the producers whom we interviewed after the programmes had been transmitted, they had each been surprised by the level of response which was considered significantly higher than the norm. Each of them also reported that the telephone lines had been jammed after the broadcasts and that they had received an unusually large post bag. In the case of *That's Life* 1,000 letters were received in the period immediately after the first programme and 40,000 people took up its invitation following the programme in May 1984, to write to MIND for a leaflet on tranquillizers (Lacey and Woodward, 1985). *Brass Tacks* and *The Cook Report* said that they had received far more letters than they normally did although the numbers did not compare with *That's Life*. In the case of *Brass Tacks* about 40 letters were received compared with 120 at *The Cook Report*. This suggests that while all three programmes had struck a chord with at least a proportion of their viewers *That's Life* had achieved the largest viewer reaction.

The institutional response. Three key institutions were frequently referred to or implicated in the different tranquillizer programmes, namely the medical profession, the pharmaceutical industry and the state. While the first two of these were criticized in all the programmes only *The Cook Report* identified them unequivocally as 'wrong doers' that needed to be brought to book for their misdemeanours. Not surprisingly they reacted more strongly to the latter programme than to the others.

In the case of the pharmaceutical industry a debate developed in its trade magazine *Scrip* (Brown, 1988; Klein, 1988) about whether companies should accept the media's invitation to participate — the view of their public relations executives and advisers — or whether they should stay away from any media discussion of the issue, as their lawyers argued. The latter approach had been adopted by Wyeth, the frontline company identified with the tranquillizer problem, when it had been approached by *Brass Tacks*, and was advocated by one commentator on the grounds that it forced the programme to concentrate on the 'real' issues — doctor diagnosis and prescribing and the cause of the patients' anxiety — instead of making the company the 'scapegoat', as was said to have happened in *The Cook Report*. The other commentator argued that 'keeping your head down' and refusing to be interviewed laid a company open to the charge of 'cover up' and had the effect of increasing rather than decreasing media and public interest in the story. Whatever the strategy, however, what was at issue here was not simply the image of the industry but how to fend off media 'attacks' in the light of legal claims for compensation from patients dependent on tranquillizers.

As for the medical profession, we have no systematic evidence about its reaction, but it seems clear from informal interviews we have conducted with GPs that they felt unjustly castigated by *The Cook Report*. This was adjudged to be the 'last straw' in a campaign which amounted to 'trial by media'. We also understand from the producer of *The Cook Report* that the Independent Broadcasting Authority felt that Roger Cook had exceeded the bounds of responsible journalism by 'door-stepping' general practitioners, and made it clear that they did not want a repetition of such behaviour with GPs in future. This reflects the mixed feelings about doctors being a target for programmes made within the exposé format. Perhaps we should also note that some doctors have responded in the medical press by trying to shift the blame from themselves and the pharmaceutical companies back to the patient (Tyrer, 1989).

The third key institution, the state, was not castigated explicitly in any of the programmes and did not feel the need to respond directly to what was transmitted. The government agency, the Committee on the Safety of Medicines, has come under considerable pressure to review the safety of Ativan in particular. As yet, however, it has not made any explicit recommendation about this drug, although it has issued general guidelines about restricting the prescribing of benzodiazepines as a class of drug. Moreover, it could be argued that the state's appreciation of the size of the audience response to these programmes has encouraged it to contribute £70,000 to the funding of a help-line on tranquillizers, run by Broadcasting Support Services in conjunction with the lunch-time BBC television magazine programme *Daytime Live*, one day a week between November 1988 and April 1989.

Cultural and ideological effects. Having sketched out the nature of individual and institutional responses we now want finally to consider the cultural and ideological effects of these programmes. At the cultural level we suggest that all three have been responsible for legitimating tranquillizer dependence as a public issue. This has been achieved by providing claims-makers with a terrain for debating the issue and an opportunity to offer ever increasing estimates about the number thought to be dependent. All of the programmes have also been responsible for amplifying this concern insofar as they have all drawn parallels between benzodiazepines and illicit drug use. As we have argued elsewhere (Gabe and Bury, 1988) the present climate in Britain is one of extreme concern if not outright panic over the use of illegal drugs, with the growth in their use being described as 'this greatest menace in peace time' (Home Affairs Committee, 1985). Given this greater sensitivity to the deleterious effects of illegal drug use, drawing parallels between them and benzodiazepines is likely to have heightened public concern about the dangers involved in taking tranquillizers and the morality of doing so.

At the same time, given the variation in media content of the programmes, one would expect some to have been more responsible for amplifying concern than others. Thus one would predict that *The Cook Report* with the exposé style would be more likely to have such an effect than, say, *Brass Tacks* with its current affairs approach. The former programme's decision to show for the first time on British television a patient withdrawing from Ativan illustrates the point nicely, though as we have noted, *Brass Tacks* did begin its coverage by showing a person preparing a 'fix' of Ativan. However *The Cook Report*, by presenting powerful images of the suffering involved in withdrawal without cautioning viewers that many benzodiazepine users (especially those taking drugs other than Ativan) do not suffer such effects, could be said to have intensified public concern unnecessarily.

As for their ideological impact we would suggest that all three programmes encouraged viewers to think primarily in individualized terms about benzodiazepines. This was achieved by presenting the users of these drugs as mainly weak and vulnerable individuals rather than as active members of particular social groups. Thus no attempt was made to explain why it is that women are twice as likely to be dependent on these drugs as men. According to Downing (1980) this may reflect a failure on the part of journalists to see women's issues as newsworthy. It may, however, simply be a direct consequence of their subordinate position in society.

It could be argued that the programmes were willing to take on the structure of power in society in the form of GPs and the pharmaceutical industry, although only one programme, *The Cook Report*, set up outright confrontation. And even here the challenge related only to the power of *individual* doctors to prescribe and a chief executive to continue marketing Ativan despite growing concern about the drug's safety. As such the programme could be said to be reinforcing viewers' faith in medical authority and capitalism by bringing to book particular 'villains', rather than questioning the more general structures in which they operate. This interpretation is given further weight when one realizes that the programme made no attempt to consider mechanisms for increasing lay participation in the 'policing' of the medical profession or alternative forms of ownership, control or accountability for the pharmaceutical industry.

Conclusion

This paper has attempted to develop an analysis of the ways in which the media have enhanced the social problem status of tranquillizers as a result of its coverage of these drugs' dependence potential and associated problems of withdrawal. Taking television as the focus for our analysis we have sought to demonstrate that it does not simply provide a vehicle for the claims-making activities of particular professional and lay groups but has its own interests and agenda. Moreover, these interests are not necessarily homogeneous as is sometimes assumed and can be influenced by the format within which the programme makers are working. In order to explore this point we have identified three formats which have been used in the television coverage of tranquillizers and have traced the ways in which these have influenced the production and diffusion of programmes and the construction of messages. Furthermore, variations in the reception and appropriation of the content of the programmes governed by these different formats have been identified where possible.

We have shown that while all three formats have encouraged a certain amount of sensationalism which has helped legitimate tranquillizer dependence as a social problem, they have differed as regards the extent to which this has been so. Thus the exposé format, with its search for villains to blame, has been the most prone to sensationalism, while the current affairs format, with its emphasis on debate, has been the least prone to this form of coverage. Despite these differences we have at this stage only been able to sketch out the variation in the responses of different audiences. It seems that these audiences have reacted to the programmes in different ways, reflecting not only the degree of sensationalism involved but also the social context they inhabit.

Clearly, more systematic research on the reactions to these different formats needs to be undertaken before we can fully substantiate our claim about the varying role of media products in the legitimation of tranquillizers as a social problem. Yet this does not undermine the point that the media have played a vital role in developing this as a public issue through their influence on different audiences. The role of the media in shaping perceptions and beliefs about health should now be firmly placed on the research agenda.

Chapter 7

Regulating our Favourite Drug

Robin Bunton

Introduction

The last twenty years have seen the emergence of a new discourse on drinking problems. The new discourse is associated with the new public health perspective on alcohol which is more ambitious than previous thinking, both in the way it conceives of the problem and the wide ranging measures it advocates to combat them. It calls for considerable expansion of operations and a coordinated, multi-sectoral programme of action. Some of the more recent elaborations of this perspective have been presented in the spate of Royal College reports on Alcohol Misuse (Royal College of Psychiatrists, 1986; Royal College of Physicians, 1987; Royal College of General Practitioners, 1986) and in recent World Health Organisation literature (WHO, 1981). It is argued here that these developments should be seen as part of broader shifts in our social regulation and control mechanisms; a move favouring more dispersed, non-segregative and community-based approaches. Such mechanisms, which are often introduced for humanitarian reasons, have significantly extended previous systems of control. This paper plots the emergence of a public health perspective on alcohol misuse and situates it within broader developments in both crime prevention and health fields. Some of the recently advocated measures are considered as mechanisms of drinking discipline. Finally, some conclusions are drawn for contemporary policy on alcohol use and misuse.

The Emergence of the Public Health Perspective

Modern societies have formulated 'the social liquor question' in different ways, exhibiting concerns for public order, productivity and public health (Makela and Viikari, 1977) as well as the desire to instil bourgeois discipline in the new proletariat (Harrison, 1971; Gusfield, 1963; Blocker, 1976). The underlying theme of addiction has dominated both the temperance movements of the nineteenth century and the focus on the 'disease' of alcoholism which developed in the 1930s (Levine, 1978). The last two decades, however, have seen the rise of the 'post addiction', or public health model of drinking problems as part of a new social regulatory mechanism. The public health perspective on alcohol misuse has four distinct features; a broader definition of the range of problems, a non-segregationistic conception of problems and solutions to them, a community focus, and advocacy of an increasingly broad range of interventions. All of these aspects can be identified in recent theoretical and policy discourse. Concepts of habituation, addiction and dependence have been refined and replaced by a more sophisticated, 'relational' concept of alcohol misuse which sees problem drinking emerging from the interaction of alcohol, the drinker and the social and physical environment (Davies and Walsh, 1983). Drinking and problem drinking are situated in a psycho/social complex and are subject to a balance of promoting and restraining forces and conflicts (Edwards and Gross, 1976; Heather and Robertson, 1981).

The new thinking and nosology brought new populations under the gaze of the alcohologist (Kreitman, 1986) and renewed concerns for the drinking of the population as a whole (Bruun, Edwards, Lumio, Makela, Pan, Popham, Room, Schmidt, Skog, Sulkunen and Osterberg, 1975; Ledermann, 1956, 1964; Skog, 1973, 1974) as well as national policy controls. A new type of public health focus emerged superseding earlier attempts to apply the prevention of infectious disease model (Gordon, 1956; Blane, 1976; Plunkett and Gordon, 1960). The 'new public health' addresses problem-prevention by manipulating the detail of the drinking individual's physical and social context on the one hand (Room, 1974, 1981; Gusfield, 1976), and the national policy on the other. More pervasive intervention measures have been developed with a concern for the detail of everyday life.

Much of the literature on problem drinking of the 1970s and 1980s has focused on community-based approaches (Stockwell and Clement, 1987) in a similar manner to drug misuse prevention and treatment policy (Stimson, 1987) and as part of overlapping movement in the mental health field (Orford 1985). In the community there have been discovered new sites for intervention and new potential for exerting force and restraint on drinking behaviour, introducing increasingly detailed regulation. The case for exploiting community resources to the full has been made in arguments for primary and secondary preventative action. 'Naturally occurring responses' may be drawn upon (Yates and Hebblethwaite, 1985) as well as a very wide variety of networks and unlikely agents which can be brought together for cumulative impact (Robinson, 1987).

Some of the impetus for this type of focus would seem to come as a reaction to over-reliance on 'control measures' such as taxation and pricing policies, licensing restrictions, bans on advertising and other national measures to influence demand and supply. Campaigning for such measures is said to divert attention from the wealth of effective local, often unrecognized, and relatively cheaply administered interventions which do not require central government involvement (Tether and Robinson, 1986). Tether (1987) argues for identifying the 'prevention potential' of communities and organizations and coordinating this to form a net of restraints and promotions to counter alcohol misuse. Such measures, he argues, impinge least on the rights and privileges of individuals and involve less state encroachment on civil or market liberties (Tether, 1987). The characterization of civil liberties, rights and state encroachment in this way may, however, oversimplify policy options. Issues of individual freedom and liberty in relation to public health action on drugs and alcohol may require a more complex moral philosophy (Bakalar and Grinspoon, 1984; Thompson, 1983). More than this, it is possible that the new discourse on alcohol misuse is itself a part of the regulatory mechanism and represents a new development in the control and regulation of our drinking.

The emergent public health paradigm on alcohol misuse encompasses and extends the fields of its predecessors, broadening the arenas of concern. Such significant and profound changes as have occurred over a relatively short period of time in the work and discourse of those working to reduce alcohol misuse are not achieved in isolation. These changes can be situated within broad changes in social and health policy and in the criminal justice system of the latter half of the twentieth century. Documentation of such changes has also voiced doubts and caution on elements of the new systems which are relevant to changes in the field of alcohol.

Changing Mechanisms of Social Control

Recent study has documented a major shift in the ideology and apparatus of social regulation and control in twentieth-century Western society. This recent change is one of two transformations linked to the development of the modern state. An initial transformation occurred at the end of the eighteenth century which introduced a highly centralized system of dealing with deviants, based upon their differentiation and segregation in institutional settings according to type — the asylum, the prison, the workhouse or the hospital. The rise of such institutional regimes and their place in early capitalist society has been well documented (Scull, 1977a; Foucault, 1967, 1973, 1977; Rothman, 1980). The second, and current, transformation has formulated a solution to deviancy which is characterized by a pervasive, dispersed or decentred social control apparatus (Cohen, 1985; Garland, 1985; Ignatieff, 1983). The move to the current, emergent system has involved a period of destructuring of older institutional forms of care and control (Cohen, 1985). Community-based forms of treatment and correction have emerged in a process Scull refers to as 'decarceration' (Scull, 1977b). This transformation has pervaded all technologies for dealing with deviance — drinking deviance included.

The move away from state centralization, from rigid professional control and from the institution characteristic of destructuring, reflected many of the concerns of the 1960s. The anti-institutionalism, anti-bureaucratism, anti-professionalism and pro-community sentiments of that period frequently drew on the work of social scientists for support (Goffman, 1961; Becker, 1963; Lement, 1967). Whilst mediated by the current political and social forms the new mechanism was to create its own dynamic and in turn mediate current social forces. Much of the analysis of the current change rests on Foucault's archeology of modern forms of discourse, particularly the birth of the modern disciplines (Foucault, 1977). Examining the birth of the prison, he documents a shift from forms of punishment that demonstrated the arbitrary power of the monarch, represented by the spectacle of the scaffold and physical torture, toward a system which separates prisoners into individual cells and subjects them to constant surveillance and regulation of movement. Epitomized by Bentham's panopticon, a new structure introduced methods of monitoring, regulating, training, dividing and classifying behaviour in increasingly more detailed ways.

An extension of these developments presents itself in the criminal justice system where a whole range of community alternatives and corrections have replaced institutional solutions. These include: pre- and post-trial diversion, releases (pre-trial, supervised and semi-supervised), pre-sentence investigation, post-adjudication units, community residential units, homes and fostering, halfway houses, outward bound projects, day centres and drop-ins, weekend detention and semi-detention, intermediate treatment, community service orders, reparation projects and reconciliation, citizen alert programmes, block watches, crime-watch style media programmes, neighbourhood watch schemes and many other intelligence and intervention measures (Cohen, 1985). As well as dealing with traditional groups of deviants these mechanisms could encompass a growing clientele of potential deviants. The new methods work in more detailed ways forming a network of corrections that in total constitute an impressively comprehensive system — especially when merged with more traditional incarceration methods.

Similar movement can be found in twentieth-century health care. Foucault himself (1973) documented the birth of modern medicine in the establishment of the clinic in and around the late eighteenth century which took individual bodies at its focus. In the early decades of the twentieth century, however, medical knowledge became located more and more in the Dispensary, taking the community as its focus (Armstrong, 1983). Social relationships were made visible and open to surveillance as medicine shifted its gaze to the social group. Patients were no longer isolated from their communities for private consultation but were treated in a newly constructed social context. New types of associated analysis emerged such as the study of health behaviour (Armstrong, 1988). A new public health emerged during the early part of this century which had new concerns including: the mother and child, nursing care, the school health service, health education, mental health services, dental health, medical social services, the handicapped child, care of the family and welfare of the elderly (Ashton and Seymour, 1988). Whereas the old public health concerns were with the environment and its effects on individuals, under the new public health relationships and social groups have become a legitimate concern. Preventative medicine has taken as its focus the community and the minutiae of social life. Health can be promoted, and concepts of positive health justify interventions aimed at the population as a whole — not simply the ill. At risk groups can be identified by epidemiologists and singled out for action. Certain illness categories (such as TB) have become subject to 'notification' to facilitate surveillance. The Dispensary has become an observing eye on the community.

Medicine, then, extended its concerns in the middle of the twentieth century and contributed, from another direction, to the web of mechanisms which constitute a new form of discipline, social regulation and control. Similar arguments to those in the criminal justice field justified and motivated this shift (Armstrong, 1983; Balint, 1957) as well concern for the crisis in health care provision in the 1970s (Allsop, 1984). Changes in criminal justice and in health care provision can be seen to be part of a broader change in society's regulatory mechanisms. In both fields the concerns of professionals extended beyond institutional walls into the body of the community, extending with them the total socio-administrative complex, and changing the ways in which individuals and groups relate to one another. Measures currently being used, or advocated, to combat alcohol related problems form part of the extended arsenal of the health and criminal justice occupations, as well as that of the alcohol worker.

Alcohol appears as one of the major features of the new public health movement. It is one of the 'new diseases' towards which health for all by the year 2000 is being directed (WHO, 1981). The broad programme of relevant intervention ranges from that of the general practitioner to the school and to the social services. Alcohol also features in major programmes aimed at crime prevention involving probation services, magistrates, prison officers, the police and lawyers. Many such areas are addressed by the report of the Home Office's Working Group on Young People and Alcohol (Home Office, 1987). The breadth of responses included in both health and criminal justice fields are summarized in the recent Government Circular on Alcohol Misuse (DHSS/Welsh Office, 1989). Current alcohol misuse policy, then, may be located within broader shifts in social and health policy and within the arrival of the disciplinary society. Though falling broadly between these two fields it would be incorrect to see these fields as rigid entities in themselves. Health and crime prevention disciplinary methods are merely a whole number of authorities to be invoked; that of the psychiatrist, the teacher, the doctor, the psychologist, etc. Foucault's political anatomy is not an item in itself for discovery but:

> It is rather a multiplicity of often minor processes, of different origin and scattered location, which overlap, repeat, or imitate one another, support

one another, distinguish themselves from one another according to their realm of application, converge and gradually produce the blueprint of a general method (Foucault 1977, p. 138).

It is in this dispersed form that the drinking disciplines find their current manifestations, and to these that they contribute. They become ideal carriers of the new disciplines.

Documentation of this profound transformation has also raised doubts and second thoughts about its direction. It has been observed that the recent changes, in almost every respect, run counter to their ideological justifications (Cohen, 1985). Scull and others argued that the shifts were not motivated simply by 'humane' intentions (Scull, 1981, 1983), and emerged from within a welfare infrastructure that was becoming too costly to justify. The moves to the community were also ahead of evaluations proving efficacy, or even cost effectiveness. Moreover, the new methods themselves had 'inhumane' elements. More disturbing was that the changes did not seem to be reducing the numbers of people under care or control. The system had simply enlarged itself, encompassing newer forms of deviance and building wider and stronger nets (Austin and Krisberg, 1981). The new mode of control was more subtle, more persuasive and more insidious. The critique raised questions about the nature of enlightened and progressive policy. Doubts cast on decarceration as a panacea for crime prevention and correction and treatment of the mentally ill can also be applied to measures to reduce alcohol related problems. The regulatory and control potential of newer measures to combat alcohol misuse also needs highlighting.

Modes of Regulation

The public health paradigm of alcohol offers enormous scope of multi-level intervention and multi-sectoral collaboration. The range of measures currently being proposed under its auspices staggers. Some of the measures put forward by the Royal Colleges in a spate of recent reports on alcohol misuse are listed in Table 7.1. The perspective gives licence to recommend national level fiscal and legal policy reform on the one hand and micro-level community measures on the other. The general question of overall consumption levels of society is of interest, as well as the detail of more specific problems of inappropriate drinking practices in the workplace. The same breadth of interest can be found in the recent report of the Ministerial Group on Alcohol Misuse which, like its establishment, enacts many of these recommendations (Ministerial Group on Alcohol Misuse, 1989).

Such recommendations would require a wide range of community agents. Orford (1987) gives a list of such agents which includes: general hospitals, health visitors, district nurses, general hospital staff, psychiatric hospital staff and community mental

Table 7.1 Some recommended measures to reduce alcohol related harm, advanced in recent Royal College reports

Prevent a further rise in any of the available indices of alcohol-related harm – such as liver cirrhosis death rate, drunkenness and drunk driving offences, and hospital admissions for alcohol dependence.

Improve consultation and working cooperation between different government departments to ensure an intergrated, effective and visible response.

Employ Government taxation policies in the interest of health.

Greatly enhance Government commitment towards public information and education (and relevant evaluative research).

Encourage public disapproval of intoxication, and foster the attitude that it is bad manners to get drunk (rather than that it is bad manners to comment on drunkenness).

Support initiatives for international recognition of the health and social implications relating to import and export of alcoholic beverages rather than accepting the dominance of the economic interest.

Set up special preventive programmes for high risk trades or professions, in collaboration with trades unions or appropriate professional organizations.

Encourage members of the community to acknowledge people who are drinking excessively and show the same active concern as they would towards any other potentially dangerous behaviour.

Ensure every person accepts responsibility for his or her own personal prevention programmes by not exceeding the daily intake level suggested. Ask every person seen in general practice or in hospital about his or her alcohol intake as a matter of routine, along with questions about smoking and medication.

Require all professions to provide training on alcohol misuse.

Ensure doctors take the lead in defining drinking habits in their practice by means of questionnaires, breath alcohol measurements and blood tests.

Encourage corporations to adopt comprehensive alcohol policies.

Reduce annual per capita consumption to about 5 litres (or 2 units a day) over the next ten years.

Increase the real price of alcohol over the next five to ten years.

Formulate more stringent rules for alcohol advertising to protect the young who are particularly vulnerable.

Restrict sponsorship of sport and the arts by the liquor industry.

Require all alcoholic drinks to show the quantity of alcohol on the container in simple measures that the average individual can understand.

Take a tougher stance on 'drinking and driving'.

Table 7.1 Continued

Avoid licensing liberalization.

Make money available from the tax on alcoholic drinks for education and research on alcohol problems; operational research especially devoted to detection and prevention should be encouraged.

Form a single Government body to coordinate all aspects of alcohol use and abuse.

(Royal College of Psychiatrists, 1986, Royal College of Physicians, 1987, Royal College of General Practitioners, 1986)

---

health staff (CMH teams, community psychiatric nurses, etc.), social services, services for children or adolescents and their families (medical, psychiatric, social and voluntary), services for the elderly, clergy and voluntary organizations (including Citizens Advice, Samaritans, Marriage Guidance, Women's Aid), local authority housing departments, probation services, magistrates, courts, prisons, police, lawyers, single homeless people and casual users of night shelters, reception centres and cheap commercial hostel accommodation, the workplace (including employers, personnel officers, industrial medical officers, company nurses and colleagues), teachers, licensed premises (especially public houses), family and friends. To effect a coordinated response new and previously unthought of groups are also being encouraged to form new alliances. Robinson makes this point in a plea to exploit five major networks; law and order, health and safety, advertising and the media, employment and education (Robinson, 1987). When confronted in total, these measures begin to assume a presence that is much more significant than the sum of the parts. A brief examination can suggest that there are already a number of regulatory mechanisms at work in numerous areas of our lives. Categorization of such measures, like any attempt at delineating social regulation and control, may be difficult. Here a suggested starting point is Foucault's modes of institutional discipline (Foucault, 1977).

In *Discipline and Punish* Foucault identifies the emergence of a diffuse set of disciplinary methods exercising control over the body through the introduction of sets of techniques which work in detailed and specific ways to optimize the capabilities of the body whilst, simultaneously, rendering it docile. The new methods were developed by the meticulous observation and recording, regulation and training of the monastery, the school, the barracks, the hospital and the workhouse, and worked by regulating the individual and group. The principles of normalization and training could be levelled not only at institutions' inmates but also at populations in general. There existed not only an 'anatomo-politics of the body' but also a 'bio-politics of the population' (Smart, 1979). It is these latter means of social regulation which have been particularly central to new public health movements of the twentieth century and the development of what Armstrong describes as the Dispensary (Armstrong, 1983). The modes of regulation which concern us here are what Foucault refers to as the art of distributions, the control of activity, the organization of genesis and the composition of forces. A systematic consideration of these categories is not possible here; however, elaborating on these, the remainder of the paper illustrates similar modes of regulation in some areas of current drinking disciplines, taking up three of these modes.

The art of distributions is described by Foucault as the means of isolation and location of individuals in space in specific functional sites — normally referring to the differentiation of the asylum, prison or similar institution. By focusing on the community the disciplinary complex (epitomized architecturally by the Benthamite panopticon design) locates individuals and groups into types and orders, suited to differentiated attention and corrective regime. As the institution physically divides and differentiates its population, equally the community gaze of the epidemiologist, alcohologist, general practitioner and the researcher, dissects, maps, codifies, and differentiates populations, according different groups varying statuses and priorities according to particular taxonomies. Groups are identified as subject to varying risk factors. They are attributed with particular qualities and allocated to particular intervention regimes. The analysis of drinking patterns is replete with increasingly more acute and detailed dissection of drinking communities.

The method of analysis is indicative of changing concerns. Recording and documenting drinking was until quite recently a matter of analyzing units of consumption — barrels, bottles and other production measures. The Royal Commission on Liquor Licensing relied on this data quality as late as 1932. In fact this method of analysis is still appropriate for much of the world's data gathering on this subject where a public perspective does not prevail (Bruun et al., 1975). Current methods of analysis, however, are no longer satisfied with quantities of alcohol production figures but require detailed and searching survey and questionnaire analysis. More recent surveys in both regular OPCS reports and the General Household Survey catalogue average consumption levels each week, the numbers of light, moderate and heavy drinkers, abstainers, when, where and which beverage is being drunk, in the presence of whom and with what consequences (Wilson, 1980; OPCS, 1989). The unit (a measure based on bodily metabolism) is used to assess quantity, similarly effecting a shift to a more detailed analysis. Attitudes towards drinking are recorded along with perception of levels of harm. This information is made available by sex, age, region and social class. Moreover, accurate contrasts can be made between each year to detail trends over increasingly short time periods. Never before has so much been known about the nature of the nation's drinking. Uniformity or record-keeping on drinking habits has been recognized as a key to international alcohol policy development in the public health perspective (WHO, 1980). It is from such figures that the numbers of problem drinkers have been estimated (Orford, 1985) and around which estimates of the extent and social cost of this harm are built (Maynard, 1985). The development of the concept of the 'at risk' group of drinkers is dependent upon this more accurate data gathering.

More reliable epidemiological evidence enabled the development of the category of 'unsafe drinking levels' now so readily accepted and a part of a consensus of medical opinion on this topic (Royal College of Psychiatrists, 1986). Such groupings of 'unsafe drinkers' have themselves entered the data gathering process, further refining the analysis of 'at risk' groups such as women, young people, the elderly, young men and particular occupations. This information spawns theories about the qualities and behaviour of such groups.

Identification of groupings and patterns of consumption cannot be separated from measures introduced to regulate them. Particular groups are the target of health promotion campaigns, law enforcement campaigns, specific early identification efforts, community-based prevention initiatives, school education programmes, workplace employee assistance programmes, drink drive campaigns and other regulatory measures. These measures can be categorized by another mode of discipline described by Foucault as the control of activity. This mechanism would seem to refer to means of regulating the body and its gestures within defined activities and temporal patterns. There is a concern with the body, the correlates of gesture, its exhastive use and temporal elaboration.

A number of features of drinking disciplines correspond to these developments. On the one hand there has been a concentration on the timing of drinking activities. It might be said that the recent relaxation of the drinking hours in Britain runs counter to this regulation, repealing much of the regulation established as a defence of the realm measure during the First World War (Dorn, 1983). Yet, these measures have not been totally swept away and new measures directed at individuals' and communities' drinking have been introduced in other areas. In Coventry, and four other cities, a ban on outdoor drinking practices in the city centre is an instance of such regulation. By far the most pervasive example of this type of regulation is the widespread adoption of a method of plotting and quantifying drinking — the drinking diary. The diary has become a standard tool of counselling and advice work but also of public education and self-help manuals (Robertson and Heather, 1986). Working with diaries individuals are encouraged to monitor daily or half daily, what, when and where drinking occurs, totalling their amounts in standard quantities or 'units' (themselves based upon average metabolism rates). The diary represents an attempt at systematized analysis and regulation of intake to within agreed-upon safe limits. It attempts to install an intoxication calculus around which personal 'choices' are made (in the case of public education work) or behavioural programmes are established (in the case of counselling and advice). The diary epitomizes a concern for the maximization of bodily potential and the eradication of harmful, inefficient drinking patterns. It is a self development device to be used in a whole variety of settings and has been applied in other areas of public health concern (Coxon, 1987).

Coupled with the concept of excessive drinking by quantity is a concern for appropriate drinking relative to place. Drinking patterns have been deemed inappropriate to certain activities and settings. Drinking and driving is the most significant single example of this in recent years, though recommendations concerning other activities are also available. Drinking whilst at work or when involved in particularly 'crucial activities' — working with machinery, or managing complex work patterns or relationships — is felt to be in need of regulation. Regulation of workplace drinking activity has manifested itself in the introduction of workplace policies and practices aimed at regulating alcohol-related production and labour problems. A large number of policies have been introduced in a whole range of industrial settings (International Labour Office, 1987). Common principles of policies include: monitoring of the labour force for early signs of a problem; provision of advice, sick leave and help for those who develop difficulties; education about alcohol; and guidelines and restrictions concerning consumption of alcohol in the workplace.

Some of the reasoning and motivation behind the introduction of such systems is obvious. The majority of problem drinkers are economically active and the use of 'constructive coercion' (the threat of unemployment) may be particularly beneficial to their prognosis. It has been recognized that the workplace is a particularly good site for the monitoring and surveillance of behaviour. There has, however, been little examination of how problems or 'at risk' groups are constructed and whose interests come to bear upon such work (Alexander, 1988). For most people, work is the most highly structured part of their daily life. The signs and symptoms of developing an alcohol problem are constant, predictable and identifiable at the workplace. A fall-off in work performance is easily recognized and problems tend to be harder to hide (International Labour Office, 1987). There are clear advantages in reduction of lost production by the introduction of such policies. By providing a more detailed monitoring of the workforce they may also add to employment disciplines in more detailed ways. Foucault has again commented on the development of such disciplines as part of industrial development. The creation of a docile labour force whose efforts may be more efficiently co-ordinated and organized around newer production processes may be another reason for the development and persistence of such methods (Lea, 1979).

A final area of parallel between drinking disciplines and institutional modes of discipline can be found around what Foucault has referred to as the composition of forces. Discipline is not simply a matter of mobilizing bodies: it must place this activity within a distribution designed to maximize and coordinate overall effect with machine-like efficiency. The composition of alcohol disciplines is necessary for the maximization of the dispersed activities referred to here. Some indication of the movement toward this is apparent in the stress on coordination. Coordinated action on alcohol is called for in a great many of the recommendations typical of public health literature on alcohol misuse. The recent Government Circular on alcohol misuse is explicit on this matter and epitomizes one approach to the development of drinking disciplines (DHSS/Welsh Office, 1989).

The Circular calls for the arrangement of local action built on a local assessment of the nature of the problems and the range of resources available to counter them. It calls for a wide range of statutory and voluntary bodies to combine with the private sector in concerted action on all fronts. Particular stress is placed upon the gathering of more detailed information to build a complete picture in more systematic records of the different manifestations of the problem. Information will be needed on health problems, crime and disorder, alcohol and work policies, medical treatment, counselling and rehabilitation facilities and professional education and training. Information, it is suggested, should be used for building 'a coordinated strategy and action plan for improving the management and deployment of resources' (DHSS/Welsh Office, 1989). Special projects and studies from around the country are recommended as illustrative of flexibly managed local solutions. These include: the Coventry City Centre Alcohol Related Crime Project, the Newport Alcohol Abuse and Social Disorder Demonstration Project, the Sussex Licensing Project, Voluntary Identity Card Schemes, and Brentwood's Pub Watch Scheme. Such schemes will be monitored and used as illustrations of good practice by the Government. As well as illustrating a national approach to the composition of forces these recommendations highlight a number of detailed drinking disciplines currently in progress. The circular gives a fairly clear indication of the direction of alcohol prevention and control measures we might expect to find towards the end of the century.

It would seem, then, that some parallels can be made between more general disciplinary development as outlined by Foucault in reference to institutional and segregation measures and those measures currently forming the public health bulwark against alcohol misuse. These measures are not usually placed within the broad framework of social control, nor are the unintended consequences in social control or regulation normally highlighted. Such questioning is difficult in the light of extensive suffering caused by alcohol consumption. It is, however, a curiously neglected area of discussion by sociologists and policy analysts considering the vigorous debate in other areas of social and health policy. This debate will raise a number of issues in alcohol policy formulation.

Discussion

Our current understanding and response to alcohol problems can be seen as a product of social structure and accepted approaches to social and health policy. Current approaches to the alcohol problem are part of more general concerns with crime prevention, health care and social care provision which contrast with previous solutions to the social liquor problem. The present dispersed disciplines that form part of drinking regulation, calling upon these forms of authority, appear in an extremely wide range of institutions and community settings. As alcohol is held to be everybody's business, it would seem that everybody's business is becoming that of the alcohologist, and all areas of our lives may be subject to his or her gaze. As such, alcohol disciplines appear to be ideal carriers of the new disciplinary measures outlined by social control analysts.

The public health perspective would appear to get to the parts that previous discourses have not reached. The post-addiction period of alcohol misuse analysis is significantly more pervasive than its predecessors. This recent transformation, however, has received little critical attention from policy analysts or sociologists. In fact, to the contrary, sociologists have in the main worked to enhance and develop both the new paradigm and the development of its recommendations. Being complicit, they have been unable to assess any unintended consequences of these new measures or plot their implications for social regulation. Such analysis is overdue and critical attention should be turned to this area as well as other related public health themes. Such analysis has much to offer the study of alcohol policy. In particular it throws into question the debate over control versus non-control. Current discourse on alcohol works with a more traditional view of the exercise of power in which control measures are assumed to work in highly centralized, top-down ways restraining and guiding individual behaviour — more usually aimed at reducing per capita consumption. It positions the state's influence on one side, in opposition, for good or bad, to individual freedom of choice in the market-place and elsewhere. This view identifies centralized responses by government, such as price and supply regulation, as control measures, yet sees localized intervention as relatively benign in control effect.

The new system of social control, described earlier, identifies dispersed, local control mechanisms instituted by a range of organizations, professionals and individuals in new more detailed and inventive ways. Under these conditions traditional oppositions are questionable, or at least make up only one axis of the control matrix. Individual freedom is not gauged simply by contrast with centralized forms of control. Whilst state control and encroachment might exist, they are only part of a broader system of control in which the individual is regulated in many different ways. Localized, community-based approaches have their own control potential. The sum of small, detailed regulation must be accounted for in any estimation of control consequences. Wilkinson (1970) is one of few authors to consider the costs of prevention measures in broad spectrum. There is a need to review the control potential of newer localized forms of intervention and to reformulate more traditional views of control. The issue of control as used by alcohologists has been developed elsewhere (Bunton, forthcoming).

In formulating such issues it might be necessary to reassess the basis of what are normally considered progressive and regressive stances. Resistance to programmes of research, to alcohol policies at work or to stricter preventative policing of the streets may often be viewed as regressive, unenlightened or otherwise unattuned to the real threat to the community posed by alcohol misuse. From another point of view this resistance might be seen as legitimate resistance to localized infringement on the rights and privileges of the community. There may be a need to address seriously the sources of such resistance and their legitimacy as oppositions to social control.

Alcohol producers and distributors have made much of issues of freedom and choice (Grindle, 1987) with their own interests in mind. They have themselves, however, also become involved in localized 'non-control' measures aimed at educating young people and the drunken driver. Currently the Government calls upon them to work collaboratively in reducing misuse of alcohol (DHSS/Welsh Office, 1989). The current drinking disciplines may serve a variety of different interests. Different forms of control and regulation may be more or less acceptable to different groups for different reasons. Accounting for such diversity should be the task of social policy analysis. Perhaps the enthusiasms of such diverse groups, including the brewers, should make us more than a little suspicious of their value.

Chapter 8

Say No to Drugs, but Yes to Clean Syringes?

Graham Hart

Introduction

The history of the non-medical use of analgesic and psycho-active drugs is marked on the one hand by governmental, medical and judicial indifference — particularly in the nineteenth century — and on the other by frenetic activity in all these arenas. It is clear that we are, in historical terms, experiencing the second of these responses to drug use — near frenzied activity. Until the mid-1980s the 'threat' of the non-medical use of opiates, particularly heroin, lay in its potentially debilitating and dependency inducing effects on 'youth', particularly young working-class men and women on the country's council housing estates (Parker, Newcombe and Bakx, 1987). Whether smoking or injecting the drug, the individual physical deterioration and negative social consequences (crime, unemployability) associated with widespread heroin use were considered self-evidently dysfunctional and to be prevented, discouraged and, for those found transgressing, punished by heavy fines and custodial sentences. A series of health education campaigns targetting young people began in 1985; the 'Heroin Screws You Up' posters were one of the more public expressions of government concern in this area. In 1987 there were 221 deaths in England and Wales registered as due to drug dependence or misuse. However, the decade has seen the appearance of a larger threat than drug use, and one which is associated with thousands rather than hundreds of deaths: AIDS.

In September 1988 the Government announced that it was making £3 million available to health authorities in England purely for the purposes of preventing the spread of HIV, the causative agent of AIDS, amongst injecting drug users. It would be naive to assume that these resources had been allocated only for the best interests of a highly stigmatized minority of people engaging in an illicit and health-threatening activity. Concern about the transmission of HIV from a predominantly heterosexual group of drug users to their non-injecting sexual partners, and subsequently into the heterosexually active population as a whole (Moss, 1987) has been sufficient to warrant what even the most critical observer would describe as a welcome addition to drug services.

This concern has had other outcomes. One of the most radical health interventions to occur in Britain in recent years in response to HIV infection amongst drug users has been the development of needle-exchange schemes. Sterile injecting equipment is dispensed free at the point of contact, as is advice on appropriate injecting sites, safer sex and condoms. How has a situation arisen that, within a matter of years — some might say months — whilst the possession of street drugs remains illegal, the Government has provided 'new' monies to ensure that the injection of these drugs is done with clean equipment? In this paper I will provide a short history of medical and government responses to drug use, from the nineteenth century to the present day, and end by describing one needle-exchange and its clients. Finally, there will be a discussion of the debates around, and implications of, the relationship between drug use and HIV infection.

Responses to drug use

During the greater part of the nineteenth century the open sale of opiate based products in pharmacies and even groceries indicate their general acceptability and use (Berridge and Edwards, 1987). Indeed, in the early years of the century opium poppies were cultivated for the express purpose of opiate production, with Mitcham in the 1830s proving to be the most congenial and successful farming area for the white poppy (*ibid.*, p. 16). How did opiate use become a social and medical problem?

Alongside the scientific development in bio-medicine which occurred at a rapid pace from the mid-nineteenth century onwards the social role of medicine changed. Medical professionalization — a process of the definition of an area of expertise over which only one group could have control — interacted with and resulted in changing notions of disease causation, its management and treatment. However, the 'clinical gaze', as described by Foucault (1973) looked beyond what was pathological in individual cell cultures to what was perceived as socially pathological. Thus disease boundaries expanded to include behaviour that had previously been considered merely perverse, sinful or criminal (Rosenberg, 1986). 'Social problems' therefore became equally amenable to the clinical gaze. Madness, sexual behaviour, alcohol and drug use all received their share of medical scrutiny and indeed state control.

Towards the end of the century the increase in subcutaneous and intravenous administration of morphine unwittingly produced so-called therapeutic addiction, with the majority of patients being middle-class. Overuse of an opiate derivative became the disease of addiction. From such a situation came the so-called 'British System' of drug maintenance which developed during the course of the twentieth century. Stimson and Oppenheimer have described the 'British System' as 'a loose collection of ideas, policies, institutions, and activities' (1982, p. 205). Its central theme, since the deliberations of the Rolleston Committee on Drug Dependence in 1926 (HMSO, 1926), has been that addicts are patients suffering from a disease, not criminals. Arriving at this label was in no small part a consequence of the professional, indeed medical, status of many addicts; they were essentially respectable, if wayward, people (Hamid Ghodse, 1983).

From 1960 onwards the complacency of the British in relation to their 'system' was severely challenged by an increasing incidence of drug use, particularly amphetamines, barbiturates and heroin, amongst a wide range of young people. The increase in heroin use and concern over its consequences led the Government of the day to reconvene the Brain Committee which had earlier reaffirmed that addicts were patients, not criminals (HMSO, 1961). In its second report (HMSO, 1965) the committee radically changed its tune; it recommended, *inter alia*:

1. Compulsory notification of addicts by doctors to the Home Office.
2. Restriction of the right to prescribe drugs such as heroin and cocaine to doctors licensed by the Home Office.
3. The setting up of Drug Dependency Units for the treatment of addicts.

The Dangerous Drugs Act of 1967, and later statutes, have ensured, in addition to these measures, heavy fines and prison sentences for the possession, production and trafficking of certain drugs; it is now also possible to have monies derived from the sale and distribution of controlled drugs seized by a court. The 'British System' now marries a medical model of addiction with a more obvious form of social control — the criminal justice system.

Heroin Screws You Up

Drug Dependency Units have only ever seen a small fraction of drug users. Even restricting discussion to those who inject — rather than smoke, sniff or take drugs orally — and to those who primarily use heroin (rather than amphetamines or barbiturates), it is undoubtedly the case that the majority of drug users have no contact with treatment agencies (Hartnoll *et al.*, 1985; Power, Hartnoll and Daviaud, 1988). The Government's awareness of the existence of a mass of drug users not in contact with agencies, and the potential health threat widespread use amongst young people posed, led them in 1985 to begin a campaign warning those who might be tempted to try heroin of the personal, health and social consequences of dependency. The first phase of the campaign had the theme 'Heroin Screws You Up'. This began in Autumn 1985 and detailed the physical deterioration associated with addiction. The second phase, running from summer 1986 to early 1987, encouraged young people to avoid peer group pressure to use heroin, and included television advertisements of a young girl being offered the drug at a party by her boyfriend and being ridiculed into accepting it ('Just say no'). The third phase, using billboards and the youth press, emphasized the immediate social consequences of frequent use. This included references to stealing from one's mother's purse or taking her jewellery, and exchanging sex for money (cf. Power in McGregor (Ed.), 1989).

Unfortunately it is said that these campaigns had negative as well as positive outcomes from a health education viewpoint. For example, the sallow youths appearing in the 'Heroin Screws You Up' posters were considered attractive enough to put on teenage bedroom walls alongside favoured pop stars. Much of the campaign was ignored by the would-be users of amphetamines and barbiturates, and drugs with similar effects to heroin, such as pethidine and palfium. The campaign had been so firmly targetted to 'smack heads' (heroin users) that other drug use appeared relatively benign. However, events were overtaking such campaigns.

HIV Infection and AIDS

In 1981 Acquired Immune Deficiency Syndrome was described and identified as a new disease. In 1984 the infectious causal agent of the disease was isolated, and it is now known as Human Immunodeficiency Virus. By the end of 1985 tests were available for the antibodies which develop as a result of infection. Late in 1985 a general practitioner serving the Muirhouse Estate in Edinburgh — an area of substantial social deprivation and high prevalence of young injecting drug users — decided to use the antibody test on blood samples he had collected and stored between 1983 and 1985 (Robertson *et al.*, 1986). The results indicated that there has been an epidemic of the infection amongst the practice's drug injectors, with by 1985 51 per cent of the sample showing antibodies. A similar study reporting from Edinburgh early in 1986 gave a prevalence of 65 per cent (Brettle *et al.*, 1986). Both studies implicated the sharing of needles and syringes as the primary cause of infection, and pointed to an earlier epidemic of Hepatitis B infection — also a blood-borne viral infection — as further proof of the likely transmission function of the activity.

Needle-sharing occurs either with the drug users' full knowledge, as when two or more people share equipment on the same occasion without sterilization between use, or in situations where there may be some uncertainty as to the sterility of equipment. This occurs when 'works' are made available, perhaps at a dealer's house, and used by different people over time. Why needle-sharing takes place at all is explored more fully by Power (in Aggleton, Hart and Davies (Eds), 1989) but there is evidence from a pre-AIDS American study (Howard and Borges, 1970) that needle-sharing may take place for social reasons. That is, the activity may serve to bond a number of individuals in a group, the prime aim of which is to enjoy the collective experience of drug-taking. However, a more prosaic explanation for needle-sharing is the simple fact of unavailability. If access to syringes is restricted but heroin (at a price) is readily available, then injecting drug users will use and reuse the equipment at hand. Apart from effectively transmitting life-threatening viral infections, such behaviour also encourages other physical morbidity amongst users, including abscesses, septicaemia and endocarditis.

In many cities such as Edinburgh where severe restrictions have been placed on the sale of needles and syringes, and indeed where these have been confiscated when found by the police, so-called 'shooting galleries' have come into being. These are places where users can inject ('shoot up') on the premises (often a dealer's house) and then after a 'fix' (successful injection) immediately leave. The practice of 'flushing', that is drawing blood into the syringe in order to flush out residual drops of heroin, also encourages the transmission of blood-borne infections. An occasional rinse of the equipment with tap water does not constitute a means of sterilization under any, but particularly these, circumstances.

It is possible to explain differences in prevalence of HIV infection between cities in the United Kingdom partly by reference to the social context of needle availability. In Liverpol, where the police have supported a needle-exchange scheme since its inception in October 1986, there is a policy of not confiscating needles and syringes; indeed on those occasions when syringes have been removed, users have been provided with credit slips to enable them to get replacement equipment on the occasion of their next visit to the needle-exchange. It can reasonably be argued that this has encouraged the low incidence of HIV seropositivity amongst injecting drug users in that city (Marks and Parry, 1987). In Glasgow, where police have not pursued an aggressive policy against small scale users (as opposed to those involved in the trafficking of drugs), and there has not been routine confiscation of 'works', prevalence is significantly lower than in Edinburgh, just forty-five miles away (Robertson *et al.*, 1986). Low rates of HIV infection amongst injecting drug users in London (Jesson *et al.*, 1986; PHLS, 1989; Hart *et al.*, 1989a) are again partly explicable in terms of the willingness of a limited number of chemists well known to users to sell needles and syringes, particularly in recent years.

The attitudes of the police and pharmacists are not the only cultural forces influencing seroprevalence. Differences between Edinburgh and London may also be explained in terms of sub-cultural differences between injecting drug users in the two cities. In Edinburgh, users constitute a fairly homogeneous population of young, white working-class and unemployed people, living on large council estates associated with multiple deprivation. If particular practices, such as needle-sharing due to unavailability, become acceptable, there is a large constituency of possible participants in that behaviour. The London drug scene, on the other hand, is more fragmented and diverse, with a heterogeneity in terms of age, background, employment, housing situation and ethnicity which is reflected in a range of routes of administration, drugs of choice and, for those who inject, needle use. This is not to say that the sharing of equipment does not occur, only that there may be fewer opportunities for blood-borne viral infections to spread through the drug-using population of the city.

A coalition of Scottish medical and public health forces in 1986 put pressure on the Scottish Office to recognize the fact of an epidemic. This resulted in a Scottish Home and Health Department Report, chaired D. B. L. McClelland (SHHD, 1986). Apart from recommending easier access to prescribed substitutes to heroin its most radical proposal was to make needles and syringes available to drug users on a one-for-one exchange basis. This was the first Government commissioned report to acknowledge the potential value of needle-exchange in preventing HIV infection. Yet Government had not accepted the proposal unreservedly. Lord Glenarthur, Minister of State at the Scottish Office with responsibility for Health and Social Work, expressed the perceived contradiction which might result from increasing access to injecting equipment. In a press statement released with the report, he said: 'Such a practice may have sound clinical advantages but it would have important implications for our policy on tackling another scourge of our times — drug misuse — to which we must also give high priority, at the same time as taking steps to prevent AIDS' (Press Release, SIO, 1986). Lord Glenarthur's dilemma, and that of many others, was this: how could Government on the one hand suggest that 'Heroin Screws You Up', and on the other provide free the wherewithal to inject the substance?

Needle-exchange

The introduction of needle-exchanges occurred with remarkable rapidity. It is an example of those in power stomaching one 'evil' — distribution of needles and syringes to drug injectors — in order to obviate others. In this instance these would be the heavy human and economic prices to pay for morbidity and mortality amongst drug users and possibly the heterosexual population as a whole from the further spread of HIV infection. The change in policy which resulted in the setting up of the needle-exchange schemes is described fully by Stimson *et al.* (in Aggleton, Hart and Davies, 1989). Essentially, by 1987 fifteen pilot schemes had been incorporated into a national evaluation directed by Gerry Stimson. Some schemes had started prior to receiving formal approval from the Government, notably those in Liverpool, Sheffield and at University College Hospital London, and indeed evaluation of the latter had also begun. The national evaluation's findings have been reported (Stimson *et al.*, 1988a; Stimson *et al.*, 1988b) and so the remainder of this paper is concerned with one scheme alone — that began at University College Hospital, subsequently transferred to the Middlesex Hospital, and known as The Exchange.

The Exchange is a shop-front street agency which is separate from the main Middlesex Hospital buildings, and is located in Cleveland St, W1. It is staffed by two drugs and health workers and several volunteers from local non-statutory drug agencies. Clients of the scheme, apart from being supplied with sterile injecting equipment, are offered practical health advice on harm minimization techniques in relation to injecting. Primary health care is also available; for example, abscesses and wounds can be dressed on the premises. Condoms are provided free, as is advice on safer sex; leaflets and posters on notice-boards also encourage the adoption of safer sex practices.

The scheme's clients are predominantly white, male (male:female ratio is 4:1) and they are long-term drug users (cf. Hart et al., 1989b). Most began injecting at about 18, and their median age on entry is 32. Most inject heroin, at least twice daily. The Exchange has proved popular with clients. From November 1987 to October 1988 the average number of clients attending per month was 257, and the numbers attending improved significantly over the course of the year (T–test $p = 0.0004$). An average of 8,950 syringes were dispensed each month, and 6,918 were returned, an average return rate of 77 per cent. Returns improved significantly during the course of the year, however; in November it was 69 per cent but by October 1988 it was 78 per cent (Chi-squared trend test: $p < 0.0001$).

During the course of interviews with a sample of clients one month and then again four months into the scheme we found reductions in sharing needles and syringes (a) as compared to reported levels prior to entry to the scheme and (b) comparing first interview (< 1 month) to second interview (< 4 months). There was also a significant reduction in the frequency of injecting after four months (Wilcoxon signed rank test: $p < 0.01$).

We asked clients about their recent sexual behaviour (< 3 months) on first and second interview. The majority of the sample had been sexually active during both time periods (77 per cent, 74 per cent). There was an increase in the proportions having non-injecting sexual partners (45 per cent vs 56 per cent), a fall in the proportions with two or more partners (26 per cent vs 20 per cent) and reduced condom use (46 per cent vs 36 per cent). Seven of the 79 men (9 per cent) who had been sexually active during the three months prior to first interview had exchanged sex for money or drugs, compared to 4 of 23 sexually active women (17 per cent); all paying sexual partners were male. Those who had prostituted had a mean of 38 sexual partners in the 3 months prior to interview (range 1–250); all but one used condoms during penetrative intercourse.

Overall, we consider the scheme to have been successful in a number of ways. Clients express satisfaction with a number of the schemes features, and their health has benefited from attendance. The proportion of clients experiencing recent abscesses — a frequent consequence of employing unsterile equipment — fell during the period of study. Although our data on clients' sexual behaviour are difficult to interpret, level of condom use is generally high compared to other predominantly or exclusively heterosexual populations (Sonnex et al., 1989). However, this is just one scheme. As Stimson et al. (1988b) have demonstrated, other schemes have not enjoyed such success. Punitive attitudes to clients, unduly strict attention to syringe return rates, inconvenient locations and opening hours have all contributed to the closure of schemes or dwindling support from clients. The success of individual schemes can easily be contrasted with the relative failure of others (Hart, Woodward and Carvell, 1989).

Conclusion

The appearance of AIDS amongst injecting drug users has resulted in a sudden increase in medical, media and political interest in this particular population. Concerned about injecting drug users acting as a source of infection within the heterosexual population, the Government in particular has acceded to a philosophy which emphasizes harm- and risk-reduction strategies, rather than the politically more acceptable but practically more difficult goal of total abstinence. This has led to a great deal of heated debate within and between drug treatment agencies, as well as amongst drug workers, as to the kind of services they should be offering to users. HIV has provided the fire for these debates.

Arguments focus on two broad areas. First, there is the issue of overall treatment policy, particularly in relation to prescribing. On the one hand there is a view that users should be offered not only free needles and syringes but also, under certain circumstances injectable drugs including heroin. Those who would provide injectable drugs are often as concerned to undercut the illicit heroin trade as to combat the spread of HIV (Marks, 1985). Some who would not go this far would yet still argue for the more liberal provision of oral methadone to a wider range of drug users than presently receive this treatment. If injecting drug users were to be offered oral methadone, it is argued, they would have less recourse to street drugs and would not inject; thus they would not be putting themselves and others at risk of HIV. The weakness in this argument centres on the fact that many drug users continue to inject even when receiving oral methadone, although they may do so less frequently than previously. However, the frequency of injecting tends to rise as methadone is reduced in dose, and so longer term prescribing of the same dose may be indicated.

Such strategies are opposed by those who do not wish to see the provision of free needles and syringes, and certainly do not under any circumstances want to see a more liberal prescribing policy. To provide needles and syringes, it is argued, is to facilitate the abuse of illicit and dangerous drugs; it should be the aim of the dependency services to help people end their drug use, not encourage it by providing the wherewithal for the administration of street drugs. In relation to more liberal prescribing policy, the only result of this will be a mass of doctor maintained — and perhaps even doctor induced — addicts, many of whom would otherwise have ended their dependency by their own efforts and/or with the help and support of professional drug workers. According to this view, HIV should be used as further encouragement to stop injecting, as one more reason not to use drugs.

Unfortunately, these arguments tend to ignore the fact that only a tiny proportion of injecting drug users are and can be seen by the dependency services, even if they wish to receive treatment. This last point is crucial; many injecting drug users do not wish to receive treatment and are going to continue to inject. With this brutal reality in mind, the practical response has been to ensure that when injection takes place, it is done safely. Thus, the introduction of needle-exchange schemes.

It is interesting to note that the process of demedicalization of the treatment of and services to drug users, which began in the 1970s, may have come to a temporary halt. During and since that decade innumerable street-based and outreach schemes have blossomed, and even within Drug Dependency Units psychiatry's place has been questioned. With the appearance of HIV infeciton, which will soon express itself as frank disease amongst many drug users, the somatization and medicalization of drug use may once again occur.

Finally, the present Government, the most sympathetic observer of which might consider antipathetic to the best interests of drug injectors, has found itself in a remarkable situation. Allocations for the financial year 1989/90 for drug services are expected to be in the region of £17 million, doubling the amount provided in 1987/88 (Druglink, 1989). New initiatives in health outreach work are to be funded, there is political pressure for drug users in prisons to be offered treatment facilities, billboard posters entreat drug injectors not to share equipment, and needle-exchanges hand out injecting equipment and condoms with alacrity. The central tenet of health education programmes — not to give out dual messages — is being openly flouted by a Government department. The Department of Health has allowed the public health initiative regarding AIDS to overcome its opposition to illicit drug use. If you don't say no to drugs, at least say yes to clean syringes.

Chapter 9

Using Alternative Therapies:
Marginal Medicine and Central Concerns

Ursula M. Sharma

The legitimacy of alternative medicine is an issue of vital public concern and the growing body of social science research on alternative healing should surely illuminate the political problems involved. I shall begin by reviewing some of the results of this research, and then outline some findings from my own investigations. These suggest that the use of alternative (or complementary) medicine is associated with many other changes in health care practice on the part of individuals and families. Alternative practitioners may be marginal (in a political sense) to the orthodox medical establishment, but the issues which are raised by the use of alternative medicine are central if we are concerned with what patients demand of the health services and how they conceive of health and well-being.

Large scale studies conducted in industrial countries suggest that the usage of alternative medicine is now substantial. The Threshold Foundation study carried out in the UK projected a rate of usage amounting to 5 per cent of the rate of consultation of GPs (Fulder 1984, p. 43). In the Netherlands a study carried out by the Dutch Institute for Preventive Health Care and the Technical and Industrial Organization was directed towards a comparison of opinions and experience of alternative medicine and official medicine; the survey found that 6.9 per cent of the sample of adults had visited one or more natural healer in the past year (Ooijendijk *et al.*, 1981, p. 44). In the absence of prior research the rate of increase in usage of alternative medicine in recent years can only be estimated, and there are problems of comparability between studies, but Fulder is probably correct in predicting a 'UK medical upheaval by the end of the decade' (Fulder, 1984, p. 44).

Who uses alternative medicine? A hypothesis which seems to have informed some research, either explicitly or implicitly, is the idea that users of alternative medicine are possibly marginal *people* as well as users of marginal *medicine*. Much American research seems to address itself to combating the notion that users of unorthodox medicine are likely to be uneducated and illiterate (McGuire, 1988, p. 10, Avina and Schneiderman, 1978). Most studies report that users come from a wide range of backgrounds and suggest no evidence that alternative medicine is the preserve of the 'crank' or hill billy. The Threshold Foundation study suggests that in Britain users of alternative medicine tend to be bunched in the young and middle-aged cohorts and, although coming from a variety of backgrounds, are somewhat more likely to be from the higher status groups (Fulder, 1984, p. 46). Research in Australia and the Netherlands has produced similar findings (Boven *et al.*, 1977, pp. 303 ff; Ooijendijk *et al.*, 1981, p. 19). A number of smaller studies in Europe, Australia and America have found either minor differences in demographic and socio-economic characteristics between samples of users of alternative medicine and control populations (generally a slightly higher proportion of educated or high status patients and a young/middle-aged age profile), or no differences at all (Furnham and Smith, 1988; Kronenfeld and Wasner, 1982; Avina and Schneiderman, 1978; Parker and Tupling, 1976). There is, however, consistent evidence that higher proportions of alternative medicine patients are female (Ooijendijk, Mackenbach and Limberger, 1981, p. 10; Fulder, 1984, p. 46). Are there characteristics of alternative medicine which render it more acceptable or accessible to women, or is it rather that women are more likely to have the kind of health problems which conventional medicine cannot cure?

Why do people use alternative medicine? There can be no doubt that the straight-forward answer to this question is simply 'Becaused they have illnesses which conventional medicine has not been able to cure'. A study of patients at the Centre for Alternative Therapies in Southampton indicated that the three complaints for which consultations were most frequently initiated were pain (arthritis, back pain, abdominal pain, headaches), allergies (eczema, urticaria, asthma, rhinitis) and non-specific symptoms such as 'feeling unwell or run down', malaise (Moore *et al.*, 1985). Very similar findings are reported for the Threshold Foundation study (Fulder, 1984, p. 47). The Australian 'Three City' study revealed that problems of the musculo-skeletal system figured most prominently among the complaints for which patients sought alternative healers (Boven *et al.*, 1977, p. 325).

It is not easy to compare data from surveys which rely on the patient's own definition of his/her problem or complaint; respondents use a variety of diagnostic vocabularies which may or may not correspond with those used by conventional doctors or alternative healers. Many alternative systems of healing have their own distinctive nosologies which are not necessarily adopted by their users. Classification by reported symptoms may be more satisfactory but leads to vagueness. 'Malaise', 'feeling unwell', are not very felicitous terms, considered as diagnostic categories. Also if individual forms of therapy are taken separately, there may be wider variation, since some medical systems are suited to (or are peceived as being suited to) particular kinds of complaint (osteopathy and chiropractic for problems of the musculo-skeletal system, for instance). However, the general picture is not at all difficult to grasp. Patients are using unorthodox medicine to deal with conditions (mainly chronic and non-life threatening) for which orthodox medicine can offer symptomatic relief rather than cure. The insistence of the BMA that alternative medicine prove its efficacy through double blind trials of medications or other methods acceptable to orthodox medical science seems therefore oddly irrelevant to these patients' perceptions of their needs. An asthma sufferer who has been unable to obtain more than temporary symptomatic relief from his/her condition under orthodox treatment and is desperate for a permanent cure is unlikely to demand this kind of proof for the efficacy of homoeopathy or acupuncture. He or she is already convinced of the inefficacy of orthodox medicine of his/her disease and has reached a stage of readiness to experiment with other systems. The same is not true of many alternative practitioners as represented through their professional associations or broad groupings like the Research Council for Complementary Medicine or the Confederation of Healing Organisations, some of which are very much concerned with the question of demonstrating the efficacy of alternative medicine in terms acceptable to the scientific establishment.

Social science research can shed little direct light on the question of whether alternative medicine actually works (or at least not in the sense that the medical profession would accept); however, it has a good deal to say on the question of customer satisfaction with the services provided by practitioners. Here again, comparability is a problem, because different studies have used different indicators of satisfaction or have questioned users at different stages of treatment, but the general picture is far from negative. Moore, Phipps and Marcer found that 59 per cent of patients interviewed at a Centre for Alternative Therapies said that they felt better after eight weeks of treatment though only nineteen had completed their treatment at the time (Moore *et al.*, 1985, p. 28). In Australia Parker and Tupling found that of a sample of chiropractic patients 45 per cent reported 'very great' or 'almost total' relief of symptoms, with another 31 per cent stating that they had 'some' relief immediately after treatment. After ten weeks a follow up enquiry indicated that 37 per cent of patients reported total improvement and 32 per cent considerable improvement, 19 per cent some improvement and only 11 per cent no improvement at all (Parker and Tupling, 1976, p. 374). An interesting American study of the perceptions of osteopaths and ordinary physicians in a small town reports a 'cognitive bias in favour of MDs (conventional doctors) but a countervailing pragmatic bias in favour of DOs (osteopaths)' (Riley, 1980, p. 1170). That is, clients had internalized the ideological notion that orthodox medicine has superior efficacy, but in practice expressed satisfaction with unorthodox practitioners whose services they had used to deal with problems the orthodox physicians could not treat. Findings such as these do not, of course, prove that alternative medicine works *better* than conventional medicine (probably most users of orthodox medicine would also be prepared to state that it effects 'some' improvement in their condition if asked) nor does it say anything about whether alternative medicine works according to its own claims or theories. What it does suggest is that levels of patient satisfaction are high enough to ensure that there will be a vigorous demand for the services of alternative healers for the foreseeable future.

I stated earlier that there was a 'simple' answer to the 'straightforward' question as to why people use alternative medicine, and my review of research so far has concentrated on researchers' answers to fairly straightforward questions (Who uses alternative medicine? For what disorders do they seek treatment?). Simple questions, however, are not always the best conceived or most interesting. We may correlate usage of alternative medicine with all kinds of demographic and medical characteristics of sample populations and compare them with control groups in all kinds of respects and still miss some very important dimensions of the demand for services. Can we treat usage of alternative medicine as a 'variable', an isolable piece of behaviour, rather than as a feature of an individual's life situation, perhaps a stage in some wider process of change in health care practice? Are individuals most appropriately taken as the units of study, given that medical sociology has made us aware that individuals frequently take decisions about health care in consultation with household members and kin?

The study which I undertook in 1986 was not designed to compare users of alternative medicine with non-users, but to discover the routes by which patients came to use it. The term 'routes' has a double sense here. It refers both to the particular experiences (ill health, dissatisfaction with NHS) through which the individual arrived at the decision to seek treatment from an alternative practitioner, and also (more literally) the path by which they came to be treated by the particular practitioner selected (the sources of information, referral, etc.). I interviewed thirty people in the Stoke-on-Trent area who had used at least one form of alternative medicine in the past twelve months. The sample was largely obtained by inviting readers of the local newspaper to volunteer their experiences of alternative medicine. We cannot draw any conclusions about the representativeness of such a self selected sample in terms of demographic or socio-economic characteristics, but this was not the purpose of the research.

The interviews were structured to the extent that they covered some standard questions and elicited a corpus of comparable data, but as far as possible I encouraged respondents to deliver this information in the context of their own 'story' of how they had come to use alternative medicine. This left them free to include in their accounts much that I would not have elicited through standardized questions in a set order. For most of the respondents the 'story of how they had come to use alternative medicine' was a narrative with a point, even a moral, which they wished to convey. In many cases the interviewee was describing a process which was by no means complete; the point at which the interviewer encounters the patient cannot be supposed to be the final point in the latter's search for satisfactory health care, and longitudinal studies of individuals (or more appropriately households) will probably be more useful in future.

Using alternative medicine is therefore part of a *process*. While some interviewees could pinpoint predisposing factors in their family background (e.g. usage of herbal medicine by parents, horrific experiences of orthodox medical treatment by a close relative) most took as their starting point their own experience of some chronic disorder and their own subsequent dissatisfaction with the treatment they received for this under the NHS. All had consulted their GP about this illness in the first place and several had seen specialists in connection with diagnosis or treatment. I did not encounter any who had used alternative medicine because they had been brought up to do so, because it was the norm in their ethnic/religious group or for other 'cultural' reasons, apart from one woman whose parents had been ardent adherents of naturopathy, though a larger sample might well identify cases of this kind of usage.

It is important to discuss users' sources of dissatisfaction with orthodox medicine at some length because many of them do not relate straightforwardly to conventional medicine's failure to 'cure' disease so much as to its failure to 'cure' disease on terms that are acceptable to the particular patient. Two individuals did report a conflictual relationship with their GP, but in most cases dissatisfaction was not focused on the perceived incompetence of individual doctors or consultants. The problems with orthodox medicine as offered under the NHS which interviewees mentioned could be grouped as follows.

The claim that conventional medicine fails to get at the 'root cause' of chronic illness or to take a preventative approach, and can therefore only treat the symptoms. For example, a young man suffering from chronic depression had been referred to a psychiatrist and had received anti-depressant drugs which had some temporary effect. But he felt that the basic cause of his state had not been discovered and that therefore he would continue to be liable to periods of depression, a prospect which he did not wish to accept. The experience of acupuncture described by friends who had used it suggested to him that this therapy might effect a long term change in his condition. When he had tried acupuncture it so fascinated him that he decided to train an as acupuncturist himself, and whilst his depression has not entirely ceased to be a problem, the periods of disability are shorter and less frequent.

This is not to say that patients always required a detailed diagnosis or a technical description of what the healer saw as the problem; patients varied very much as to the degree of interest they took in the actual rationale or theory of the forms of healing used. What was more often reported was relief that their dissatisfaction with symptomatic 'cures' had been acknowledged as legitimate and reasonable, and an appreciative sense that the healer was tackling the problem at a more fundamental level that conventional doctors had managed to do.

The fear of drugs which might become habit forming, or the dislike of side effects of particular drugs. Sometimes this took a rather diffuse concern about drugs that are too 'strong' — an imprecise fear of the body being interfered with too drastically. Sometimes there was general anxiety that prolonged or frequent use of drugs would interfere with the body's ability to react to drugs in acute situations, especially with regard to the use of antibiotics for childhood ailments. In other cases the dissatisfaction was based on a very specific experience. For instance, one interviewee's consultant had prescribed drugs for high blood pressure which, she said, made her feel exhausted and weak, 'like an old woman'. When she discovered a herbalist who could treat her she was relieved to be offered medicine which, she said, controlled her condition with no side effects whatsoever. The same interviewee expressed concern over the state of health of her sister who suffered from arthritis and who, she said, had been given ever stronger drugs to control the condition without any real improvement.

The editors of a recent volume on chronic illness point out that, for many patients, living with long term illness involves coping not only with the discomfort or disability caused by the illness itself but also coping with the physical or social demands made by the medical regime prescribed to deal with the illness (Anderson and Bury, 1988, p. 250). Another way of presenting this point might be to say that some patients find the cost of the regime prescribed for an illness outweighs the benefit it confers in terms of increased well-being or ability to live a normal life, and therefore they seek alternative regimes in the hope that their costs will be more acceptable.

Fear or dislike of forms of treatment which are seen as too radical or invasive. A middle-aged woman who suffered from back pain had been offered surgery under the NHS without, however, any guarantee that her condition would be cured. Indeed, she had been told that there was a slight risk that it might become worse. A major operation which did not have any certain outcome seemed to her too drastic a step to take and the risk of a deterioration dismayed her as her work required her to move and lift inmates in an old people's home. She visited a chiropractor at the suggestion of a colleague of her husband and after a fairly lengthy (and at first painful) course of treatment reported an almost complete recovery.

The perceived inability of conventional medicine to cope with the social and experiential aspects of illness. There is now more awareness of the need for personal support in severe or terminal illness, yet even apparently trivial conditions like eczema pose a need for personal support when they are chronic (as patients' self-help groups recognize). The sufferer needs to feel that the healer (of whatever kind) appreciates and does not dismiss the forms of distress or inconvenience which the illness causes. Some interviewees emphasized a desire for practical advice in the day-to-day management of their illness (useful adjustments to diet, suggestions for patterns of rest and exercise, stress management techniques, etc.). It is not by any means the case that all conventional doctors are unable to offer this personal interest and support, nor is it the case that all sufferers found alternative healers willing to provide it. Many healers, however, allow for much longer consultation times than do GPs, especially for a first consultation which may (especially in systems like homoeopathy) involve taking a very detailed case history. A time-consuming form of treatment may be acceptable to the sufferer if s/he feels it is producing some lasting effect.

Dissatisfaction with the kind of relationship between doctor and patient which interviewees feel that conventional medicine requires or presupposes. In many of the interviews, patients communicated a conscious appreciation of the more active role they felt able to play in the management of their illness or the general pursuit of health. Usually this feeling of being in control was described as a by-product of their experiences rather as the goal they had been seeking in the first place. A woman who had suffered from asthma for many years described her encounters with conventional and numerous forms of alternative medicine by saying: 'I am not criticizing other people . . . but I think that very often they go to the doctor and they just accept what the doctor says. I would advise anybody to go to the doctor first, but now I would always use alternative medicine to get a second opinion and treatment if you are not satisfied.' Many took an explicitly consumerist approach; one young man who had recently begun to consult an iridologist and to use herbal medicine described his and his wife's attitude to conventional medicine thus: 'If we need to, then we do go to our GP — we are not totally blinkered. We aim to get the best out of both systems.'

Yet some interviewees recognized that this active, critical and perhaps eclectic approach to health care might be incompatible with the model of the doctor–patient relationship in which the doctor has total responsibility for the treatment and the patient has only to trust and comply. Most interviewees had avoided telling their GPs about any alternative treatment they had received becaused they intended to continue to use the GP's services and did not wish to be seen to violate this model of the GP–patient relationship.

So far I have concentrated on the critical point at which the patient decides for the first time to seek alternative treatment and I have stressed that this decision is compounded of desire for treatment for a specific and (usually) chronic condition and dissatisfaction with the form of treatment received under the NHS, which may not simply relate to conventional medicine's failure to *cure* as much as with failure to cure *on terms acceptable to the patient*. The search for a satisfactory cure for a chronic illness or disorder does not always lead a sufferer directly to the door of an alternative practitioner. Many respondents recounted what can best be described as a programme of self education about their disorder which they had undertaken once they had realized that a quick cure was not likely. One patient had read and assimilated a large number of popular medical books on diet obtained from local bookshops and the public library to inform herself about her dietary allergy before she sought treatment from a herbalist. A woman with chronic asthma had obtained a great deal of information from the popular media, mainly television programmes and women's magazines, before contacting a spiritual healer about whom she had read a magazine article.

Many interviewees described this process of self education as one which changed some of their views on health in general, as well as their views on a specific health problem. A young husband who had suffered from chest problems described how the dietary recommendations of an iridologist caused him and his wife to think more in general about what they ate: 'There has been a lot of information on television and so forth about additives. I started to notice this sort of information more. And I began to talk to Jennifer (a family friend who used the same healer) and I began to wonder whether our diet had always been at fault.' His wife continued: 'It (i.e. the changes in diet which they had made) has improved the quality of our life. We think more about the effects of ageing; one day we shall be at the wrong end of thirty, then forty, then fifty . . . we have been eating wholefoods for two years now, but it is all too easy to abuse your body.'

Most interviewees in the sample, however, described the initial decision to use alternative medicine as prompted by a recommendation to a specific practitioner by a specific member of their network (see Table 9.1). This confirms what many other researchers have found, i.e. that most users come to alternative healing via personal recommendation obtained through informal networks rather than via GPs' referrals or formal channels of information. Table 9.1, however, refers to the *first* experience of alternative medicine, and many patients had used more than one form of alternative medicine, either for the same disease at different times, or more usually, for different diseases. If we include sources of information used for all consultations (not just the first) we find more diverse sources of information, with cultural and political organizations playing a greater part (for example, the Soil Association, vegetarian cookery classes, feminist groups).

Table 9.1 How respondents heard about the 'alternative' healer they used first

Source of information	Number of respondents
'Public' sources:	
Advertisements/Yellow pages	3
GPs' recommendation	1
Local association/organization	1
'Private' sources:	
Friends/acquaintances/colleagues	23
Relatives	2
Total	30

Most patients, however, seemed to have gained the confidence to approach a non-orthodox healer in the first place after hearing some kind of success story about that healer from a relative, friend or colleague, and only used information from more impersonal sources once a personal recommendation had yielded some kind of useful experience. This confirms an observation which practitioners whom I have interviewed have often made, namely that advertisement is hardly an issue. Recommendations circulate by word of mouth and most practitioners interviewed so far have stated that a satisfactory level of clientele can be built up very quickly in this way.

What is striking about the interviewees' stories is that initial usage of one form of alternative medicine is often followed by use of other forms, either serially or simultaneously, for the same or for different illnesses. Some patients had used as many as five types in as many years (see Table 9.2). In only one case was this due to continued failure to obtain any relief. A young man who had a skin condition affecting his scalp and had seen a consultant dermatologist, but without any significant improvement, announced to me his dogged intention of trying as many different forms of medicine in turn until he found one which had some effect. What seemed more common was that some degree of satisfaction (not necessarily total) with the particular form of alternative medicine first sampled led to a more experimental attitude and eventually to trials of other kinds of healing.

Table 9.2 Number of types of alternative medicine used by respondents (either serially or simultaneously)

Types of alternative medicine used:	1	2	3	4	4 +	
Number of respondents	9	8	4	7	2	(Total 30)

In many cases this change to a more eclectic approach to health care was one which affected the whole family. This could happen in several ways. In some cases the interviewee had recommended a form of treatment which s/he has used to other members of the family or had used it for children. In other cases the treatment involved the family indirectly insofar as the patient had to observe some regime (usually dietary) which affected the family. A woman who used a particular kind of diet recommended by a herbalist in treating chronic arthritis said that whilst she could not insist that her family eat the diet prescribed for herself, it was convenient to plan meals so that her work was not unnecessarily duplicated. Her family had accepted these changes in family eating patterns, indeed had come to appreciate them. In other cases the regime presented more problems, but only one patient reported downright uncooperative or dismissive attitudes on the part of household members to their usage of alternative medicine. In a few cases patients reported that a spouse or children had regarded their usage of alternative medicine in the light of an eccentric aberration but had not put any obstacles in the way of the interviewee's sticking to the regime prescribed.

When looking at the effects of use of alternative medicine on family health care practices it is important to place these changes in a broader context. Some of the dietary changes and shifts in lifestyle reported by patients as stemming from the recommendations of alternative healers are changes which are being recommended by many other sources of medical authority or information (GPs, popular medicine journals, health promotion campaigns) and are by no means peculiar to alternative medicine 'sub-cultures'. Reduced consumption of animal fats, high fibre diets, regimes of exercise and use of relaxation techniques might be examples. Such changes should be seen as part of more general shifts in thinking about personal and family health care voiced particularly effectively, but not exclusively, by holistic healers.

More significantly, there is little evidence that users of alternative medicine cease entirely to use orthodox medicine, though they may use it less, or for different purposes, or more critically. A sceptical attitude to orthodox medicine did not lead to its abandonment. Usually patients used alternative medicine for specific illnesses or problems and GPs for others. Interviewees had not abandoned the NHS even though dissatisfied with it. In Table 9.3 I have tried to summarize some of the main patterns of usage which I found among the individuals I interviewed. This is not a very satisfactory exercise since it is clear that what we are looking at is a very fluid scene in which many people are in the process of changing the pattern of their 'health seeking behaviour' either as individuals or at the household level, and many of the people I interviewed are likely to change their patterns further in future. But from this table we can see that we do not have to treat users of alternative medicine and users of the health service as two discrete sets of people. Use of alternative medicine generated in a particular situation of illness may continue but alongside orthodox medicine. In some cases initial use of alternative medicine had eventually led to committed devotion to a particular system of alternative medicine to the virtual exclusion of all other systems. This was the case with a farmer who had become convinced of the efficacy of homoeopathy in his twenties, after a severe and painful ear infection. He has, he claimed, never consulted an ordinary doctor since, except once to have a broken arm X-rayed and immobilized, and is an enthusiastic evangelist for homoeopathic treatment.

This degree of exclusive commitment, however, was unusual. Most interviewees could think of occasions during the past twelve months when they had consulted their GP for themselves or for other members of their family, and could envisage other times in the future. Of course, it is possible that users of alternative medicine continue to consult their GPs whilst failing to comply with their prescriptions or instructions for treatment. A study of users of ritual healing groups in America notes that many respondents in the study did consult their doctors about symptoms and might value some aspects of their services (in particular their diagnostic skills) but would reserve the right not to follow the doctor's suggestions for treatment. As the author points out, the very notion of 'compliance' implies a power relationship which some users of alternative medicine have (either explicitly or implicitly) called into question (McGuire, 1988, p. 194).

One very widespread idea which seems to me to be a misconception (at least so far as this country is concerned) is that users of alternative healing are naively attracted by the ideological claims of alternative medicine. Johathan Miller suggested in a recent newspaper article that 'much alternative medicine on offer — acupuncture or homoeo-

Table 9.3 Types of usage of alternative medicine

Conflictual relationship with GP plus occasional or regular use of alternative medicine	2
'Experimental' or eclectic use of alternative medicine	12
Stable and regular use of one form of alternative medicine	9
'Restricted' use of one form of alternative medicine (for a single illness)	7
Total	30

pathy, for example — appeals to soft primitivism', a concept which he defines as 'a belief that there was a time when men were harmonious and happy — the myth of the Golden Age — and possessed with wisdoms we are foolish to ignore and idiotic to forget' (Miller, 1989). Possibly this is so: certainly such ideas are frequently expressed in a variety of quarters. But this would not in itself suffice to explain the increasing use of alternative medicine, which seems related to quite pragmatic objectives such as obtaining a cure for a specific illness or leading a more active and healthy life. Only a very few of the people I interviewed gave explicitly ideological reasons for their initial attraction to alternative medicine, though some, as I have indicated, have altered their way of looking at care of the body and mind as a result of their encounter. So ideological commitment might explain why some people *continue* to use alternative medicine having once used it successfully, insofar as they are convinced by what they learn about it from practitioners, but it would not account for the initial resort to unorthodox medicine itself.

Yet most patients using alternative medicine would seem to be (negatively) dissatisfied with the service offered by orthodox medicine, coming on the whole from its areas of notable failure, rather than (positively) attracted by any alternative world view the former may claim to offer. Two themes recur very frequently in the interviews, and receive widespread mention in the literature on the subject:

1. The demand that the patient's experience and understanding of his or her disease should be acknowledged and treated with respect. Not all interviewees spoke in terms of a more 'equal' relationship with the doctor or healer, but many wanted to be better informed so that they could exercise more control in the management of their illness. Where alternative practitioners took the trouble to explain the rationale of treatment to the patient this was appreciated, and often contrasted with the failure of orthodox doctors to take time to provide information about treatment, or to take account of the patients' experience of his/her illness.

137

2. The demand for what could loosely be called a more 'holistic' approach on the part of doctors. Patients do not always use the term holism, and when they do, they do not always refer to exactly the same thing. However, a recurrent theme in the interviews was the desire that the personal context of illness should be taken into account. The treatment by drugs, which is all that many patients can obtain under the NHS, was often seen as too narrow even where it was 'effective' in terms of sheer relief of symptoms.

The first demand appears to correspond to a feature of the health philosophy of the present Government, namely that the patient should be in a position to 'choose' treatment and to take a high measure of responsibility for his or her own health. Health education is seen very largely in terms of campaigns to modify aspects of life-style which are held to carry risks of ill health. The 'choice' which the patient is to exercise seems at the moment to refer to the choice between private and public medicine or between different private doctors practising orthodox medicine, but the terms of the rhetoric are not dissimilar. The consumer movement, as expressed through journals such as *Which?* and *Self Health*, also implicitly expouses a philosophy of individual responsibility and choice in health matters. All these voices imply the possibility of a demand-led health system, even if they are coming at the idea from different directions. The logic of the free market is that alternative medicine should be allowed to flourish; it will prosper or decline according to the state of demand for its services. Many doctors currently practising orthodox forms of medicine already offer forms of alternative medicine to their patients or take an interest in the holistic health movement. How long will the generally extremely conservative attitude of the medical profession (as expressed officially through the BMA) be able to withstand the effects of a growing market in a political climate dominated by the ethic of the market?

As regards the second demand, the need for a more holistic approach is evidently recognized by many members of the medical profession, even those who are by no means in favour of alternative medicine itself. The British Holistic Medicine Association has many general practitioners among its members and one may find contributions from medical doctors as well as healers and lay people in journals such as *Cadduceus*. Jonathan Miller, in the article already mentioned, admits that the mechanistic model of the human person espoused by modern medicine, and its consequences for treatment, are repulsive to many patients. Many of the patients I interviewed attributed the aspects of NHS treatment which they did not like to the mode of delivery rather than to the system of medicine itself. That is, they recognized that pressures of time and organization make it impossible for doctors to deal with them as whole persons even if they wish to. It is curious that only one of the patients I interviewed had actually obtained orthodox treatment from a private consultant for the condition for which they subsequently sought alternative healing. Perhaps a larger sample would throw light on why some patients consider private medicine such an option and others do not. It has to be remembered that in an area like the one in which I have researched, use of alternative medicine is not necessarily more expensive than use of a private consultant. In fact some of it is remarkably cheap. (At the time of writing £15 for an initial session of three-quarters of an hour to one hour is not unusual for many healers; if one feels better after one or two sessions this may be a cheaper option than visiting a consultant.) So, again, it is difficult to disentangle ideological factors affecting patient's choice of treatment from other more practical considerations.

Use of alternative medicine is still a minority choice, but from what I have said here, it will be clear that it is not a marginal issue. If sociologists are to make a positive contribution to the debate about its legitimacy then they should study it both from the point of view of the patient and that of the practitioner. Alternative medicine is best researched and discussed in the context of concepts such as help/health seeking behaviour or 'treatment strategies'. Though some patients do change their cultural expectations about what doctors or healers should do, or about how illness is caused, as a result of their encounters with alternative medicine, most cannot be said to belong to a separate cultural group; where they express unease over the way in which orthodox medicine delivers its services, they are generally voicing anxieties which they share with many who do not use alternative medicine. Users of alternative medicine are making certain kinds of consumer choice, albeit choices which may have radical consequences for the entire household's lifestyle and habits. As with other patients, their choices derive from the interaction between the nature of their illnesses (chronic, difficult for orthodox medicine to treat) and the nature of their lay referral networks (access to information about specific healers, cultural and political resources).

Alternative medicine therefore is 'marginal' medicine (cf. Wallis and Morley, 1976) only in the obvious sense that it is still used by a minority (albeit a substantial one), and in the political sense that it has limited recognition by the state. Its study has raised issues concerning changes in household health care practice, consumer eclecticism and sources of dissatisfaction with orthodox medicine which should be of central concern to the medical professionals and social scientists alike.

Chapter 10

Caribbean Home Remedies and their Importance for Black Women's Health Care in Britain

Nicki Thorogood

Introduction

This paper looks at the use of bush and other home remedies amongst Afro-Caribbean women in Britain. This seems currently to have received little sociological attention. Rather, there have been analyses of lay beliefs and folk remedies amongst white Britons (Helman, 1984; Blaxter *et al.*,1982; Dunnell and Cartwright, 1972) and of 'cultural' differences in the experience of mental illness (Littlewood and Lipsedge, 1982), or 'guides' for health workers, written with varying degrees of awareness, about differences in the experience of health and health care amongst Britain's ethnic minorities (Mares *et al.*, 1985; Henley, 1979; Fuller and Toon, 1988). There have also been studies of Caribbean folk systems *within* the Caribbean (Kitzinger, 1982; Littlewood, 1988) but seemingly little about whether or how these practices are maintained amongst Afro-Caribbeans in Britain (Morgan, 1988).

The findings in this paper are based on in-depth interviews with thirty-two Afro-Caribbean women living in Hackney. The sample was drawn equally from two age groups (16–30 years and 40–60 years) and two locations (a local Health Centre and by 'word of mouth' in the local community). The research methodology aimed to make visible aspects of the subject's lives as they saw them. In this manner it was hoped to distance this research from assumptions made by other work based on notions of ethnicity and culture. This neglects any consideration of racism — that is, the structural manifestation of power inequalities — and reduces everything to the shortcomings of individuals and their cultures (Pearson, 1986).

The research on which this paper is based (Thorogood, 1988) suggests that this is an area worth considering. For although most of the interviewees felt that 'bush' was very much a thing of their past, certain attitudes and practices remained nevertheless. Further, it is a fascinating and comprehensive system which by its very existence in their past necessarily informs this group's experience of and response to the present. Indeed, I would suggest it plays a considerable part in helping to understand the actions of these people in relation to the medical establishment, whether state or private. This paper aims to conceptualize 'bush' not as an exotic or totally independent system but like other lay systems, as part of a multi-faceted strategy for managing health. It is suggested that the use of 'bush' is rooted in historical experience but can also illustrate contemporary relationships in health care.

Caribbean 'Folk Medicine': Bush and other Home Remedies

Perhaps the best way of understanding how the remedies were (and are) used, and what they are used for is to 'catalogue' those mentioned by the women (Table 10.1). There were three main groups: (a) bush (herbs), (b) proprietary remedies bought from a chemist or shop and (c) home remedies — concoctions made at home that were neither bush nor bought. Several remedies were used for more than one 'complaint', and most 'complaints' had more than one remedy (see also Littlewood, 1988). Several were often mentioned by the same woman. Most of these remedies were those they had used in the West Indies although some were still used in Great Britain. Many women remarked on how their children or grandchildren in this country would not drink the bitter herbs. (Indeed, in general, the women used their GP more and their own remedies less in this country (Thorogood, 1988)).

The remedies listed have been grouped according to the 'complaint' they were used for. There is of necessity some overlap and some areas which are less clear. One of the largest groups by far were 'washouts' and they were taken as diversely as daily or once a year. This inventory shows the wide range of remedies in use as well as the categories of illness which were considered suitable for home treatment. This is not to suggest that they did not use doctors and hospitals — they did; but to suggest that there were constraints upon this use and that these constraints were (and are) structured by race, class and gender.

The list of complaints and remedies often covers three generations and spans two places. The list includes all those self-administered remedies mentioned, whether they referred to children, mothers or grandmothers and whether they were used here or 'home'. However, whilst there were some remedies that belonged specifically to the Caribbean or to Britain, there was a great deal of overlap and many differences were a consequence of the differing times and circumstances rather than a change of attitude. To uncover more about these women's attitudes to, and experience of, bush and home remedies both as children and adults, here and in the West Indies, I shall turn to what they said.

Table 10.1 Bush and other home remedies

Washouts	Cerasee
Cerasee (also called Miraculous Bush)	Wincarnis or Halls 'tonic wine'
Camomile tea	Sarsparilla
Benjamin Herb	Stout & condensed milk & nutmeg
Bush tea (herb unspecified)	Brandy, milk & water
Senna & Sennakot	Guinness
Castor Oil	Malt
Syrup of figs	Vitamins – multivits, Vit C, Seven Seas
Exlax	Cod Liver oil
Epsom Salts	Metatone (proprietary brand)
Fynnon Salts	Complan (proprietary brand)
Glauber Salts	Nutriment (proprietary brand)
Shark Oil	Nu-nu Balsam (spelling uncertain)
Phsyic	
Scotts Emulsion	*Stomach aches*
Liquid of Life (proprietary tonic)	Cerasee
	Camomile
Headaches	Peppermint
Turpentine Bark (cooling poultice)	Angostura Bitters
Cudgil or Bat root (tea & a rub)	Cod Liver oil
Ice Poultice	Andrews Liver Salts
Limeacol	Blue Bush root (to prevent billiousness
Laite	from Mangoes)
Bay rum	Boiled orange peel tea
'Whizz' (a brand of analgesic)	
Aspirin	*Asthma & bad chests*
Panadol	Ganja (as tea)
	Warm Vaseline & Menthol rub
Rashes	Camphor
Meths	'Steam trap' from chemist
	Vick
Eczema	Mucron
Calomine lotion	
	Faintness
Skin care	Limeacol
Cocoa butter	Smelling salts
Shark liver oil (drunk as tonic)	
Soft candle (for babies)	*Toothache*
Olive oil (rubbed in to prevent stretch	Vinegar in salt water
marks during pregnancy)	Brandy
	Teething powder (babies)
Tonics	
Tree & Bush roots (collected, dried,	*Mumps*
mashed & boiled, then bottled)	Warm ash on flannel & tied round cheek
Liquid of Life (proprietary tonic)	

Table 10.1 Continued

Scarf tied round cheek
Corn meal poultice
Tobacco leaf poultice

Colds (with no temperature)
Cerasee
Peppermint
Red Bark
Leaf of life
English Plantain
Aniseed
Indian root pills
Honey, lemon & sugar
Lime juice
Coconut oil & garlic (for chest colds)
Ganja (for chest colds)
Salt water gargle (sore throats)

Worms
Worm medicine
Yeast food

Calming down
Limeacol
Bay rum
Ganja tea
Laite
Vinegar in warm water
Cerasee

Period pains
Cerasee
Ginger tea
Anadin (sent from WI at first)
Bush (unspecified)

Whooping Cough
Bush rat

Chicken-pox
Bush rat soup
Jeyes fluid (diluted in bath)

Nourishment
Soup
Beef, Iron & Bone broth
Greens
Orange juice
Sunshine (Vit.D)

Cuts and Grazes
Antiseptic cream
Iodine

Fevers
Thimble Bush with egg whites & brandy
Thimble bible steam bath of field weeds
   (made with odd number of herbs, e.g.
   3, 5, 7)
Quinine (malaria)
Fevergrass
Limeacol (cooling rub)
Laite (cooling rub) (particular to St Lucia)
Bay rum

Jaundice
'Billiousness powder'

Muscle Pains
Bay rum
Limeacol
Sacron (proprietary 'rub')
Deep Heat
Canadian healing oil
Jamaican healing oil
Caribbean healing oil
Soft candle, nutmeg/rum

Measles
Measle Bush (tea & to bathe skin)
Pimento bush
Fever grass root
Tamarind leaf tea (& bath)
Calomine lotion
Parched corn tea (i.e. dried maize)

Table 10.1 Continued

After birth	Benylin (all from chemist) (UK only)
Corn meal porridge	*For children – UK only*
Metatone	Phensic
	Junior Aspirin
Coughs	Beechams powders
Linctuses (all from chemist)	Lemsip
Syrups (all from chemist)	Benylin
Ferral compound (all from chemist) (UK only)	Vicks
	Antiseptic

All of the thirty-two women interviewed were familiar with bush and twenty-nine of the women had used it at some point in their lives. The remaining three consisted of one city-born older woman, who perhaps had not had such easy access to bush, and two British-born younger women both of whom had grandmothers in Britain who regularly still used bush. Bush is exactly what it sounds like. The leaves, stalk and sometimes the root of bush is boiled in water with the resulting liquid used as a 'tea' or to bathe with. In the West Indies the appropriate plants are to be found growing in fields as uncultivated bush or in many people's backyards (either planted or wild) along with other vegetables and fruits, the odd chicken or two and maybe even a pig. Thus the leaves can simply be picked and boiled:

> If you are not right back home, you just go out, take of a leaf, boil it, make a tea and you are all right. (Dorothy)

Along with the easily available bush were the proprietary tonics and washouts and some foods mentioned specifically as being used to maintain and promote health. I have grouped them together because they are used in similar ways. All were at least perceived as traditional (either to the family or the Caribbean), were self-administered and were controlled by the interviewee or her mother. No men were mentioned in relation to the decision-making about or administering of appropriate treatment, although Littlewood (1988) notes: 'Men are believed to know more about bush than women, and they treat themselves when working in the bush.' Similarly, Morgan and Watkins (1988) in their study of hypertension note the use of bush remedies amongst their West Indian (*sic*) respondents with no apparent distinction between genders.

The most frequently mentioned bush was Cerasee. Everyone had heard of this and most women had used it, many regularly. It was clearly 'good' for just about anything and was perceived as both preventative and curative. It was frequently mentioned as good for period pains but it was also attributed cleansing and purifying properties which were related to menstruation (Thorogood, 1988). Thus, Ann said:

A little goes a very long way and it's very good for the blood as well. They say it purifies the blood.

And Pearl, a younger woman, said:

A form of washout, that cleanses not only your digestive system but it cleanses your womb and everything. Washes you out when you are having trouble with menstruation. It's quite useful. It's good for everything really.

Nevertheless, she doesn't drink it herself and many of the younger women said it was too bitter. Many of the women, both young and old, said they could not get the children to drink it:

I just couldn't be bothered. It's easier to go to the shop and buy a bottle of linctus and then again, I don't think the children would have drank it because it's bitter. It's very, very bitter. You have to drink a cupful of it and you can imagine . . . these kids take one spoonful of a nasty tasting medicine and they want to spit it out, so definitely I couldn't get them to take a cupful. (Marie)

However, it was still popular amongst older women and the mothers and grand-mothers of the younger group.

It was often suggested that there was a 'proper' (i.e. in accordance with the Western 'scientific' medical model) medicinal or health-giving content of these herbal remedies and that they were in some way the 'raw material' of 'much modern medicine'; that is, tablets and 'medicine' (liquid in bottles) (see also Littlewood, 1988). As one older woman said:

I think that most of those things, because if you get the medicines from the . . . you go to the chemist and buy something sometimes and if you read the contents you will find that a lot of those things are what we used to have. And these health foods and health shops, a lot of these things that they sell are the same things that we used to have to take. (Dorothy)

The cleansing aspect of Cerasee was repeated in many descriptions of home remedies. It is worth now turning to some of the most frequently mentioned categories and considering in more detail how home remedies are used.

Washouts

'Washouts' constituted the most frequently used (and mentioned) remedies as well as the longest list of both herbs and proprietary brands and most of the women (twenty-six) had, at some point during their lives, used a washout regularly. All of the twenty-six who had used washouts had used them regularly in childhood. However, the regularity with which they were given and taken varied enormously. Three older women remembered the whole family being given a dose on August Bank Holiday; four women's (three older and one younger) families had theirs on the first Sunday of the month; two (one older and one younger) had fortnightly doses and four women (two older and two younger) took a washout daily. Others (four older and one younger woman) said they had been given washouts 'occasionally' (although in two cases this still involved the whole family taking them together), and finally some women (one older and four younger) had been given a washout 'when necessary'.

Many women took more than one sort of washout, the most popular combinations including senna, castor oil, salts and 'physic'. The daily doses tended to be either castor oil, salts or syrup of figs and were often combined with a 'tonic' or vitamin supplement such as 'Seven Seas' or Cod Liver Oil. One of the older women recalled having Shark Oil daily. However, washouts taken less frequently tended to consist of more than one thing — e.g. once a month: doses of salts and senna and herb tea (Evelyn); Caster Oil, Epsom salts and camomile tea (Beryl); Senna and Castor oil (Edna); Caster oil and 'physic' every two weeks (Sandra). For two families the August Bank Holiday ritual consisted of taking three types of washout on three consecutive days.

It seems that for the most part life in Britain has changed these habits. Some of the women (five, all older) continue to use washouts, though apparently not very often. Many women said they had stopped as soon as they grew up and their parents stopped forcing them — although this did not always prevent them from forcing their own children! Those that continued abandoned bush from necessity and resorted instead to the more readily available proprietary brands such as Sennakot and Epsom salts. Some women felt washouts were no longer necessary as they had a healthy diet (see below), and others felt that there was no time in this country. This is because after taking a washout it is wise not to go too far away from home for a day or two (hence the Bank Holiday ritual) and as Yvonne says, this is a hard condition to fulfil in this country:

> Because she is with a childminder I don't like the idea of her having diarrhoea and that. If I didn't work Saturday, I'd have the whole weekend and then I could give it to her Saturday and then Sunday we are at home I don't mind. I just try to leave her and give her fresh orange juice or something like that will keep her loose.

In general, those children of the older group who were born in the West Indies, were the most likely to have been given washouts.

Suffice to say here that during the interviews the West Indian diet was generally praised as being 'fresh', 'natural', 'healthy', etc. It is something of a contradiction to find this emphasis on good diet in Britain to some extent compensating for washouts. I suppose that 'fashions' in health care change and it is generally the younger women who talk about diet in this way. As they have said, purgatives no longer fit in with their routine. Neither are children in this country disciplined to take nasty medicine.

What these comments and descriptions show is, I believe, the commonly held view that keeping your 'insides clear' is important whether through washouts or diets. There may be a number of reasons for this. Firstly, taking purgatives and laxatives is a widespread practice. It may also be historically related in that it is more fashionable in some periods than in others. Nevertheless, it seems there is a qualitative difference in attitude between keeping 'regular' or responding to constipation and 'washing your insides out' (although the outcome might be much the same). Washouts, I suggest, indicate different theories and beliefs about the body and ways of treating it and this is consistent with the views of diet outlined above. Central to this set of beliefs is the conceptualization of the body as containing a central passage running from top to bottom, which has to be kept free from 'blockages'. Kitzinger (1982) discusses this, and the possible origins of this type of belief, in her article:

> Jamaican concepts of sickness are composed of two in some ways disparate body cosmologies, one derived from the mediaeval European 'humours' and the other from West African concepts of blockage by objects which whether by sorcery or other means, have obstructed passages so that body substances can no longer flow ... This is related to the bodily concept in which there is one passage leading between the mouth and the lower orifices, passing through the uterus and the stomach on the way (1982, pp. 198–9).

As the white women in the study to which this research was linked (Gabe and Lipschitz-Phillips, 1982) were regular users of laxatives it would seem likely that their cultural heritage derived from that of mediaeval 'humours'. It is, I suggest, the combination of this and the West African cosmology which leads to the very particular meaning and use of washouts I found amongst Afro-Caribbean women in Britain. Although the women were well aware of the laxative properties of the washouts, there were other elements to it, purifying, cleansing, body maintenance ideas, something like 'Dyno-rod' for humans:

Arlene: ... it was more like maintenance, just making sure you had it a certain time every week and that was it. Like you have a wash every day, you have that every week or every month.

NT: A kind of washing you inside?

Arlene: Yes, it's not because anything was wrong with you. No it was a regular thing.

Rather more emphasizing the cleaning out aspect was this comment:

> She would give us a regular washout, basically before we went back to school, because she said we ate too much junk at school. I think just once a year. (Joy)

This makes it almost seem like spring cleaning! Stressing the element of purification and cleansing were these remarks:

> Liquid of Life . . . you can buy it in the chemist, it kind of purifies the body or something, it wash all the rubbish away, cleans out the body. (Norma)

and

> Cerasee — that's a form of washout. That cleanses not only your digestive system but it cleanses your womb and everything. (Pearl)

This last comment shows a very clear conception of the linking of internal organs by a central passage. It also seems to me that there are two strands running through these comments, not only that of cleaning or clearing out in a practical sense, but also of cleansing and purifying in a ritualistic way, symbolizing a fresh start, renewal or re-creation, particularly of the reproductive organs.

Tonics

One further kind of internal treatment frequently mentioned, was that of 'tonics'. Some of these were also washouts (Cerasee, Liquid of Life) and therefore cleansing but most were presented as strengthening, 'body building' and nourishing. Tonics were also presented as being a useful pick-me-up:

> I think she (mother) used to take a tonic. Beef, iron and wine, that was it.
> They used to take it if they feel a bit run down. (Thomasina)

This mixture, therefore, contains 'strength' and 'nourishment' and there were a number of other references to alcohol as tonic.

Alcohol as tonic is implied in Ivy's description of the drink that goes with the steambath for malaria — egg white, brandy and Thimble bible bush; and Marie drank Guinness whilst breast-feeding for nourishment as well as to 'make the baby a little tranquil'. Littlewood (1988) also suggests that alcohol belongs to the hot/cold system, and notes that stout is used to build women up again after childbirth which is seen as purging (and therefore cooling).

The clearest indication of tonic as nourishment was when it was perceived as a direct substitute for food:

> . . . as I said, I've never really felt that down when I was in the West Indies to say I have to take tonics for sickness, you know, or body building or anything. We just normally have the proper meal from day to day and as I said, everything is fresh you know. In my family we never specially had to have tonic to sort of build us up or anything like that. (Ann)

Ann's denial that they needed tonics in her family (since they had proper meals) is contradicted by the detailed description of making tonics that she had given a minute or two earlier:

> Well, we make our own tonics in the West Indies and we more or less make it from roots of trees, certain types of roots that you can get from the bushes, and you get them, dry them, wash them properly and boil that, and then you store that in bottles for a certain amount of time and we use that for tonic and apart from that we have lots of fruits and things and we sort of blend them together, you know.

This is told in a continuous and collective past as if it is commonplace and customary, not only to her family.

Helman (1981) categorizes tranquillizers according to whether they are perceived as 'tonic', 'fuel' or 'food'. The basis for the distinction is made on (a) the level of control over the drug the user feels they have and (b) whether they perceive the drug effect as acting on themselves or (indirectly) on their relationships. Helman also suggests that: '*all* "chemical comforters" — from coffee, alcohol, tobacco and "vitamins" to more powerful psychotropic drugs — can be fitted into this classification' (1981, p. 521).

The descriptions and explanations of 'tonics' amongst these women do fit Helman's category of 'tonic' (episodic, self-administered, acting on the taker) although they are not necessarily reserved for the treatment of illness. Helman (1986, p. 218) adds that prior to the easy availability of psychotropic drugs the symptoms described by 'tonic' users had frequently been treated by patent 'Nerve Tonics', 'Restoratives' and 'Elixirs of Life'. However, the descriptions of 'tonics' given by the women in my sample do not particularly relate to low spirits, loss of vitality, anxiety or tension. They are, it seems, perceived more as a means of 'restoring balance' to 'the system', of providing nourishment and strength, either as an addition or as a means of 'keeping going' (see also Dunnell and Cartwright, 1972; Blaxter and Paterson, 1982). In this sense they are more akin to 'fuel' or 'food', although Helman associated with these categories a loss of personal control and an effect on social relations. These elements are missing from these women's accounts.

This example highlights cultural differences in the experience and perception of illness and therefore the appropriate ways for dealing with it. Whilst it might be possible to fit all 'chemical comforters' into the categories of 'tonic', 'fuel' and 'food', the meanings of these categories is culturally specific. The use of tonics amongst these Afro-Caribbean women was as a source of nourishment, for restoring balance and (occasionally) to keep going and was largely episodic: therefore crossing all three of Helman's categories (see also a discussion of their use of benzodiazapines in Gabe and Thorogood, 1986a). This way of conceptualizing health and illness perhaps has more in common with the Chinese and West African systems described above.

It is interesting to note, however, that there was not very much mention of hot and cold in relation to remedies and none at all in relation to illness. None were referred to as 'hot' or 'cold' as in Chinese or Moslem systems. Again although I never specifically asked about this, I think that if it had been a central feature of their health beliefs it would have surfaced in the classifications and categories in the same way that those about passages and blockages did.

Discussion

How then do bush and other home remedies act as a resource, and what impact do they have on the health behaviour of these women in other domains, e.g. the private and state health services? They act as a resource because they form a body of knowledge about the way the body works and the sources of risks and dangers to it (symbolic and actual) which has grown out of the historical experiences of these women. The way they experience health and illness and the appropriate ways of dealing with this are an expression of their 'culture', their history and their current experience as black women. In this way 'culture' can be reappropriated and seen as part of a dynamic interactive process. Bush and home remedies are completely under the control of the women in my sample (or their mothers) and as such mediate their relationships with both health and illness (structurally experienced) and the institutional health care systems.

What is it that defines an illness as sometimes suitable for treatment by common sense and sometimes worthy of a doctor's attention? It may be that doctor's medicine is sometimes 'unavailable' with the doctor acting as gatekeeper either because surgery hours are short and inconvenient or because he or she (but mostly he) is unwilling to prescribe anything (Stimson and Webb, 1975). Graham suggests that: 'These meetings typically occur at the point where the resources of informal caring have been exhausted' (1984, p. 165). This implies that the same 'illnesses' or at least the same set of symptoms that were once suitably treated at home shift into the public sphere at the point where 'normal' life cannot be maintained (Blaxter and Paterson, 1982). There are also categories of illness which demand instant medical attention (e.g. broken limbs) and are thus clearly outside the common sense boundaries and yet others which may never require a doctor (e.g. colds) (Cornwell, 1984, p. 130). The content of these categories, as we have seen, is not fixed but varies with the social, cultural and historical contexts. The decision to 'see a doctor' is a complex process involving advice, consultation, help and caring from friends and relatives (Friedson, 1961).

Dingwall (1976) also suggests that the 'interests of others may also be taken into account' when deciding whether even to define oneself as ill. This has obvious significance for women and I would further suggest that it is not only family duties and responsibilities (the interests of others) which either prompt or hinder help seeking but also the kind of *treatment* (social and medical) one is given to expect. Clearly, the ascription of illness and subsequent action are socially constructed. Where, when and how treatment is sought will be based on what is available, acceptable and appropriate to the help seeker. Whatever the possible explanations for making the move to seek help from a doctor these will all be structured by the experience of race, class and gender. I suggest 'appropriate treatment' is constructed not only out of historical and cultural knowledge but also by present day experiences.

West Indian women carry out 'routine maintenance' for themselves and their families using bush and home remedies for washouts, tonics, childhood illnesses, minor 'everyday' (Cornwell's 'normal') illness and somewhat more ambivalently, for antenatal care and childbirth. In general, home remedies treat conditions not worthy of a doctor. As we have seen these may be culturally specific as with the older women in this group, some of whom regarded malaria as an everyday complaint to be dealt with at home. The use of bush and other home remedies may also be seen as an extension of women's work within the home. This knowledge and its application is yet another expression of their 'caring' and again constitutes the 'hidden' material base to what appears as emotional labour — tending the sick, routine preventative measures. This is health and illness in the private sphere, learnt and practised by women within the home. Thus, most aspects of health and illness for which bush and home remedies are used are those aspects which would not be considered appropriate to go to the doctor with anyway. In addition to this, there were tales of home remedies succeeding where doctor's medicines had failed, at least as far as the story-teller was concerned.

This might be seen to provide external evidence of the efficacy of home remedies and of the ability of the 'ordinary' people to know better than doctors (Cornwell, 1984, p. 174), particularly on issues of 'normal' illness. It might also be seen as further proof of the remedy being the 'natural', 'unrefined', 'raw' (Levi-Strauss, 1986) form of 'scientific', 'unnatural' doctor's medicine, or at least a constituent of it, particularly in the case of bush (see Dorothy's comments about Cerasee on p. 145. Still further, there are times when home remedies and doctor's medicine are complementary, the former relieving symptoms and 'building up strength' whilst the latter effects a cure.

This no doubt has parallels both in other classes and other cultures. However, the particularity of these women's relation to home treatment has implications for institutional medicine. Bush and home remedies may be seen as constituting an alternative to 'real medicine' as a way of both treating and thinking about 'illness'. When a decision to consult a doctor is made a number of changes take place: a different status is conferred on the 'illness'; control and responsibility, in theory at least, (see Stimson, 1974) shift from the private (women's) to the public (doctor's) sphere; different behavioural rules apply and are legitimated. Consequently a new set of social relations is constructed and with them a new relation to the ideology.

Finally, it is worth noting that the relationship of these women to medicine as a resource was not limited to the state sector. Their experience of the NHS as both workers and patients, again both a consequence and an expression of their class, race and gender positions, informs their reactions and responses to it. This, combined with their historical experience, leads them to take a very consumer-oriented approach towards health care. Equal and appropriate treatment (both medical and personal) cannot be taken for granted but must be sought out (Thorogood, 1989). This view, combined with their realistic appraisal of the politics of NHS finance, means for many of them that private medicine presents a practical alternative. This generally consisted of a paid-for consultation with a GP used in tandem with the NHS. This relationship to private medicine has been considered in detail elsewhere (Thorogood, 1988); however, it is pertinent to note it here. For, as the foregoing more detailed discussion has shown, bush, along with private medicine and the NHS, constitute a range of alternatives in health care available to this group of women. Their use is not discrete and we cannot simply label these practices (both bush and private medicine) as relics of tradition (or 'culture'). It is, I hope, clear that their use by this group of women is an active part of managing their contemporary lives and best understood when analyzed in terms of the women's structural position.

Chapter 11

Health and Work in the 1990s: Towards a New Perspective

Norma Daykin

Introduction

The connected themes of 'health' and 'work' are not new for sociology. However, fifteen years after the passing of the 1974 Health and Safety at Work Act (HSW), there is a need for a new perspective on occupational health in the UK. This need arises as a result of changes in industrial and economic processes, and needs to build upon theoretical developments of the 1970s and 1980s. Some of these changes and developments are discussed in the first part of this paper. Changes in the economy, in the labour process and in patterns of employment have raised new questions about occupational health for the 1990s. As well as responding to the continuing problem of industrial accidents and acute ill health, there is a need for effective policy and theoretical approaches to problems of chronic ill health and occupational stress, neither of which are adequately dealt with by existing policies. In addition, perspectives and definitions of occupational health problems have broadened during the 1980s, raising questions about the nature of risks and hazards, as well as the groups of workers affected. The development of a feminist perspective has been important, and attention needs to be paid to the problems faced by women in both their paid and their unpaid work. Finally, the changed political climate of the 1980s raises questions about the future of health and safety policy in the UK.

This paper contributes towards the development of a new perspective, drawing upon policy analysis as well as empirical work. The focus is upon a group of workers not usually at the centre stage of the sociology of occupational health: young women. It is argued that for young people, especially young women at work, the development of effective health and safety strategies is impeded both by institutional and ideological weaknesses within the current policy approach to work and health. The data upon which the reported findings are based was gathered over a period of two years, beginning in the summer of 1986. Approximately fifty young people from two comprehensive schools in the south west of England were interviewed before leaving school. Two-thirds of the original sample were interviewed again one year later, after they had entered jobs, YTS schemes or unemployment.

Problems in Health and Safety Policy

The 1974 Health and Safety at Work Act (HSW), which followed the Robens Report of 1972, remains in place as the dominant piece of legislation on the subject in the UK. The HSW set down minimum standards of safety and health provision, and established legal duties of employers, employees, and the manufacturers of industrial products. The Health and Safety Commission (HSC), a tripartite body involving representatives of the state, employers and trade unions, was appointed to oversee the new legal arrangements. The aims of the legislation were twofold: to work towards prevention of, or compensation for, major industrial accidents and prescribed diseases.

During the 1970s, critical perspectives on health and safety policy tended to focus upon the ideology which underpinned the Robens approach to workplace health. The Robens Report stated the belief of the Committee that 'individual apathy' was the cause of most workplace accidents. In addition, the primary responsibility for preventing occupational accidents and disease was seen to lie with those who create and work with the risks. The Committee sought, therefore, to encourage self regulation and personal responsibility (DOE, 1972). It has been argued that this perspective has led to the development of hazard prevention strategies which have emphasized the behaviour of individual workers, at the expense of the working environment itself (Kinnersley, 1973; Doyal, 1979; Watterson, 1986). This tendency to problematize individual behaviour, rather than dangerous processes and structures, is linked to a tendency to blame the victims of occupational injury and disease. Marxian commentators have suggested that this tendency obscures the real cause of occupational hazards: industrial processes which result from capital's control over labour (Walters, 1985). These critics also suggested that the individualistic approach led to the development of inadequate workplace health strategies. These, according to Doyal (1979), have developed within the constraints of a capitalist economy, and their overall thrust has been 'towards the adjustment of workers to the pace and the physical conditions of the productive process, rather than the reverse', (p. 71). Hence instead of seeking to eliminate hazards at source, health and safety programmes have often been limited to the provision of protective clothing, together with exhortations to workers to behave responsibly.

Within the individualistic perspective, young people are seen as particularly 'at risk' because of inexperience and other characteristics associated with youth. Hence the HSE has produced special guidelines which aim to educate young people about appropriate workplace behaviour (HSE 1984). The extent to which the causes of workplace accidents are behavioural or structural is difficult to assess, since these two sets of factors are interrelated in ways which are rarely acknowledged or highlighted in survey research. A study of accidents on YTS, for example, drew attention to factors associated with accidents, including 'improper access', running, improper behaviour and lack of skill (Glendon and Boyle, 1987). A more detailed, qualitative analysis would be needed, however, in order to explore the underlying causes of accidents. Whilst running at work is clearly an example of improper behaviour, more needs to be known about the context in which running takes place. Are trainees likely to rush to meet productivity targets, or to follow instructions set by superiors? Young people at work usually lack the autonomy which is required to determine standards of appropriate behaviour, a fact which a purely individualistic approach tends to ignore.

A second area of concern during the 1970s and 1980s has been the priority given to acute occupational illness, and in particular, industrial accidents, over other patterns of ill health. The inadequacy of existing arrangements in relation to the prevention and reporting of chronic disease and occupational ill health has been widely noted (Doyal, 1979; HSE, 1988). This inadequacy in part stems from the underdevelopment of occupational health services in Britain. Employer's statutory obligations in this area remain limited. Despite a recent increase in interest in US-style health promotion programmes, at the end of the 1980s it was found that over half of Britain's workers, and 80 per cent of workplaces, had no access to even basic occupational health services other than first aid (Webb *et al.*, 1987).

Hence a concern with accident rates and acute illness continues to dominate policy and practice. The HSE has recently introduced new, more comprehensive regulations for the reporting of occupational ill health. At the same time, however, economic and social trends have served to reinforce traditional concerns. Firstly, an increase during the mid 1980s in the reported number of serious accidents at work has been cause for alarm. One commentator has estimated a 23.6 per cent increase in serious industrial accidents in the UK during the mid 1980s (Nichols, 1986). This trend has been linked to changing industrial processes and patterns of working generated by recession, and by the character of recovery in certain sectors. The HSE has, for example, expressed concern about the number of small firms and the emergence of sub-contractors often carrying out hazardous activities formerly undertaken by larger companies with established safety traditions, especially in the construction industry (HSE, 1988). At the same time, the increasing complexity of industrial processes and the use of chemicals creating more toxic hazards has led to the development of a specialized capacity within the Factory Inspectorate.

The effect of these two trends has been to reduce the visiting capacities of the inspection authorities. In addition, the responsibilities of the HSE have been increased during the 1980s, with the addition of gas safety, for example, to its remit. Yet the HSE's income has, in real terms, declined. The HSE has been a victim of the New Right's economic and political strategy of reducing public expenditure and encouraging self regulation and voluntary effort. The Factory Inspectorate has had its numbers reduced by 213 between 1980 and 1986. These trends have inevitably affected both traditional visiting and the order of official priorities. The Executive was able to claim in its 1986/87 report that whilst commitments in respect of nuclear and other more hazardous plant had been met, this was at the expense of other work. The report drew attention to a rising backlog of 'median' hazard companies which had not been inspected for a substantial period, and a large number of newer companies which had not been inspected at all (p. 2).

In addition to the trends outlined above, the enforcing authorities are influenced by public perception of risk, which is in turn influenced by major disasters reported in the media. Fatalities and major injuries are more quantifiable, and therefore more newsworthy, than chronic disease or long term stress. Public perceptions of risk have helped to shape the agenda, particularly for the discussion of young people's health and safety at work. After some well publicized fatalities, concern about the adequacy of health and safety on the Youth Opportunities Programme (YOP) — the forerunner of YTS — was widespread (Featherstone, 1985). The Manpower Services Commission (MSC) was prompted to conduct it own research into health and safety on YTS during 1985 and 1986 (Glendon and Boyle, 1987). The overwhelming concern was, however, with accidents, and broader questions of workplace hazards or stressors were not addressed.

The emphasis upon acute as opposed to chronic ill health at work in official policy has also been reflected in academic research. Some commentators have attempted to justify this approach by arguing that accident rates provide a useful proxy measure of wider problems with working conditions. This is because accident rates have been positively correlated with other measures of the quality of working life, such as voluntary absence or strike frequency (Beaumont and Leopold, 1983). However, to focus solely upon accident rates carries the risk of obscuring more complex patterns of ill health from analysis. It also implies that these patterns are of less importance, and therefore less deserving of an input of resources.

The broadening of perspectives on workplace health is necessary if an adequate response to the issues is to be developed in the 1990s. Whilst trends in the economy have increased the risk of acute ill health in some sectors, the problems of chronic illness have also been compounded by the increasing complexity of industrial processes, and the continual introduction of new chemicals and toxic hazards into the labour process. At the same time, labour market trends, such as the 'casualization' of work, may have increased the psychosocial pressures of work for many people. During the 1980s there has been an increase in the numbers of part-time and casual workers, and growing numbers of young people and adults are now recruited into temporary government training schemes which offer no guarantee of secure employment. The number of self employed workers has also increased, and there has been an increase in 'flexible' working patterns which make use of shiftworkers and homeworkers

(Wilson and Bosworth, 1987; Allen and Wokowitz, 1987). Many casualized employees lack the benefits of protection under existing health and safety legislation. These changing conditions of employment, which are underlined by the constant fear of unemployment for many workers, provide fertile ground for an increase in stress-related occupational ill health. Yet the British law, in contrast with, for example, Swedish legislation, remains silent on questions of psychosocial risk factors (Shipley, 1987).

During the 1970s, critics of health and safety policy and practice concerned themselves mainly with class issues. The need for a broader definition of workplace health issues in the 1990s is aligned to the need for a broader theoretical perspective. The needs of women workers, for example, can only be partially addressed by a focus on acute ill health and accidents. This is because of the sexual division of labour, which results in the concentration of males in 'high risk' and priority areas such as mining and quarrying. In these industries, the rates of fatal and major injury are five or more times the rate for all industries (HSE Annual Report, 1986/87). Three-quarters of the accidents which featured in the MSC survey of young people on YTS occurred to male trainees (Glendon and Boyle, 1987). Male workers are much more likely to suffer from a serious accident at work, and a narrow focus on accidents and injuries therefore results in the 'masculinization' of workplace health issues.

During the 1980s, there has been a growing interest in questions of women's health and work amongst feminist commentators (Lewin and Oleson, 1985; Doyal, 1984). A feminist perspective on occupational health needs to take into account not only the ideological biases which characterize current arrangements, but the effects of institutional sexism in health and safety policy making.

The emphasis upon worker participation through trade union safety committees and representatives has been seen as one of the main strengths of the 1974 Act. The 1970s legislation did result in the formation of many new joint safety committees, and the appointment of many new safety representatives (Beaumont and Leopold, 1983). Glasner and Travis (1987) have suggested that these institutional arrangements have enabled trade unionists to influence policy, and to set the agenda for the debate around health and safety issues. For example, trade unionists have participated in the 'social construction' of VDUs as a potential health hazard, against a consensus of scientific and official opinion. As a result of such trade union activity, attention has been focused on an occupational health issue which affects many women. However, women themselves have tended to be marginalized from this process of negotiation. Women have traditionally been underrepresented in the workers' organizations which help to reinforce dominant health and safety concerns. (Wickham, 1986). Trade union health and safety committees and representatives have been concentrated in larger firms, and in high risk industries which have high levels of unionization, and which employ mainly men (Beaumont and Leopold, 1983). As a result of the underrepresentation of women in health and safety 'negotiating' apparatus, women's issues have been taken up only selectively and unevenly. This highlights the importance of women's involvement in trade unions during the 1990s.

It should be pointed out, however, that women have also been marginalized within the official policy making apparatus, and as a result, policy priorities have developed which fail to address many of their needs. The Robens committee, which took advice from a range of concerned parties, did not hear from any organization concerned specifically with women's employment. Although women make up over 40 per cent of the workforce, the profile of women throughout the 1980s remained low. In 1986/87 there was only one woman, along with nine men, on the HSC, and research conducted in the early 1980s indicated that only about one in ten inspectors are female. Female factory inspectors tend to work in 'female' employment such as health and education, and rarely in 'masculine' areas such as construction and industry (Tydeman, 1983). Hence a complex pattern of both institutional and ideological weaknesses serves to marginalize workers, particularly women workers, from debate and action around workplace health and safety issues. The second part of this paper examines the effects of ideology and institutional provision on a group of young workers and trainees during their first year in the labour market.

Young People and Health and Safety at Work

A total of thirty-four young people — twenty-five young women and nine young men — were interviewed during the second stage of the study. Almost three-quarters of the sample were YTS traineees. Eight young women were in employment, and a further two were unemployed. The types of training and the jobs performed by males and females in the sample followed a similar pattern of gender segregation to that observed in the labour market more generally (Cockburn, 1987; Wickham, 1986). The young men were spread across a range of manual and non-manual occupations, including the jobs of garage mechanic, draughtsman, bricklayer and cook. In contrast, over half of the young women were doing some kind of office work, whilst a further fifth were working or training as sales assistants. The remaining young women were involved in service or industrial work.

The young people in this sample seemed to have largely absorbed the individualistic assumptions of policy, and this was illustrated by their descriptions of workplace hazards, as well as in their strategies for coping with these. During the interviews, eighteen young people were able to identify occupational hazards, such as risks from chemicals, the dangers of manual handling and falls, and the use of dangerous or unguarded machinery. Comments often revealed a belief that workplace hazards were the result of improper behaviour, and that accidents only occurred to irresponsible individuals. Hence Gillian, a YTS secretarial trainee, described accidents which had occurred in her workplace:

There might be a danger of accidents down in the workshop. One boy cut his thumb off . . . he was sawing, and he wasn't watching what he was doing, so it was his own fault . . . and a few boys got hit on the head with hammers, that's because they left 'em on the shelf, and the shelf wasn't safe, and they knew it but they still left 'em there.

The individualistic assumptions which underpin this comment also influenced young people's strategies for dealing with workplace hazards. Those who had identified hazards were asked to describe ways in which the problems could be overcome within their work. Collective strategies, or those which necessitated the reorganization of work processes and environments, were not mentioned by this group. The commonest response, made by five young men and three young women, was to suggest the wearing of protective clothing as the best way of dealing with the hazard. The remaining respondents fell into two categories: those who stated that 'being careful' was the only way of coping; and those who simply stated that nothing could be done about hazards.

The limitations of individualistic approaches are aptly demonstrated by the experiences of this group. Personal protection, the main method of dealing with hazards, often proved unworkable in practice. Whilst young people recognized in theory the need for protective clothing, in practice this was not always supplied by the employer. Only three of these young people had been supplied by an employer with protective clothing which they actually wore. This ranged from rubber gloves for cleaning in the case of a female shop trainee, to overalls, safety boots, glasses and hat in the case of a male engineering trainee. In three cases, although protective clothing was provided, it was seldom worn because it was cumbersome and impeded efficient working. For example, Andrea, a hairdressing trainee, described the problem of trying to work whilst wearing rubber gloves:

We're supposed to wear gloves for tinting, and when we're using perm lotions and bleaches and things . . . but it's a a bit difficult wearing gloves for perming because it's harder to wind up the curlers, so we just don't bother using them.

When employers failed to provide protective equipment, this was unlikely to be challenged by the young people. Fear of standing out, and of being seen as causing trouble, were important influences on this group of young workers. Women like Elaine, a factory worker, accepted hazards with an alarming sense of resignation.

N: Are there any hazards in your job?
E: Cleaning fluids, smells 'orrible.
N: What can you do about that?
E: We're meant to be wearing gloves, but there ain't none. Says on the bottle, wear gloves when using this . . . Everyone just uses it with their hands, so it don't really matter . . .

The individualism internalized by these young people prevented them from challenging the situations which many found themselves in, and even more from developing alternative, collective strategies. This pattern was reinforced by health and safety training, when it was provided. Few of the young people in this sample had access to occupational health services beyond the minimum. YTS trainees were, however, more likely than young people in employment to have received some form of health and safety training. This training was nevertheless limited in scope, emphasizing individual behaviour and basic housekeeping routines, and rarely raising broader questions about the control of workplace hazards.

Membership of trade unions might have provided the young people with a forum in which to discuss their concerns about occupational health issues. However, only two out of thirty-four young people were members of trade unions. Reasons for this were complex: only four young people stated that union membership was not allowed or approved of in their workplace. Few young people voiced anti-union sentiments. After a year in the labour market, they were largely ignorant about the role and function of a trade union.

Hence after a year of work and training, the ideological and institutional weaknesses of current approaches to health and safety had effectively combined to disempower these young workers, and to limit their development of effective workplace health strategies. This process affected male and female workers in similar ways. The difficulties experienced by young women were, however, compounded by the process of 'masculinization' of health and safety issues. The young people's accounts reflected the official preoccupation with acute ill health and accidents at work, as well as a tendency to attribute gender to different types of work hazard. Young men were more likely than young women to be able to identify workplace hazards. Eight out of the nine young men did this, compared to less than half of the female respondents. This difference in perception between males and females, and the tendency for young women to label their work as 'safe', can partly be explained by the effects of occupational segregation. This places men and women in different settings, with different hazards. However, occupational segregation cannot alone explain the fact that in young people's accounts, 'masculine' hazards were attributed greater importance than 'feminine' ones.

Young women who did identify potential workplace hazards often qualified their remarks by stating that the real hazards affected other, usually male, workers. For example, Sharon, an office worker in a large engineering company, stated that

> The only hazard I would ever worry about is if you've got to walk down on the shop floor, and go near the machines . . . sometimes you've got to walk through where the chaps are working . . .

Hence notions of 'hazards' were associated with machines and masculinity. Young women were therefore dismissive of the question of hazards, to which males responded with more than a touch of bravado and pride.

Whilst young women were dismissive of the language of hazards, they did tend to embrace the language of comfort and convenience. A total of twenty-three complaints about heating, lighting, ventilation and noise were made by the twenty-four young women currently in employment or training. Amongst the nine young men, a total of five similar comments were made. Young men tended to be dismissive of these issues, however, often responding to questions about comfort and convenience with a shrug or a laugh. When describing cold conditions of the garage at which he worked, Stephen added,

> It's all right . . . we just do some hard work to keep warm.

This identification of males and females with different types of occupational hazard would be unproblematic if not for the fact that the young people's accounts reflected a *hierarchy* of concerns. For both sexes, issues of 'comfort' were seen as more trivial and less important that 'real' hazards. Health and safety training, which concentrated almost exclusively upon the risk of accidents, reinforced this hierarchical understanding of workplace health issues. This left young people at a disadvantage when attempting to develop strategies for dealing with 'comfort' issues, which were unrecognized and ignored.

The issues raised in relation to workplace comfort and convenience were, in fact, far from trivial for many of the young women. Young women who had insisted that their jobs were 'safe' often went on to describe chronic symptoms related to the work environment. Hence Alison, a secretarial trainee, stated that

> I get headaches every day when I'm in the college. I think its to do with the lights. They're long strip lights, you know, and I'm sure they give me a headache . . . it starts every day about dinner time.

The fact that five young women actually left jobs because of poor working conditions testifies to the seriousness of some of the complaints. Two young women had left the labour market completely, and others had been forced into jobs or YTS schemes after failing to survive the jobs they had initially chosen. Jennifer, who had changed jobs twice, described this process:

> My first job was in G. supermarket, but I had to leave because I could not physically cope with all the heavy lifting. My second job was a live-in job as a kennel maid. The living accommodation was an old caravan with no running water or toilet or washing facilities. The pay was £35 per week for 45–50 hours.

Another young woman had left her YTS hairdressing scheme after a failed attempt to raise the issue of working conditions with the responsible managing agent.

I know they all say that hairdressing's long hours, and that, but I'd just had enough. We worked all day, with no dinner breaks or tea breaks, from 9 a.m. to 9 p.m., and it was only YTS. But when I told the college I was doing those hours, 'cause they said if you do more than 40 hours a week you've got to tell 'em, they just turned round and said it was my fault, sort of thing, what do you expect? So I didn't want that, so I got out of it.

The fact that issues of health and working conditions were often unrecognized, therefore, impeded the development of positive health strategies by young women. These strategies were further weakened by the individualistic assumptions which characterized male and female responses to health hazards. Hence young women and men developed personalized, informal strategies for dealing with the effects of poor working conditions. For some young people, personalized strategies were reasonably effective. For young women whose VDU work formed only a part of wider clerical duties, personalized strategies entailed making use of opportunities for 'natural breaks', and alternating their VDU use with other tasks. However, where young women had been employed solely as VDU operators, such an approach proved impossible. Susan described the stress of such work.

I work for quite long periods, fifty or sixty client letters have to be put on every day . . . I try and get off, but we've been getting piles of work from other branches, having to get it all done in one week. And our manager's entered us for this 'superbranch' competition, to get the most plans processed, so it's non-stop . . .

The effectiveness of young people's occupational health strategies was further weakened by their general lack of control over basic features of the working environment, such as temperature, ventilation and lighting. In most cases, decisions about these issues, like decisions about work pacing, were made by employers and supervisors who were themselves less personally affected by the consequences. These aspects of the working environment were particularly important for young women, who were more likely than young men to be employed in sedentary or close-up work. Susan described the way in which decisions about workplace 'comfort' were made in her workplace.

S: The lighting's not very good, because it's artificial lights that are on all day, I don't get any natural light.
N: Why's that?
S: Because the boss likes the blinds shut.
N: Is there anything you can do about that?
S: Just grin and bear it.

In the absence of effective personal strategies, young women continued to 'grin and bear' poor working conditions for as long as they could. When conditions became intolerable, young women left their jobs because this seemed to be the only strategy open to them.

As well as highlighting the inadequacies of individualized approaches to occupational health and safety, the young people's accounts demonstrate the narrowness of conventional notions of what constitutes workplace 'hazards'. An approach which concentrates upon, or prioritizes, acute illness and accidents to the detriment of issues of chronic ill health and stress leaves large areas of occupational health experience unexplored. These areas are particularly important in determining the quality of working life for women workers, who do not immediately identify with the masculine language of 'hazards'. The experiences of this sample group demonstrate the need for a broader perspective on workplace health issues than that represented in current policy. Such a perspective needs to accommodate an understanding of issues of stress and health as they affect women workers. These stressors are often underlined by gender at work. Gutek and Morash (1982) have analyzed sexual harassment as one end of a continuum of behaviour which characterizes male–female interaction in the workplace. This interaction, they argue, is infused with gender stereotypes. Hence the jobs done by women are infused with aspects of the female stereotype such as nurturance or perceived physical attractiveness. The jobs performed by young women in this sample were indeed infused with expectations of femininity, and as a result, young women often found themselves responsible for maintaining the comfort and convenience of other workers, bosses and clients. Hence young women described making coffee, running errands, and generally supporting other people at work as a natural extension of their work. These work roles raise further questions about the relationships between 'health' and 'work' for women. Graham (1984) has identified many of women's caring functions within the family as a form of hidden health maintenance. The accounts of the young women in this sample suggest that this process of health maintenance spills over into the workplace when women are employed. Research needs to be carried out to explore in more detail the hidden health functions of women's paid work, and the implications of these for their own health. For the young women in this sample, responsibility for the comfort and convenience of others was paradoxical, given the lack of attention given to their own quality of working life. At the same time, this responsibility increased the stress of work, which was usually performed in circumstances over which the young people exercised little control.

Summary and Conclusions

This paper has demonstrated the need for a new perspective on issues of 'health' and 'work', which builds upon the theoretical insights of the 1970s and 1980s. Problems identified in the decade after the 1974 Health and Safety at Work Act remain, and throughout the 1980s, new problems and issues have arisen. The individualistic assumptions of policy and practice, and the imbalance which has led to the prioritizing of acute ill health at the expense of other issues, continue to limit the effectiveness of health and safety policy. The empirical findings reported here highlight some of the practical limitations of the individualistic, accident centred approach.

New perspectives on work and health must take into account the changes in employment patterns as well as shifts in ideology and policy which have occurred in recent years. The insecure employment status of young people like the ones described above is an important factor which may influence occupational health strategies in ways which are difficult to chart. It is unsurprising, given the threat of unemployment and the low status of young people at work, that this group did not develop the assertive response to health and safety problems envisaged in the Robens Report. Hence the principles of self regulation and personal responsibility embodied in the Robens approach are increasingly inappropriate in the economic climate of the late 1980s and early 1990s.

New perspectives on health and safety policy must also take into account the insights gained from a feminist analysis of work and health. This analysis reveals aspects of health at work which are not accounted for when the focus is purely on acute and quantifiable ill health. Most importantly, responses to health and work in the 1990s must tackle the difficult question of work stress as it affects men and women.

The future of health and safety policy in the UK is, in a sense, in question. This under-resourcing of the HSE and the HSC throughout much of the 1980s has to some extent limited the effectiveness, and the scope, of current policy. However, various positive influences will also be at work during the 1990s, including that of European legislation. Current policy is paradoxical. On the one hand, the 1980s have witnessed deregulation and fragmentation within industry, trends which have clear negative implications for health and safety. On the other hand, the increased involvement of the state in employment and training offers at least the possibility of new, collective responses to occupational health. For young people in this sample, participation in YTS did increase access to, albeit limited, health and safety training. This feature of government-led training and employment schemes could, arguably, be built upon, providing the basis of a positive approach to work and health in the 1990s.

Chapter 12

Where was Sociology in the Struggle to Re-establish Public Health?

Thomas Acton and David Chambers

Human endeavours to postpone death and moderate pain provide endless material for the sociologist. The pace of addition to that literature is so great as to disguise the fact that amid the welter of health policy and outcome studies, there are not only no *new* sociological directions, but little sociological direction of any kind.

The papers in this book derive from a conference on sociology in action. An active sociology is one that alters the social action that it studies, one whose sociological directions in some sense cut across the conventional wisdom of existing practice, providing new understandings which make change inevitable.

The 'new public health' does presuppose new understandings of social action, even though professional sociologists have contributed little to them. During 1988 a new pressure group, the Public Health Alliance, brought together the community physicians grouped around the journal *Radical Community Medicine*, environmental health officers, senior administrators, health authority members and others. They hoped to tap a new governmental wholism in health, embodied in a report from a Committee of Inquiry chaired by the Chief Medical Officer (Acheson, 1988a), which made the first official assessment of overall health needs since the Report of the Royal Sanitary Commission of 1871. Acheson's (1988b) more personal view encouraged this hope of a broader vision.

The publication in January 1989 of the White Paper on the NHS, *Working for Patients*, ended such optimism. There was no mention of Acheson's recommendations for an integrated health strategy directed by a powerful new corps of public health physicans replacing the wimpish 'community physicians'. The case for public health made out by Acheson is not rebutted in *Working for Patients*: it is simply ignored.

The core of Acheson is its call 'to recognise above all the need for continuing co-operation and collaboration between the two main statutory agencies — health and local authorities (and others, e.g. MAFF, HSE as appropriate)' (Acheson, 1988a,

p. 45). This collective and social approach to health planning is the exact opposite of the atomistic market-clinical ideology embodied in the White Paper: ' . . . the Government is taking the next logical steps by delegating as much decision-making as possible to the local level. Hospitals and other management units will be expected to carry more direct responsibility for running their affairs . . . The Government intends ensuring . . . that money flows to those hospitals which treat most patients' (Department of Health, 1989, p. 11).

The failure of Acheson to make any impact on the conventional thinking embodied in the White Paper marks for us the failure of the sociology of health to be an active sociology. It seems a passive sociology, condemned to follow in policy's wake, ignored if it strays from a narrow path, peddling explanations, justifications, and critiques of problems defined from within existing policy perspectives. We ask two questions. First (compare Acton and Chambers, 1986), why environmental perspectives, obvious to us, from our involvement in environmental health training, have taken so long to percolate through to policy debates; second, why the knowledge marshalled by Acheson failed to be utilized or even acknowledged by the Government.

The Sociology of Health

Our explanations of parallel blindnesses in policy, medicine and mainstream sociology, depend on a theoretical framework for the sociology of health that we have been forced to develop for B.Sc. and M.Sc. Environmental Health courses.

Ideas of health and cleanliness are vital and fundamental components in the social construction of symbolic and physical order in society. We emphasize both that they are in society, and that they are socially constructed. This has two consequences. First — and this may sound a cliché, but we had to rediscover it for ourselves through complaints of superficiality from students — we have to tackle the classic problems of order, conflict and change in society. Our students need real sociology, and not a filetted version for health students. Secondly we have to go behind mainstream medical sociology to question categories like dirt, using anthropologists like Douglas (1966). Having presented health as a socially constructed category intimately connected with social order in general, the problem of health policy becomes the classic sociological one of how order in society is maintained, resisted, and changed. In the UK state action to assure this order is in three institutional areas: clinical medicine, community medicine, and environmental health.

Clinical medicine occurs where medical doctors or other clinical specialists under the general political control of doctors intervene in the bodies of 'patients', that is persons displaying symptoms (i.e. physical manifestations deemed pathological). Clinical medicine is organized through the NHS, which is responsible to the Department of Health.

Community medicine occurs where medical doctors or other clinical specialists under the general political control of doctors intervene in the bodies of broad categories of humanity (e.g. pregnant women, children, male smokers) without regard to whether they exhibit symptoms. Examples might be vaccination, or ante-natal classes. Community medicine was transferred from local authorities to the NHS in 1974.

Environmental health measures occur where material conditions in the physical and spatial ordering in our habitat are adjusted to minimize a threat to the health of anyone who might be affected. The point is to lessen the need for doctors doing things to people's bodies. Environmental health is administered by local authorities. Of all the auxiliary health professions started by doctors, environmental health officers are the only ones to have escaped from the political and educational control of the doctors.

Much confusion exists about these categories. Community physicians often insist, against all logic, that theirs is a 'clinical speciality' (Macara, 1976), and subsume what environmental health officers do under the title 'preventive medicine', even though the use of medicine is exactly what environmental health officers try to avoid. In practice, of course, the three may be intimately connected. If, for example, someone is asked to stop smoking because they develop lung cancer, that is clinical medicine. If we request them to stop because they might develop lung cancer, that is community medicine. If we ask them to stop because they are creating a hazard for anyone else nearby, that would be an environmental health measure.

Public Health, Old and New

In nineteenth-century Britain, as a part of the reconstruction of the social order to secure the bourgeois industrial state against the threat represented as 'poverty', an integrated policy on 'public health' was built up in the practice of the medical officers of health employed by the newly created network of elected local government. In the twentieth century that vision disintegrated, despite the despairing way in which the ever more powerless medical officers of health (now renamed community physicians) clung, and still cling to it (Acton, 1984). It is in that tradition that Acheson stands. In 1975, a year after community medicine had been removed from local government, Brockington (1975, p. 178), the doyen of academic community medicine, wrote: 'The future in Europe and the New World may well become a fight to prevent the hospital taking control.'

Working for Patients underlines the failure of that fight. It ignores community physicians. Indeed, when it refers (p. 54) to 'the reforms of the Hospital and Community Health Services set out in this White Paper', the words 'Community Health' are a terminological mistake. They do not actually refer to anything within the sphere of community medicine as defined in the NHS but to the clinical work of general practitioners. The report has four chapters on hospitals, two on general practitioners, and nothing whatsoever on community medicine in the NHS. In practice, 'working for patients' means 'hospitals first!' The report never questions the assumption that doctors must only consider the interests of people already sick. There is no notion that an integrated planning approach might lead to a health service in which reducing the number of people in hospital was a badge of success; in future the rewards will go to hospitals who can 'attract' most patients. The White Paper's writers do not even appear to have read Acheson, let alone be aware of the community medicine responsibilities which remain in the NHS or the important local government functions carried out by environmental health officers.

The Acheson Committee was set up following a chain of events rooted in the medical empire's concentration on cures and neglect of its overall responsibilities. In 1984 a scandal over the food poisoning outbreak at Stanley Royd Hospital in Wakefield (DHSS, 1986) led to an outcry which two years later forced the ending of 'crown immunity' of hospitals from important aspects of environmental health law; environmental health officers were given the right to prosecute hospitals and health authorities for endangering their clients just as they can restaurants and supermarkets. The government, however, felt that public concern was not allayed, and, citing Stanley Royd and an outbreak of Legionnaires' Disease in Stafford, set up the Acheson Committee of Inquiry. At first it included no environmental health officers, though one was appointed later, and some environmental health officers jumped to the conclusion that a 'revenge of the MOHs' for the loss of crown immunity was being planned.

The environmental health officers had seen removal of crown immunity from hospitals as a famous victory. Although they studiously avoided any triumphalism against doctors, it remained true that for the first time since they themselves had shaken off the formal control of the medical profession in 1974, they had brought a doctor-controlled institution to book, and established their right to apply some, at least, of the law and their professional skills to hospitals (even if prisons, and military and civil service canteens remain beyond their reach). They feared that the community-physician-dominated Acheson committee would draw on medical chagrin at the loss of crown immunity to recommend that the processes of environmental inspection be put back under medical control, by restoring the old powers of the medical officer of health to their NHS successors, the community physicians. They need not have worried. Oddly, for an inquiry set up over a health problem in a hospital, the Acheson report barely mentions hospitals. Acheson was interested in Stanley Royd not as environmental health officers are, as a failure of technical and administrative responsibility (the duty of care), but just as an example of a notifiable condition — which could happen anywhere. There is no indication that they have even noticed that it was seen as a victory over medical indifference to environmental health.

Nonetheless, its initial terms of reference forced the Acheson Committee to a broader set of questions than any official health document for a century. There was an opportunity to consider not merely how to redefine the public health function, but all the professional inputs and expertise necessary to achieve health in the World Health Organisation's definition: 'a state of complete physical, mental and social well being and not merely the absence of disease or infirmity' (WHO, 1948). (This is not to suggest that this 'definition' is adequate — the social construction of notions of 'well being' is where sociology comes in!) Indeed, the Acheson Inquiry took as its benchmark such a broad based notion of health:

> In the past, the term 'public health' has commonly, if mistakenly, been rather narrowly interpreted and associated with sanitary hygiene and epidemic disease control. We prefer our broader definition based on that formulated by the World Health Organisation (WHO) in 1952 (*sic*). These definitions give as much weight to the importance of lifestyle as to environmental hygiene in the preservation and promotion of health and leave no room for rivalry between preventive and curative medicine (Acheson, 1988a, p. 1).

This statement of intent not only attempts to cut through the implied rivalry between curative and preventive medicine, but also unequivocally appeals for a new breadth of vision. The report which emerged, however, betrays a continuation of the habit of mind which assumes that public health is an unassailable medical domain, and is impervious to the critiques of those who remain outside the culture of medicine or who threaten its self-perception. This failure to match the breadth of the question by the breadth of the answer can be found right at the beginning of the report. Acheson's recognition (1988a, p. 1) of the wide-reaching scope of any overall consideration of health is followed by an immediate retreat into a much narrower examination, largely limited to the role of community physicians within the medical establishment. This reflects the redefinition and narrowing by the Secretary of State for Social Services of the terms of reference from:

> To consider the future development of the public health function; including the control of communicable diseases and the speciality of community medicine, following the introduction of general management into the Hospital and Community Health services, and recognising a continued need for improvements in effectiveness and efficiency . . .

to:

> a broad and fundamental examination of the role of public health doctors including how such a role could best be fulfilled.

From the outset, then, we agree that, as the Public Health Alliance (1988, p. 2) suggest, Acheson is circumscribed. Public health is a far wider issue than communicable disease control. The inquiry's analysis is partial in its coverage, reflecting the fragmented nature of public health issues which have, ever since the decline of the Victorian sanitary ideal, failed to stimulate any truly strategic national policy initiatives.

Why has Acheson's Impact been Limited?

The apparent speed with which Acheson has been lost from the health debate is only in part attributable to countervailing Government policies such as its public relations concern with the NHS, its reduction of the independence of local authorities and its drive for public economies. The shift in the focus of policy discussions also reflects the weak positions of the community doctors during their fourteen years of relegation from the front line after their separation from local authorities in 1974 (Acton, 1984). The local authority is the very tier of the state which Acheson correctly asserts has carried the primary responsibility for public health (Acheson, 1988a, para. 4. 38). It is during this period that the environmental health profession has come to the fore in the delivery of public health. The community physicians' weak position has been exacerbated by various issues which, in the minds of the public, are not immediately identifiable with medicine and doctors, whether curative or preventative. Salmonellosis in eggs, listeriosis in dairy and precooked foods, water quality, and lead-free petrol — all these issues and others besides, have highlighted environmental health. Increasingly environmental health officers are being termed the 'health experts', a term reflecting both their actual involvement, as well as the media's perception of their involvement, with those factors identified, but not considered in detail, by Acheson (1988a, p. 24) as part of the public health function, namely: 'those problems relating to the impact upon health of the natural and man made environment'.

The modification of 'crown immunity' after Stanley Royd clearly marked a degree of acceptance of environmental health officers as bona fide professionals. It remains to be seen, however, whether this is merely a sop offered to the environmental health profession out of pragmatism and the need to re-establish public confidence, or whether the passing acknowledgment granted to their 'specialised scientific knowledge' and 'specialised post-graduate qualifications' by Acheson (1988a, p. 25) will lead to their real acceptance as partners by community physicians.

Several factors came together to enable environmental health officers to extend their challenge to medical domination beyond their own sphere of professional activity to broader aspects of health policy. The reorganization of the health service in 1974 removed the then medical officers of health from local government and thus cleared the decks for the expansion of environmental health. Securing graduate status removed the stigma of being second class professionals. Environmental health officers have become a natural group to which the public turn for advice, whether it be on the hazards of fallout fron Chernobyl, noise from the high speed chunnel link or the safety of their food

(Ackerley and Jones, 1985). Environmental health officers are closely involved in policies to rehabilitate the inner cities (Chambers and Gray, 1988). Their accessibility to the public has dictated their destiny; indeed, some environmental health officers argue that, in terms of professional development, environmental health has arrived at a point where its momentum is such that community medicine is caught in its slip-stream. The agenda for the corporate development of the environmental health profession is, then, how far and how fast they can capitalize upon their role in the implementation of policies to take on a much more influential role in policy formulation. Partisans of 'the new public health' argue, however, that this role must be secured in collaboration with those doctors who will recognize the interdependence of medical and environmental health perspectives.

The failure of the community medicine tradition, the reason why environmental health officers tend to criticize it as narrowly epidemiological, is not a failure to *raise* environmental questions which challenge the clinical tradition intellectually, but a failure to analyze the possibilities of environmental health *practice*, which can challenge clinical control (or neglect) in health policy in a practical way. Not until the new Public Health Alliance do we really find any community physicians working together with environmental health officers to construct a critique of health practice (Rayner, 1988). In the work of the Public Health Alliance one can indeed find the beginning of a sociological explanation of the failure of Acheson to take adequate account of the local authority environmental health services, but it is a beginning in which the participation of professional sociologists was limited to informal discussions with the founding group. Public Health Alliance documents do not cite the literature of medical sociology. Debates at its first Annual General Meeting in 1989 explicitly raised social questions about such matters as the balance between government action on the environment, and on poverty, and individual responsibility in smoking and dietary matters, and the political independence of state health education in challenging industry. Two MPs, distinguished academics, leading doctors, environmental health officers, and environmental campaigners, health authority members and a representative of the Commission of the EEC contributed to these debates, but no sociologists. Young radical professionals have joined forces with 'the great and the good' of the old progressive establishment.

Ten years ago such a grouping would certainly have felt the need to recruit a few leading sociologists. Part of the reason why they have not done so is political; few of the candidates one might try to recruit among sociologists have any 'pull' in Downing Street today. But part of the reason is also intellectual. The Public Health Alliance have located the failure of impact of the Acheson Report in its failure to carry through the concept of public health to an achievable social practice; their critique is, at heart, based on sociological questions. But the conventional sociology of medicine has no more answers to offer than traditional community medicine.

Implications for the Conventional Sociology of Health

The self-image of 'sociology in action' is one of sociology making a contribution to policy, rather than vice versa. The sociology of medicine, however, although it has made some progress in the last decade, still seems a reflection of, rather than a stimulus to, medical thinking. When one of the present writers attended the 1976 BSA Conference, the theme of which was the Sociology of Health and Illness, the most striking and disconcerting fact was that the total failure to mention environmental health seemed quite invisible to everyone else there. Sociological studies then seemed to concentrate on medical and nurse training, the ethnography of treatment, the organization of the NHS (with comparative sidelights on radical alternatives in the Third World), and epidemiology, the latter actually being carried out more by doctors than sociologists. These problematics developed naturally out of the growth of medical sociology to meet the demands of reforms in medical training after 1945. Sociologists often tackled these problems both radically and critically, annoying doctors in the process, but because they were still fundamentally working to problems defined by clinical medical practice, they were unable to transcend them.

This failure to transcend was not a simple consequence of absence of critical thought. There is a perfectly viable Marxist critique of inequity in the organization and delivery of health care (Navarro, 1979) but while class analysis tackled questions of the distribution of value, and social relations in production, it did not tackle the question of the social construction of value itself. Such questions tended to be left to liberals like Laing or Illich. Sometimes this has led Marxists to interpret liberal questioning of the value of medical services as an indication that the questioner was indifferent to inequalities of distribution. This mutual incomprehension was only possible because of the invisibility of alternative sources of values offered by environmental health policy and practice. Perhaps one reason why medical students have traditionally found sociology so annoying, is that the sociology offered them merely accentuates the worries they already have about the practice of medicine, without actually offering them any practical solutions.

Concern for inequality in health since the mid-1970s has breathed some new life into the traditional critiques of medicine without, however, having any effect on government policy whatever. Since the Townsend and Davidson (1982) reworking of the Black Report (a really spectacular failure to influence state action), questions about environmental factors have been raised in some, though by no means all, medical sociology texts, as they have been by community physicians. But social scientists have mirrored the failure of community physicians to come to terms with the practice of environmental health. They tuck it away in a neat little black box labelled 'the contribution of local authorities to health', which is rather like summing up all that doctors do as 'the DHSS contribution to health'. A dimension of reality is missing.

A striking example of this is the work of Ruth Levitt. Levitt's (1980) text on the

Control of Pollution Act 1974 is the favourite 'sociology' book of many of our environmental health students, because of its painstaking consideration of the administrative problems of implementing that Act. Levitt is rare among social scientists in that as well as having written a book on an environmental health issue, she has also written (1976, 1980) on clinical health organization, a standard text on the 1974 NHS reorganization; and yet our students have difficulty believing that both books are written by the same person. The two Acts seem hermetically sealed in different administrative sectors, and no thought seems given to the concept of health which underlies both policies; the difference is taken for granted, and the practice of those who enforce the implemented sections of the Control of Pollution Act remains unexamined; and Levitt seems to feel no strain.

Speculation about the relationship between sociology and health policy must presuppose some more general theory of the utilization of research and scholarship. It is beyond the scope of this Chapter (and that perhaps is part of the problem of health sociology!) to examine in detail the aspirations of the rather incoherent literature of research utilization (Bulmer *et al.*, 1986; Cherns, 1979; Bryant, 1975; Payne *et al.*, 1981). The general assumption, however, of those who attempt to theorize the role of sociological contributions to policy, is that new directions in any field of sociology will result from the independent sociological critique of institutional practice, and that sociologists will be there somewhere engaged in the social policy process, even if unsuccessfully. We have argued, however, that in the case of health policy a social critique has emerged which even though it has had no policy impact so far, presents a serious challenge, different in kind from other critiques of the past forty years. Professional sociologists, however, have made little contribution to that critique.

It might be asked from what lofty viewpoint we presume to make such sweeping criticisms. We can only repeat that we are led to them by the contradictions posed by the task of retailing the sociology of health to environmental health officer students whose work it renders invisible. Our position is an organic outgrowth ('organic' in the Gramscian sense) of our connection with the reproduction of environmental health practice. It remains marginal to mainstream sociology because the knowledge of environmental health officers remains marginal to the medical-doctor-dominated 'public myth' of health policy.

The Gramscian theory of the role of intellectuals (Gramsci, 1971) distinguishes between those 'traditional' intellectuals whose critique of capitalism comes from within the practice of a bourgeois life-style, and those organic (or home-grown) intellectuals of the working class whose critique is not the mere dialectical inversion of bourgeois reasoning but an alternative reality derived from the living practice of proletarian life. One may cavil at the extent to which bourgeois reality and proletarian reality are genuinely independent, but surely it is useful to make the distinction between a critique derived solely from the perceived internal contradictions of one ideology and practice, and a critique of one practice-ideology from the standpoint of another which comprehends it. The unfortunate corollary of this is that it is very hard for those caught up in the debate over the internal contradictions of one practice to address themselves to questions derived from another practice. We would present this as a general explanation for the failure of social policy research utilization. Insofar as the funders of sociological research want solutions to the problems of their existing practice, large-scale sociological research is locked into existing perspectives, and endless worrying at the problems which are not able to be easily resolved within those perspectives (or else they would hardly have been handed to the sociologists). Sociological policy research cannot make an impact by answering unasked questions.

Our criticisms of both medicine and sociology are not, therefore, based on some special claim to superior ability in sociological analysis or insight; we are ordinary scholars who happen to be caught up in the process of education for environmental health practice, and whose critique derives from this experience. Neither we nor any other scholars as sociologists are contributing a fresh understanding of health; it is the partial opening of community medicine to cross-fertilization with environmental health that has done that.

References

ABBOTT, P. (Ed.) (1988) *Deprivation and Health Inequalities in the Plymouth District*, Plymouth, Plymouth Polytechnic.

ABBOTT, P. and SAPSFORD, P. (1987) *Women and Social Class*, London, Tavistock.

ABBOTT, P. and SAPSFORD, R. (1988) 'The Body Politic: Health, Family and Society', Unit 11 of Open University Course D211, *Social Problems and Social Welfare*, Milton Keynes, Open University Press.

ABRAMS, P. (1980) 'Social Change and Neighbourhood Care', in *Social Work Service*, 22.

ACHESON, Sir E.D. (1988a) *Public Health in England: The Report of the Committee of Inquiry into the Future Development of the Public Health Function*, Cmnd 289, London, HMSO.

ACHESON, Sir E.D. (1988b) 'On the State of the Public Health', *Public Health*, 102, pp. 431–7.

ACKERLEY, L. and JONES, A. (1985) 'Food Poisoning — Fact or Fiction? An observation of the current interpretation of the term "Food Poisoning" ', *Journal of International Medical Research*, 13, 4, pp. 241–4.

ACRE (1988) *Affordable Homes in the Countryside*, Gloucester.

ACTON, T. (1984) 'From Public Health to National Health: The Escape of Environmental Health Officers from Medical Supervision and Fragmentation of Nineteenth Century Concepts of Health', *Radical Community Medicine*, 19, pp. 12–23.

ACTON, T. and CHAMBERS, D. (1986) 'The Decline of Public Health', *Nursing Times*, 13 August.

AGGLETON, P., HART, G., DAVIES, P. (Eds) (1989) *AIDS: Social Representations, Social Practices*, Lewes, Falmer Press.

ALEXANDER, J. (1988) 'The Ideological Construction of Risk: An Analysis of Corporate Health Promotion Programmes in the 1980's, *Soc. Sci. and Med.* 26, 5, pp. 559–67.

ALLAN, G. (1979) *A Sociology of Friendship and Kinship*, in Studies in Sociology No. 10, London, George Allen and Unwin.

ALLEN, S. and WOLKOWITZ, S. (1987) *Homeworking: Myths and Realities*, London, Macmillan.

ALLEN, S. (1982) 'Gender inequality and class formation', in GIDDENS, A. and MACKENZIE, G. (Eds) *Social Class and the Division of Labour*, Cambridge University Press.

ALLSOP, J. (1984) 'Politics for Prevention', in *Health Policy and NHS*, London, Longman.

ALUN, E.J. and PHILLIPS, D.R. (1984) *Accessibility and Utilization*, New York, Harper and Row.

AMBROSE, P. (1977) 'Access and Spatial Inequality', Unit 23 of Open University Course D204, *Fundamentals of Human Geography*, Milton Keynes: Open University Press.

ANDERSON, R. and BURY, M. (Eds) (1988) *Living with Chronic Illness*, London, Unwin Hyman.

ARBER, S. (1987) 'Social Class, non-employment, and chronic illness: Continuing the Inequalities in Health debate', *British Medical Journal*, 294, pp. 1069–73.

ARBER, S. (1989a) 'Gender and class inequalities in health: Understanding the differentials', in FOX, A.J. (Ed.) *Inequalities in Health in European Countries*, Aldershot, Gower.

ARBER, S. (1989b) 'Class consumption, unemployment and role', *Social Sciences and Medicine* (under submission).

ARBER, S., GILBERT, G.N. and DALE, A. (1985) 'Paid employment and women's health: A benefit or a source of role strain?', *Sociology of Health and Illness*, 7, 3, pp. 375–400.

ARBER, S., DALE, A. and GILBERT, G.N. (1986) 'The limitations of existing social class classifications for women', in JACOBY, A. (Ed.) *The Measurement of Social Class*, Social Research Association.

ARMSTRONG, D. (1983) *Political Anatomy of the Body: Medical Knowledge in Britain in the Twentieth Century*, Cambridge, Cambridge University Press.

ARMSTRONG, D. (1988) 'Historical Origins of Health Behaviour', in ANDERSON, R., DAVIES, J., KICKBUSCH, I., McQUEEN, D. and TURNER, R. (Eds) *Health Behaviour Research and Health Promotion*, Oxford, New York, Tokyo, Oxford University Press.

ARMSTRONG, P. (1982) 'If it's only women it doesn't matter so much', in WEST, J. (Ed.) *Work, women and the labour market*, London, Routledge and Kegan Paul.

ASHTON, J. and SEYMOUR, H. (1988) *The New Public Health*, Milton Keynes, Open University Press.

ASSOCIATION OF COUNTY COUNCILS (1979) *Rural Deprivation*, London, HMSO.

ASSOCIATION OF DISTRICT COUNCILS (1979) *Rural Recovery: Strategy for Survival*, London.

AUSTIN, J. and KRISBERG, B. (1981) 'Wider, Stronger and Different Nets: the Dialectics of Criminal Justice Reform', *Journal of Research in Crime and Delinquency*, 18, 1, pp. 165–96.

AVINA, R.L. and SCHNEIDERMAN, L.J. (1978) 'Why Patients Use Homoeopathy', *Western Journal of Medicine*, 128, pp. 366–9.

BAKALAR, J.B. and GRINSPOON, L. (1984) *Drug Control in a Free Society*, Cambridge, Cambridge University Press.

BALINT, M. (1957) *The Doctor, His Patient and the Illness*, London, Pitman.

BALLARD, R. (1983) 'Racial Inequality, Ethnic Diversity and Social Policy: Applied Anthropology in Urban Britain', revised version of a paper presented at The British Sociological Association Conference, Cambridge.

BARRETT, M. and ROBERTS, H. (1978) 'Doctors and Their Patients: the social control of women in General Practice', in SMART, C. and SMART, B. (Eds) *Women, Sexuality and Social Control*, London, RKP.

BARTHES, R. (1972) *Mythologies*, London, Jonathan Cape.

BATH, S.S.D. (1970) 'Publicity Effectiveness Survey', *Intergovernment Clearing House*, Vol. 5.

BEAUMONT, P.B. and LEOPOLD, J.W. (1983) 'The State of Workplace Health and Safety in Britain', in JONES, C. and STEVENSON, J. (Eds) *Yearbook of Social Policy in Britain*, London, RKP.

BECKER, H. (1963) *Outsiders: Studies in the Sociology of Deviance*, Glencoe, Free Press.

BERRIDGE, V. and EDWARDS, G. (1987) *Opium and the people: Opiate use in 19th century England*, London, Yale.

BERNARD, J. (1971) *Women and the Public Interest*, Atherton, Mcline.

BLANE, H.T. (1976) 'Education and the Prevention of Alcoholism', in KISSIN, B. and BEGLEITER, H. (Eds) *The Biology of Alcoholism (Vol 4)*, New York, Plenum Press.

BLAXTER, M. (1985) 'Self-definition of health status and consulting rates in primary care', *Quarterly Journal of Social Affairs*, 1, 2, pp. 131–71.

BLAXTER, M. and PATERSON, E. (1982) *Mothers and Daughters: a three-generational study of health attitudes and behaviour*, London, HEB.

BLOCKER, J.S. (1976) *Retreat from Reform: The Prohibition Movement in the United States 1890–1913*, Westport, Greenwood Press.

BLUMER, H. (1971) 'Social problems as collective behaviour', *Social Problems*, 18, 3, pp. 298–306.

BOND, M. (1980) *Women's Work in a Woman's World*, unpublished MA Dissertation, Department of Applied Social Studies, Warwick University.

BOVEN, R., LUPTON, G., NAJMAN, J., PAYNE, S., SHEEHAN, M. and WESTON, J. (1977) 'Current Patients of Alternative Healthcare — a Three Cities Study', appendix of a *Report of the Committee of Inquiry into Chiropractice, Osteopathy, Homeopathy and Naturopathy*, Australian Parliamentary Paper no. 102.

BRADLEY, T. and LOWE, P. (Eds) (1984) *Locality and Rurality*, Norwich, Geo Books.

BRETTLE, R.P., DAVIDSON, J., DAVIDSON, S.J., GRAY, J.M.N., INGLIS, J.M., CONN, J.S., BATH, G.E., GILLON, J., MCCELAND, D.B.L. (1986) 'HTLV-VI antibodies in an Edinburgh Clinic', *Lancet*, I, p. 1099.

BRITTEN, N. and HEATH, A. (1983) 'Women, men and social class', in GARMARNIKOV, E. *et al.* (Eds) *Gender, Class and Work*, London, Heinemann.

BROCKINGTON, C.F. (1975) *World Health*, London, Churchill Livingstone.

BROGDEN, G. (1984) 'Deprivation in Urban and Rural Areas: Needs, Identification and Policy', in LISHMAN, J. (Ed.) *Social Work in Rural and Urban Areas*, Aberdeen, Aberdeen University Press.

BROWN, P.J. (1988) 'When the media attacks, what do you do?' *Scrip*, 1306, pp. 8–10.

BROWN, G. and HARRIS, T. (1976) *The Social Origins of Depressions*, London, Tavistock.

BRUUN, K., EDWARDS, G., LUMIO, M., MAKELA, K., PAN, L., POPHAM, R., ROOM, R., SCHMIDT, W., SKOG, O., SULKUNEN, P. and OSTERBERG, E. (1975) *Alcohol Control Policies in Public Health Perspective*, Finland, The Finnish Foundation for Alcohol Studies.

BRYANT, C.G.A. (1975) *Sociology in Action*, London, Allen and Unwin.

BULMER, M. *et al.* (1986) *Social Science and Social Policy*, London, Allen and Unwin.

BUNTON, R. (forthcoming) 'Changes in the Control of Alcohol Misuse', *British Journal of Addiction*.

BURNS, T. (1977) 'The organisation of public opinion', in CURRAN, J. *et al.* (Eds) *Mass Communications and Society*, London, Edward Arnold.

BUTLER, J.E. and FUGUITT, G.V. (1970) 'Small Town Population Change and Distance from Larger Towns: a Replication of Hassinger's Study: The Quality of Life'., *Rural Sociol.*, 35, pp. 396–402.

CAB (1985/86, 1986/87, 1987/88) *Annual Report: Devon and Cornwall*, Area Office, Newton Abbot.

CASSELL, J. (1976) 'The Contribution of the social environment to host resistance', *American Journal of Epidemiology*, 104, pp. 107–23.

CASTELLS, M. (1976) 'Theory and Ideology in Urban Sociology', in PICKVANCE, C. (Ed.) *Urban Sociology: Critical Essays*, London, Tavistock.

CHAMBERS, D and GRAY, F.G. (1989) 'Public Intervention in Private Sector Housing: The British Experience', in VAN VLIET, W. and VAN WESSEP, J. (Eds) *The Deregulation of Housing*, London, Sage.

CHERNS, A. (1979) *Using the Social Sciences*, London, Routledge and Kegan Paul.

CLARKE, L. (1984) *Domiciliary Services for the Elderly*, Beckenham, Croom Helm.

COCKBURN, C. (1987) *Two Track Training: Sex Inequalities and the YTS*, London, Macmillan.

COHEN, A.P. (1977) 'For a political ethnography of everyday life: sketches from Whalsay, Shetland', *Ethnos*, XLII, pp. 3–4.

COHEN, A.P. (1982) 'Belonging: the experience of culture', in COHEN, A.P. (Ed.) *Belonging*, Manchester, Manchester University Press.

COHEN, S. (1985) *Visions of Social Control: Crime, Punishment and Classification*, Cambridge, Cambridge University Press.

COLES, O. (1978) 'Transport and Rural Deprivation', in WALKER, A. (Ed.) *Rural Power*, London, CPAG.

CORNWALL, S.S.D. (1983) 'Going Local', Truro, LA paper, 29 March.

CORNWELL, J. (1984) *Hard Earned Lives: Accounts of Health and Illness from East London*, London, Tavistock.

COX, K.R. and REYNOLDS, D.R. (1974) 'Locational Approaches to Power and Conflict', in COX, K.R. *et al. Locational Approaches to Power and Conflict*, Beverley Hills, California, Sage.

COXON, T. (1988) 'Something Sensational: The Sexual Diary as a research method in the study of sexual behaviour of gay males', *Sociological Review*, 36, 2, pp. 352–67.

COYLE, A. (1982) 'Sex and skill in the organisation of the clothing industry', in WEST, J. (Ed.) *Work, Women and Labour Market*, London, Routledge and Kegan Paul, pp. 10–26.

CRAWFORD, R. (1984) 'A cultural account of "health", control, release and the social body', in MCKINLAY, J.B. (Ed.) *Issues in the Politics of Health Care*, London, Tavistock.

DALE, A. (1986) 'A note on differences in car usage by married men and married women', *Sociology*, 20, pp. 91–2.

DALE, A. (1987) 'The effect of life cycle on three dimensions of stratification', in BRYMAN, A., BYTHEWAY, B., ALLATT, P. and KEIL, T. (Eds) *Rethinking the Life Cycle*, Macmillan.

DALLEY, G. (1984) 'Rural Urban differences in health care, some research evidence', in LISHMAN, J. (Ed.) *Social Work in Rural and Urban Areas*, Aberdeen, AUP.

DALLEY, G. (1988) *Ideologies of Caring: Rethinking Community and Collectivism*, London, Macmillan Education.

DALY, A. (1975) 'Measuring Accessibility in a Rural Context', in WHITE, P.R. (Ed.) *Rural Transport Seminar*, London Transport Studies Group, Polytechnic of Central London.

DAVIES, P. and WALSH, D. (1983) *Alcohol Problems and Alcohol Control in Europe*, London, Croom Helm.

DEACON, B. (1987) *Poverty and Deprivation in the South West*, London, CPAG.

DENNIS, N., HENRIQUES, F. and SLAUGHTER, C. (1956, 2nd edn 1969) *Coal is Our Life*, London, Eyre and Spottiswoode (2nd edn Tavistock).

DEPARTMENT OF EMPLOYMENT (1972) Report of the Committee 1970–1972 (Robens Report) *Safety at Work*, Cmnd 5034, HMSO.

DEPARTMENT OF EMPLOYMENT (1987) *Family Expenditure Survey, 1986*, HMSO.

DEPARTMENT OF HEALTH (1989) *Working for Patients: The Health Service Caring for the 1990s*, Cmnd 555, London, HMSO.

DEPARTMENT OF HEALTH AND SOCIAL SECURITY (1980) *Inequalities in Health*, London, DHSS.

DEPARTMENT OF HEALTH AND SOCIAL SECURITY (1986) *Report of the Committee of Inquiry into the Outbreak of Food Poisoning at Stanley Royd Hospital*, Cmnd 9716, London, HMSO.

DEPARTMENT OF HEALTH AND SOCIAL SECURITY/WELSH OFFICE (1989) *Interdepartmental Circular on Alcohol Misuse*, HN (89) 4 LAC (89) 6 WOC 8/89 WHC 89 (14).

DEXTER, M. and HARBERT, W. (1983) *The Home Help Service*, London, Tavistock.

DILLMAN, D.A. and TREMBLAY, K.R. (1977) 'Rural America', *Annals of the American Academy of Political and Social Science*, 429, pp. 115–29.

DINGWALL, R. (1976) *Aspects if Illness*, London, Martin Robertson.

DOBBS, B. (1979) 'Rural Public Transport: The Economic Stranglehold', in HALSALL, D.A. and TURTON, B.J. (Eds) *Rural Transport Problems in Britain*, Transport Geography Study Group, Institute of British Geographers, University of Keele.

DORN, N. (1983) *Alcohol, Youth and the State; Drinking Practices, Controls and Health Education*, London, Croom Helm.

DOUGLAS, M. (1966) *Purity and Danger*, London, Routledge and Kegan Paul.

DOUGLAS, M. and NICOD, M. (1974) 'Taking the Biscuit: the Structure of British Meals', *New Society*, 30, pp. 744–7.

DOWNING, J. (1980) *The Media Machine*, London, Pluto Press.

DOYAL, L. (1979) *The Political Economy of Health*, London, Pluto Press.

DOYAL, L. (1984) 'Women, Health and the Sexual Division of Labour: A case study of the Women's Health Movement in Britain', *Critical Social Policy*, 3, 1, pp. 21–33.

DRUGLINK (1989) '£17m for drug services in 1989/90' *Journal on Drug Misuse in Britain*, March/April, 4.

DUNCAN-JONES, P. (1981) 'The Structure of Social Relationships: Analysis of a Survey Instrument, Part I', *Social Psychiatry*, pp. 55–61.

DUNLEAVY, P. (1979) 'Rehabilitating Collective Consumption', unpublished paper cited in SAUNDERS, P. (1981) *Social Theory and the Urban Question*, London, Hutchinson.

DUNNELL, K. and CARTWRIGHT, A. (1972) *Medicine Takers, Prescribers and Hoarders*, London, RKP.

EDWARDS, G. and GROSS, M.M. (1976) 'Alcohol Dependence: Provisional Description of Clinical Syndrome', *British Medical Journal*, 1, pp. 1058–61.

EGINGTON, A. (1983) 'Knowing Where to Draw the Line', in *Community Care*, 2 June, pp. 16–17.

ELIAS, N. (1978) *The Civilising Process: Volume One, The History of Manners*, Oxford, Basil Blackwell.

ERICKSON, R. (1984) 'Social class, men, women and families', *Sociology*, 18, 4, pp. 500–514.

EUROSOCIAL Report No: 16 (1985) *Youth and the Life in Remote Rural Areas*, Vienna, Berggasse.

FEATHERSTONE, E. (1985) 'Young Women and YTS Training', *Critical Social Policy*, 13, pp. 103–7.

FEATHERSTONE, M. (1987) 'Lifestyle and consumer culture', *Theory, Culture and Society*, 4, 1, pp. 55–70.

FEJES, F. (1984) 'Critical mass communications research and media effects: the problem of the disappearing audience', *Media, Culture and Society*, 6, 3, pp. 219–32.

FISKE, J. (1987) *Television Culture*, London, Methuen.

FOGELMAN, K., FOX, A.J. and POWER, C. (1989) 'Class and Tenure Mobility: do they explain social inequalities in health among young adults in Britain?', in FOX, A.J. (Ed.) *Health Inequalities in European Countries*, Aldershot, Gower.

FOUCAULT, M. (1967) *Madness and Civilization*, London, Allen Lane.

FOUCAULT, M. (1973) *The Birth of the Clinic*, London, Tavistock.

FOUCAULT, M. (1977) *Discipline and Punish; the Birth of the Prison*, London, Allen Lane.

FOX, A.J. and GOLDBLATT, P. (1982) *Socio-demographic mortality differentials from the OPCS Longitudinal Study 1971-75*, (series LS no. 1), London, HMSO.

FOX, A.J., GOLDBLATT, P. and JONES, D.R. (1985) 'Social class mortality differentials: Artefact, selection or life circumstances?', *Journal of Epidemiology and Community Health*, 39, 1, pp. 1–8.

FRANKENBERG, R. (1966) *Communities in Britain*, Harmondsworth, Pelican.

FRANSELLA, F. and FROST, K. (1977) *On Being A Woman*, London, Tavistock.

FRIEDSON, E. (1961) *Patient's Views of Medical Practice*, New York, Russell Sage Foundation.

FULDER, S. (1984) *The Handbook of Complementary Medicine*, Sevenoaks, Coronet Books.

FULLER, J.H.S. and TOON, P. (1988) *Medical Practice in a Multi-cultural Society*, Heinemann, London.

FURNHAM, A. and SMITH, C. (1988) 'Choosing Alternative Medicine. A comparison of the beliefs of patients using a GP and a homoeopath', *Social Science and Medicine*, 26, 7, pp. 685–9.

GABE, J. and BURY, M. (1988) 'Tranquillisers as a social problem', *The Sociological Review*, 36, 2, pp. 320–52.

GABE, J. and LIPCHITZ-PHILLIPS, S. (1984) 'Tranquillisers as social control?', *The Sociological Review*, 32, 3, pp. 524–46.

GABE, J. and LIPCHITZ-PHILLIPS, S. (1982) 'Evil necessity? The meaning of benzodiazapine use for women patients from one general practice', *Sociology of Health and Illness*, 4, 2, pp. 201–9.

GABE, J. and THOROGOOD, N. (1986a) 'Prescribed drugs and the management of everyday life: the experiences of black and white working class women', *The Sociological Review*, 34, 4, pp. 737–72.

GABE, J. and THOROGOOD, N. (1986b) 'Tranquillisers as a resource', in GABE, J. and WILLIAMS, P. (Eds) *Tranquillisers: Social, Psychological and Clinical Perspectives*, London, Tavistock.

GALLIE, D. (1988) 'Employment, unemployment and social stratification', in GALLIE, D. (Ed.) *Employment in Britain*, Oxford, Blackwell.

GARLAND, D. (1985) *Punishment and Welfare: A History of Penal Strategies*, Aldershot, Vermont, Gower.

GEERTZ, C. (1975) 'Thick Description: Towards an Interpretative Theory of Culture', in *The Interpretation of Cultures*, London, Hutchinson.

GENERAL HOUSEHOLD SURVEY (1986) *General Household Survey: Supplement A*, London, HMSO.

GIARCHI, G.G. (1984) *Between MacAlpine and Polaris*, London, Routledge and Kegan Paul.

GIARCHI, G.G. (1986) 'De-industrialisation of the Rural Areas', paper and NACAB Conference, Nottingham University.

GIARCHI, G.G. (1987) 'Cornwall's Gaza Strip: Administrative and Cultural Constraints to Geriatric Care in a Peripheral Rural Area', DI GREGORIO, S. (Ed.) *Social Gerontology: New Directions*, London, Croom Helm.

GIARCHI, G.G. (1988) *Responding to Need in a Rural Area*, Liskeard, NACAB Report.

GIGGS, R. (1983) 'Health', in PACIONE, M. (Ed.) *Progress in Urban Geography*, Beckenham, Croom Helm.

GILBERT, G.N. (1986) 'Occupational class and inter-class mobility', *British Journal of Sociology*, 37, 3, pp. 370–91.

GILDER, I. (1984) 'State Planning and Local Needs', in BRADLEY, T. and LOWE, P. (Eds) *op. cit.*

GIRT, J.L. (1973) 'Distance to General Medical Practice and its effect on revealed ill-health in a rural environment', *Canadian Geographer*, 17, pp. 145–66.

GLASNER, P. and TRAVIS, G.D.L. (1987) 'The Social Construction of a Health Hazard: Trade Unions and Visual Display Units'. Paper presented at the British Sociological Association Annual Conference, Leeds.

GLENDINNING, C. and MILLAR, J. (1987) (Eds) *Women and Poverty in Britain*, Brighton, Wheatsheaf.

GLENDON, A.I. and BOYLE, A.J. (1987) *YTS Accident Injuries April 1983 – September 1986: Final Report*, Sheffield, Health and Safety Technology and Management Ltd.

GOFFMAN, A. (1961) *Asylums*, Harmondsworth, Penguin.

GOLDTHORPE, J.H. (1983) 'Women and Class analysis: In defence of the conventional view', *Sociology*, 17, 4, pp. 465–88.

GOLDTHORPE, J.H. (1984) 'Women and Class analysis: A reply to the replies', *Sociology*, 18, 4, pp. 491–9.

GORDON, J.E. (1956) 'The Epidemiology of Alcoholism', in KRUSE, H.D. (Ed.) *Alcoholism As A Medical Problem*, New York, Meobor.

GOVE, W.R. (1978) 'Sex differences in mental illness among adult men and women', *Social Science and Medicine*, 12, pp. 187–98.

GOVE, W.R. (1984) 'Gender differences in mental and physical illness: The effects of fixed roles and nurturant roles', *Social Science and Medicine*, 19, 2, pp. 77–91.

GOVE, W.R. and HUGHES, M. (1979) 'Possible causes of the apparent sex differences in physical health', *American Sociological Review*, 44, pp. 126–46.

GRAHAM, H. (1983) 'Caring: A Labour of Love', in FINCH, J. and GROVES, D. (Eds) *A Labour of Love: Women, Work and Caring*, London, Routledge and Kegan Paul.

GRAHAM, H. (1984) *Women, Health and the Family*, Brighton, Wheatsheaf.

GRAMSCI, A. (1971) *Selections from the Prison Notebooks*, Ed. HOARE, Q. and SMITH, G.N., London, Lawrence and Wishart.

GRANT, G. (1979) 'Approaches to social welfare delivery in rural areas', paper at European Centre for Social Welfare Delivery in Rural Areas, Portugal, Sesimbra.

GRINDLE, R. (1987) *Exploding the Myth: The Truth About Alcohol Misuse*, six articles reprinted from the *Morning Advertiser*.

GUPTILL, S.C. (1975) 'The Spatial Availability of Physicians', *Proceedings of the Association of American Geographers*, 7, pp. 80–84.

GUSFIELD, J.R. (1963) *Symbolic Crusade*, Urbana, University of Illinois Press.

GUSFIELD, J.R. (1976) 'Alcohol and Alcohol Problems: New Thinking and New Directions', in FILSTEAD, W.J., ROSSI, J.J. and KELLER, K. (Eds) *The Prevention of Drinking Problems*, New York, Ballinger Pub. Co.

GUTEK, B.A. and MORASH, B. (1982) 'Sex Ratios, Sex-Role Spillover and Sexual Harassment of Women at Work', *Journal of Social Issues*, 38, 4, pp. 55–74.

HAGERSTRAND, T. (1970) 'Transport', in HOUSE, J.W. (Ed.) *The UK Space*, London, Weidenfeld and Nicolson.

HAM, C., DINGWALL, R., FENN, P. and HARRIS, D. (1988) *Medical Negligence: Compensation and Accountability*, London, Kings Fund Institute.

HAMID GHODSE, A. (1983) 'Treatment of drug addiction in London', *Lancet* I, pp. 636–9.

HARPER, S. (1986) 'The Kinship Network of the Rural Aged'. Paper presented at the British Society of Gerontology Conference, Glasgow.

HARRISON, B. (1971) *Drink and the Victorians: The Temperance Question in England, 1815–1872*, London, Faber.

HART, G.J., CARVELL, A.L.M., WOODWARD, N., JOHNSON, A.M., WILLIAMS, P., PARRY, J.V. (1989a) 'Evaluation of Needle Exchange in Central London: Behaviour Change and Anti-HIV Status Over One Year', *AIDS Care*, 3, pp. 261–5.

HART, G.J., SONNEX, C., PETHERICK, A., JOHNSON, A.M., FEINMANN, C., ADLER, M.W. (1989b) 'Risk Behaviour for HIV Infection Amongst Injecting Drug Users Attending a Drug Dependency Clinic', *British Medical Journal*, 298, pp. 1081–3.

HART, G.J., WOODWARD, N. and CARVELL, A. (1989) 'Needle-Exchange in Central London: Operating Philosophy and Communication Strategies', *AIDS Care*, pp. 237–45.

HART, J.T. (1971) 'The Inverse Care Law', *Lancet*, I, pp. 405–12.

HARTNOLL, R., MITCHESON, M., LEWIS, R. and BRYER, S. (1985) 'Estimating the Prevalence of Opioid Dependence', *Lancet*, I, pp. 203–5.

HARVEY, D. (1970) 'Social Processes and Spatial Form: an Analysis of the Conceptual Problems of Urban Planning', *Papers and Proc. of Regional Sc. Assoc.*, 25, pp. 47–69.

HARVEY, D. (1973) *Social Justice and the City*, London, Edward Arnold.

HAYNES, R.M. and BENTHAM, C.G. (1982) 'The Effect of Accessibility on General Practitioner Consultations, Outpatient Attendances and Inpatient Admissions in Norfolk, England', in *Social Science and Medicine*, 16, pp. 561–9.

HEALTH AND SAFETY COMMISSION (1983) Health and Safety (Youth Training Scheme) Regulations, London, HMSO.

HEALTH AND SAFETY EXECUTIVE (1984) *Mind How You Go!*, London, HMSO.

HEALTH AND SAFETY EXECUTIVE Annual Reports 1986/67; 1987/8, London, HMSO.

HEATHER, N. (1985) 'Introduction', in HEATHER, N., ROBERTSON, I. and DAVIES, P. (Eds) *The Misuse of Alcohol*, Beckenham, Croom Helm.

HEATHER, N. and ROBERTSON, I. (1981) *Controlled Drinking*, London, Methuen and Co. Ltd.

HEDLEY, R. and NORMAN, A. (1982) *Home Help: Key Issues in Service Provision*, London, CPA.

HELMAN, C. (1981) 'Tonic, Fuel and Food: social and symbolic aspects of the long term use of psychotropic drugs', *Social Science and Medicine*, 15B, 4, pp. 521–33.

HELMAN, C. (1984) 'Feed a cold, starve a fever', in BLACK, N., BOSWELL, D., GRAY, A., MURPHY, S. and POPAY, J. *Health and Disease, A Reader*, Milton Keynes, Open University Press.

HELMAN, C. (1986) 'Long term use of psychotropic drugs', in GABE, J. and WILLIAMS, E.P., *op. cit.*

HENDERSON, S. (1977) 'The Social Network, Support and Neurosis', British Journal of Psychiatry, 131, pp. 185–91.

HENDERSON, S. (1974) 'Care-eliciting behaviour in man', *Journal of Nervous and Mental Disorders*, 159, pp. 172–81.

HENDERSON, S. (1980) 'A development in Social Psychiatry: the systematic study of social bonds', *Journal of Nervous and Mental Disorders*, 168, pp. 63–9.

HENLEY, A. (1979) *Asian Patients – In Hospital and at Home*, King Edward's Hospital Fund for London, Tunbridge Wells, Pitman Medical Publishing Company Limited.

HERBERT, D.T. and THOMAS, C.J. (1982) *Urban Geography: a First Approach*, Chichester, John Wiley.

HIRST, P. and WOOLLEY, P. (1982) *Social Relations and Human Attributes*, London, Tavistock.

HM STATIONERY OFFICE (1926) *Report of the Departmental Committee on Drug Dependence (Rolleston Committee)*, London, HMSO.

HM STATIONERY OFFICE (1961) *Interdepartmental Committee on Drug Addiction: Report*, London, HMSO.

HM STATIONERY OFFICE (1965) *Interdepartmental Committee on Drug Addiction: Second Report*. London, HMSO.

HOME OFFICE (1987) *Young People and Alcohol: Report of the Working Group of the Standing Conference on Crime Prevention*, London, Home Office.

HOUSING CORPORATION (1988) *West Region Policy Statement, 1987–88*, Exeter, West Region Office.

HOWARD, J. and BORGES, P. (1970) 'Needle-Sharing in the Haight: Some Social and Psychological Functions', *Journal of Health and Social Behaviour*, 11, pp. 220–30.

HUGHES, J. (1985) 'Some dimensions of regional inequality', *Poverty*, 61.

HUNT, A. (assisted by FOX, J.) (1970) 'The Home Help Service in England and Wales', *The Government Social Survey*, London, HMSO.

IGNATIEFF, M. (1983) 'State, Civil Society and Total Institution: A Critique of Recent Social Histories of Punishment', in COHEN, S. and SCULL, A.T. (Eds) *Social Control and the Modern State: Comparative and Historical Essays*, Oxford, Martin Robertson.

ILLICH, I. (1981) *Shadow Work*, Boston, Marion Boyars.

INTERNATIONAL LABOUR OFFICE (1987) 'Alcohol and Drugs', *Conditions of Work Digest*, 6, 1.

JESSON, W.J., THORP, R.W., MORTIMER, P.P. and OATES, J.K. (1986) 'Prevalence of Anti-HTLV-III in UK Risk Groups 1984/85', *Lancet*, I, p. 155.

JOSEPH, A.E. and BANTOCK, P.R. (1982) 'Measuring potential physical accessibility to general practitioners in rural areas: a method and case study', *Social Science and Medicine*, 16, pp. 85–90.

JOSEPH, A.E. and BANTOCK, P.R. (1983) 'Rural Accessibility of General Practitioners. A Canadian Perspective', IBG Conference, Edinburgh.

JOSEPH, A.E. and PHILLIPS, D.R. (1984) *Accessibility and Utilization*, London and NY, Harper and Row.

KINNERSLEY, P. (1973) *The Hazards of Work and How to Fight Them*, London, Pluto.

KITZINGER, S. (1982) 'The social context of birth', in MACCORMACK, C.P. (Ed.) (1982) *An Ethnography of Fertility and Birth*, London, Academic Press.

KLEIN, T. (1988) 'When keeping your head down can lead to decapitation', *Scrip*, 1320, pp. 20–1.

KNOX, P.L. (1978) 'The Intraurban Ecology of Primary Medical Care: Patterns of Accessibility and their Policy Implication' *Environment and Planning*, A, 10, pp. 415–35.

KNOX, P.L. (1982) 'The Geography of medical care delivery: an historical perspective', *Geoforum*, 12, pp. 245–50.

KREITMAN, N. (1986) 'Alcohol Consumption and the Prevention Paradox', *British Journal of Addiction*', 81, pp. 353–63.

KRONENFELD, J.J. and WASNER, C. (1982) 'The Use of Unorthodox Therapies and Marginal Practitioners', *Social Science and Medicine*, 16, pp. 1119–25.

LACEY, R. and WOODWARD, S. (1985) *That's Life Survey on Tranquillisers*, London, BBC Publications.

LAND, H. (1976) 'Women: supporters or supported?' in BARKER, D.L. and ALLEN, S. (Eds) *Sexual Divisions and Society: Process and Change*, London, Tavistock.

LARKIN, A. (1978) 'Housing and the Poor', in WALKER, A. (Ed.) *Rural Poverty*, London, CPAG.

LATTO, (1980) 'Help Begins at Home, Part I', *Community Care*, 24 April, pp. 15–16.

LEA, J. (1979) 'Discipline and Capitalist Development', in FINE, R. *et al. Capitalism and the Rule of Law*, London, Hutchinson.

LEDERMANN, S. (1956) *Alcool, Alcoolisme, Alcoolisation, Données scientifiques de caractère physiologique, economique et social*, Paris, Presses Universitaires de France.

LEDERMANN, S. (1964) *Alcool, Alcoolisme, Alcoolisation, mortalé. morbidité, accidents du travail*, Paris, Institute de'Études Demographiques.

LEMENT, E.M. (1967) 'Paranoia and the Dynamics of Exclusion,' in SCHEFF, T.J. (Ed.) *Mental Illness and Social Processes*, New York, Harper and Row.

LESCHINSKY, D. (1977) *Health Sevices in Rural Areas*, London, National Federation of Women's Institutes.

LEVINE, H.G. (1978) 'The Discovery of Addiction: Changing Conceptions of Habitual Drunkenness in America', *Journal of Studies on Alcohol*, 39, pp. 143–74.

LEVI-STRAUSS, C. (1978) *Structural Anthropology*, London, Allen Lane.

LEVI-STRAUSS, C. (1986) *The Raw and the Cooked. Introduction to a Science of Mythology*, Harmondsworth, Peregrine Books, Penguin.

LEVITT, R. (1976) *The Reorganised National Health Service*, Beckenham, Croom Helm (2nd edn 1977, 3rd edn (with A. Hall) 1984).

LEVITT, R. (1980) *Implementing Public Policy*, Beckenham, Croom Helm.

LEWIN, E., and Oleson, V. (1985) *Women, Health and Healing: Towards a New Perspective*, London, Tavistock.

LISHMAN, J. (Ed.) (1984) *Social Work in Rural and Urban Areas*, University of Aberdeen, Research Highlights, No. 9.

LITTLEWOOD, R. (1988) 'From vice to madness: the semantics of naturalistic and personalistic understandings in Trinidadian local medicine, *Social Science and Medicine*, 27, ,2 pp. 129–48.

LITTLEWOOD, R. and LIPSEDGE, M. (1982) *Aliens and Alienists, Ethnic Minorities and Psychiatry*, Harmondsworth, Penguin.

LOVELOCK, D. (1984) *Review of the National Association of Citizens Advice Bureaux*, Cmnd. 9139, HMSO.

LOWE, C.R. (1969) 'Industrial Bronchitis', *British Medical Journal*, February, pp. 463–86.

MACARA, A.W. (1976) 'How can community medicine help the clinician?' *The Practitioner*, 217, p. 577.

McGREGOR, S. (Ed.) (1989) *Drugs and Society*, London, Tavistock.

McGUIRE, M.B. (1988) (with assistance of Debra Hunter) *Ritual Healing in Suburban America*, New Brunswick and London, Rutgers University Press.

McLAUGHLIN, B. (1983) *Country Crisis*, London, Media Services Unit, National Extension College, Channel 4, ATV.

McLAUGHLIN, B. (1985) *Deprivation in Rural Areas*, A Research Report to the DOE and the Development Commission.

MAKELA and VIIKARI, (1977) 'Notes on Alcohol and the State', *Acta Sociologica*, 20, pp. 155–79.

MANNING, N. (1985) 'Constructing social problems', in MANNING, N. (Ed.) *Social Problems and Welfare Ideology*, Aldershot, Gower.

MANNING, N. (1987) 'What is a social problem?', in LONEY, M. *et al.* (Eds) *The State or the Market: Politics and Welfare in Contemporary Society*, London, Sage.

MANPOWER SERVICES COMMISSION (1987) *Health and Safety on YTS Report, 1 January 1985 to 31 December 1986*, Sheffield, MSC.

MARCUS, A.C., SEEMAN, T.E. and TELESKY, C.W. (1983) 'Sex differences in reports of illness and disability: A further test of the fixed rule hypothesis', *Social Science and Medicine*, 17, 15, pp. 993–1002.

MARES, P., HENLEY, A. and BARKER, C. (1986) *Health Care in Multi-racial Britain*, London, HEC/NEC.

MARKS, J. (1975) *Home Help*, Occasional Papers on Social Administration, No. 58, London, G. Bell and Sons.

MARKS, J. (1985) 'Opium, the Religion of the People', *Lancet*, I, pp. 1439–40.

MARKS, J. and PARRY, A. (1987) 'Syringe-Exchange Programme for Drug Addicts', *Lancet*, I, pp. 691-2.

MARS, G. and NICOD, M. (1984) *World of Waiters*, London, George Allen and Unwin.

MARTIN, J. and ROBERTS, C. (1984) *Women & Employment: A Lifetime Perspective*, London, HMSO.

MARTINEZ-BRAWLEY, E. (1984) 'In Search of the Common Principles in Rural, Social and Community Work', in LISHMAN, J. (Ed.) *op. cit.*

MARX, K. (1867) *Das Capital*, Volume 1, Hamburg, Ottomeissner.

MASSAM, B.H. (1974) 'Political geography and the provision of services', *Progress in Geography*, 6, pp. 179–210.

MASSAM, B.H. (1974) *Spatial Search*, Oxford, Oxford University Press.

MAYNARD, A. (1985) 'The Role of Economic Measures in Preventing Drinking Problems', in HEATHER, N., ROBERTSON, I. and DAVIES, P. (Eds) *The Misuse of Alcohol*, Beckenham, Croom Helm.

MILLER, J. (1989) 'Neither fish, fowl nor red herring', *The Independent*, 7 January.

MINISTERIAL GROUP ON ALCOHOL MISUSE (1989) *First Annual Report 1987-1988*, London, Home Office.

MOORE, J., PHIPPS, K. and MARCER, D. (1985) 'Why do people seek treatment by alternative medicine?', *British Medical Journal*, 290, 5 January, pp. 28–9.

MORGAN, M. and WATKINS, C.J. (1988) 'Managing Hypertension: Beliefs and responses to medication among cultural groups', *Sociology of Health and Illness*, 10, 4, pp. 561–78.

MORROW, A. (1983) 'Finding Solutions Together', in *Community Care*, 1 September, pp. 18–19.

MOSER, K. and GOLDBLATT, P. (1985) 'Mortality of women in the OPCS Longitudinal Study: Differentials by own occupation and household and housing characteristics', *Social Statistics Research Unit Working Paper No. 26*, London, City University.

MOSER, K., PUGH, H. and GOLDBLATT, P. (1988a) 'Inequalities in women's health: Developing an alternative approach', *British Medical Journal*, pp. 1221–4.

MOSER, K., PUGH, H. and GOLDBLATT, P. (1988b) 'Inequlaities in women's health in England and Wales: Mortality among married women according to social circumstances, employment characteristics and life cycle stage', *Social Statistics Research Unit Working Paper, No. 57*, London, City University.

MOSS, A.R. (1987) 'AIDS and Intravenous Drug Use: the Real Heterosexual Epidemic', *British Medical Journal*, 294, pp. 389–90.

NATHANSON, C. (1975) 'Illness and the feminine role: A theoretical review', *Social Science and Medicine*, 9, pp. 57–62.

NATHANSON, C. (1980) 'Social roles and health status among women: the significance of employment', *Social Science and Medicine*, 14A, pp. 463–71.

NATIONAL CONSUMER COUNCIL (1978) *The Right to Know, A Review of Advice Centres in Rural Areas*, London, Bedford Square Press.

NATIONAL CONSUMER COUNCIL (1977) *The Fourth Right of Citizenship, A Review of Local Advice Services*, London, NCC.

NAVARRO, V. (1979) *Medicine under Capitalism*, Beckenham, Croom Helm.

NICHOLS, T. (1986) 'Industrial Injuries in British Manufacturing in the 1980s – a Commentary on Wright's Article', *Sociological Review*, 34, pp. 290–306.

NICHOLSON, S. (1985) *Out of Town: Out of Mind*, Leicester, Gartree Rural Unemployment Project.

NORFOLK, S.S.D. (1976) 'Team "Social Indicators" ', SSRG Symposium, *Social Indicators and Community Profiles in Rural Areas*.

OAKLEY, A. (1974) *Housewife*, London, Allen Lane.

OAKLEY, A. (1980) *Women Confined: Towards a Sociology of Childbirth*, Oxford, Martin Robertson.

OAKLEY, A. (1987) 'Fieldwork up the MI: Policy and Political Aspects', in JACKSON, A. (Ed.) *Anthropology at Home*, ASA Monograph 25, London, Tavistock.

O'DONNELL, K. (1989) *The Impact of Job Losses in the Coal Mining Industry on Wakefield Metropolitan District, 1981–88*, Wakefield Metropolitan District Publication.

OFFICE OF POPULATION CENSUSES AND SURVEYS (1980) Classification of Occupations, London, HMSO.

OFFICE OF POPULATION CENSUSES AND SURVEYS (1984) *General Household Survey*, 1982, London, HMSO.

OFFICE OF POPULATION CENSUSES AND SURVEYS (1986) *Occupational Mortality: The Registrar General's Decennial Supplement for Great Britain, 1979–80 1982–83*, London, HMSO.

OFFICE OF POPULATION CENSUSES AND SURVEYS (1986) *General Household Survey, 1984*, London, HMSO.

OFFICE OF POPULATION CENSUSES AND SURVEYS (1988a) *General Household Survey, 1985*, London, HMSO.

OFFICE OF POPULATION CENSUSES AND SURVEYS (1988b) *Regional Trends 1987*, London, HMSO.

OFFICE OF POPULATION CENSUSES AND SURVEYS (1989) *General Household Survey 1986*, London, HMSO.

OKLEY, J. (1983) *The Traveller-Gypsies*, Cambridge, Cambridge University Press.

OOIJENDIJK, W.T.M., MACKENBACH, J.P. and LIMBERGER, H.H.B. (1981) *What is Better? An investigation into the use of, and satisfaction with, complementary and official medicine in the Netherlands*, London, Threshold Foundation.

ORFORD, J. (1985) *Excessive Appetites: A Psychological View of Addictions*, Chichester, Wiley and Sons.

ORFORD, J. (1987) 'The Need for a Community Response to alcohol related problems', in STOCKWELL, T. and CLEMENT, S. (Eds) *Helping the Problem Drinker; New Initiative in Community Care*, London, New York, Sydney, Croom Helm.

PACIONE, M. (1984) *Rural Geography*, London, Harper and Row.

PAHL, J. (1989) *Money and Marriage*, London, Macmillan.

PAHL, R. (1970) *Patterns of Urban Life*, London, Longman.

PAHL, R. (1975) *Whose City?* Harmondsworth, Penguin Books.

PAHL, R. (1979) 'Socio-Political Factors in Resource Allocation', in HERBERT, D. and SMITH, D. (Eds) *op. cit.*

PAHL, R. (1984) *Divisions of Labour*, Oxford, Basil Blackwell.

PARKER, G. and TUPLING, H. (1976) 'The Chiropractic Patient: Psychosocial Aspects', *Medical Journal of Australia*', 4, September, pp. 373–9.

PARKER, H., NEWCOMBE, R. and BAKX, K. (1987) 'The New Heroin Users: Prevalence and Characteristics in Wirral, Merseyside', *British Journal of Addiction*, 82, pp. 147–57.

PARKER, R. (1981) 'Tending and Social Policy', in GOLDBERG, E.M. and HATCH, S. (Eds) *A New Look at the Personal Social Services*, London, PSI.

PEARSON, M. (1986) 'Racist Notions of Ethnicity and Culture in Health Education', in RODMELL, S. and WATT, A. (Eds) *The Politics of Health Education*, London, Tavistock.

PHILLIPS, D. (1981) *Contemporary Issues in the Geography of Health Care*, Norwich, Geo Books.

PHILLIPS, D. and WILLIAMS, A. (1984) *Rural Britain*, Oxford, Blackwell.

PLUNKETT, R.J. and GORDON, J.E. (1960) *Epidemiology and Mental Illness*, New York, Basic Books.

POLAND, F. (1986) 'Minding and Mothering. The Tension Between "Work" and "Care" ', in The Social Care and Research Seminar, *On Researching the Topic of Care*, Studies in Sexual Politics, 11, Manchester Department of Sociology, Manchester University.

POPAY, J. and JONES, G. (1988) 'Gender inequalities in health: Explaining the sting in the tail', paper presented to the Social Policy Association Annual Conference, July, University of Edinburgh.

PORTER, M. (1983) *Home, Work and Class Consciousness*, Manchester, Manchester University Press.

POWER, R., HARTNOLL, R. and DAVIAUD, E. (1988) 'Drug Injecting, AIDS and Risk Behaviour: Potential for Change and Intervention Strategies', *British Journal of Addiction*, 83, pp. 649–54.

PUBLIC HEALTH ALLIANCE (1988) *Beyond Acheson: An Agenda for the New Public Health*, Birmingham, Public Health Alliance (PO Box 1156, Kings Norton, Birmingham B30 2AZ).

PUBLIC HEALTH LABORATORY SERVICES WORKING GROUP (1989) 'Prevalence of HIV Antibody in High and Low Risk Groups in England', *British Medical Journal*, 298, pp. 422–3.

QURESHI, H. and WALKER, A. (1986) 'Caring for Elderly People: The Family and the State', in PHILLIPSON, C. and WALKER, A. (Eds) *Ageing and Social Policy*, London, Gower.

RAYNER, G. (1988) 'Health Goals into the next century', *Environmental Health*, 196, 4, pp. 10–16.

REID, I. and WORMALD, E. (Eds) (1982) *Sex Differences in Britain*, London, Grant McIntyre.

REX, J. and MOORE, R. (1969) *Race, Community and Conflict: A Study of Sparkbrook*, Oxford, Oxford University Press.

RICHIE, J. et al. (1981) *Access to Primary Health Care*, London, OPCS.

RIKKINEN, K. (1968) 'Change in Village and Rural Population with Distance from Duluth', *Economic Geography*, 44, pp. 312–25.

RILEY, J.N. (1980) 'Client choices among osteopaths and ordinary physicians in Michigan community', *Social Science and Medicine*, 14B, 2, pp. 111–20.

ROBERTS, H. (1984) *The Patient Patient*, London, Pandora.

ROBERTS, H. and BARKER, R. (1986) 'The social classification of women', *Social Statistics Research Unit Working Paper No. 46*, City University.

ROBERTSON, I. and HEATHER, N. (1986) *Let's Drink to Your Health*, London, British Psychological Society.

ROBERTSON, J.R., BUCKNAL, A.B.V., WELSBY, P.D., ROBERTS, J.J.K., INGLIS, J.M., PEATHERER, J.R. and BRETTLE, R.A. (1986) 'Epidemic of AIDs-Related Virus (HTLV-III/LAV) Infection Among Intravenous Drug Abusers', *British Medical Journal*, 292, pp. 527-30.

ROBINSON, D. (1987) 'Alcohol Problems: Prevention at the Local Level', *Health Trends*, 19.

ROOM, R. (1974) 'Minimising Alcohol Problems', *Alcohol Health and Research World*, ,3 pp. 12-77.

ROOM, R. (1981) 'The Case for a Problem Prevention Approach to Alcohol, Drug and Mental Problems', *Public Health Reports*, 96, pp. 26-33.

ROSENBERG, C.E. (1986) 'Disease and Social Order in America: Perceptions and Expectations', *The Millbank Quarterly*, 64, pp. 34-55.

ROSENTHAL, M. (1987) *Dealing with Medical Malpractice*, London, Tavistock.

ROTHMAN, A. (1980) *Conscience and Convenience*, Boston, Little Brown.

ROYAL COLLEGE OF GENERAL PRACTITIONERS (1986) *Alcohol - A Balanced View*, London, Royal College of General Practitioners.

ROYAL COLLEGE OF PHYSICIANS (1987) *A Great and Growing Evil*, London, Tavistock.

ROYAL COLLEGE OF PSYCHIATRISTS (1986) *Alcohol Our Favourite Drug*, London, Tavistock.

RURAL VOICE (1987) *A Rural Strategy*, Fairford, Rural Voice Policy Statement.

RUSSELL, A. (1986) *The Country Parish*, London, SPCK.

SAUNDERS, P. (1981) *Social Theory and the Urban Question*, London, Hutchinson.

SCHULTZ, R.R. (1975) 'A space potential analysis of physician location', *Proceedings of the Association of American Geographers*, 7, pp. 203-8.

SCOTTISH HOME AND HEALTH DEPARTMENT (1986) *HIV in Scotland: Report of the Scottish Committee on HIV Infection and Intravenous Drug Misuse*, Edinburgh, SHHD.

SCOTTISH INFORMATION OFFICE (1986) News Release, 24 September 1986; Publication of Scottish Committee Reports on AIDS and Drugs Misuse.

SCULL, A. (1977a) *Museums of Madness: The Social Organisation of Insanity in Nineteenth Century England*, New York, St Martin's Press.

SCULL, A. (1977b) *Decarceration: Community Treatment and the Deviant - A Radical View*, Englewood Cliffs, NJ, Prentice Hall.

SCULL, A. (1981) 'Progressive Dreams, Progressive Nightmares: Social Control in Twentieth Century America', *Stanford Law Review*, 33, pp. 301-16.

SCULL, A. (1983) 'Community Corrections: Panacea, Progress or Pretence?', in GARLAND, D. and YOUNG, T. (Eds) *The Power to Punish*, London, Heinemann.

SEED, P. (1984) 'Residential and day services, Change in a changing context', in *Social Work in Rural and Urban Areas*, op. cit.

SHANNON, G.W. (1977) 'Space, time and illness behaviour', *Social Science and Medicine*, 11, pp. 683-9.

SHANNON, G.W. amd DEVER, G.E.A. (1974) *Health Care Delivery: Spatial Perspectives*, NY, McGraw Hill.

SHARPE, S. (1984) *Double Identity: The Lives of Working Mothers*, Harmondsworth, Penguin.

SHIPLEY, P. (1987) 'The Management of Psychological Risk Factors in the Working Environment, UK Law Compared', *Work and Stress*, 1, pp. 43-8.

SILVERSTONE, R. (1988) 'Television, myth and culture', in CAREY, J.W. (Ed.) *Media, Myths and Narratives: Television and the Press*, London, Sage.

SKOG, O.-J. (1973) *A Contribution to a Theory of the Distribution of Alcohol Consumption*, 1, National Institute for Alcohol Research, Oslo.

SKOG, O.-J. (1974) *A Contribution to a Theory of the Distribution of Alcohol Consumption*, 2, National Institute for Alcohol Research, Oslo.

SMART, B. (1979) 'On Discipline and Social Regulation: A Review of Foucault's Genealogical Analysis', in FINE, R. et al., *Capitalism and the Rule of Law*, London, Hutchinson.

SMITH, D.M. (1974) 'Who gets what, where and how: a welfare focus for human geography', *Geography*, 59, pp. 289-97.

SMITH, D.M. (1977) *Human Geography: A Welfare Approach*, London, Edward Arnold.

SOLOMAN, D.N. (1968) 'Sociological Perspectives on Occupations', in BECKER, H.S., *et al.* (Eds) *Institutions and the Person, papers presented to Everitt C. Hughes*, Chicago, Adline Publishing Co.

SONNEX, C., HART, G.J., WILLIAMS, P., ADLER, M.W. (1989) 'Condom Use by Heterosexuals Attending a Department of Genitourinary Medicine: Attitudes and Behaviour in the Light of HIV Infection', *Genitourinary Medicine*, 65, pp. 248–51.

SPECTOR, M. and KITSUSE, J. (1977) *Constructing Social Problems*, Menlo Park, California, Cummings Publishing Company.

STACEY, M. (1976) 'The Health service consumer: a sociological misconception', STACEY, M. (Ed.) *The Sociology of the Health Service*, Sociological Review Monograph 22, London, Routledge and Kegan Paul.

STACEY, M. (1977) 'People who are affected by the Inverse Law of Care', *Health and Social Services Journal*, 3 June, pp. 898–902.

STACEY, M. (1981) 'The Division of Labour Revisited, or Overcoming the Two Adams', in ABRAMS, P., DEEM, R., FINCH, J. and ROCK, P. (Eds) *Practice and Progress: British Sociology 1950-1980*, London, Allen and Unwin.

STANDING CONFERENCE OF RURAL COMMUNITY COUNCILS (1978) *The Decline of Rural Services*, London, SCRCC.

STANWORTH, M. (1984) 'Women and class analysis: a reply to John Goldthorpe', *Sociology*, 18, 2, pp. 159–70.

STELLMAN, J.W. (1977) *Women's Work, Women's Health: Myths and Realities*, New York, Pantheon Books.

STERN, J. (1983) 'The relationship between unemployment and morbidity and mortality in Britain', *Population Studies*, 37, pp. 61–74.

STEVENSON, G. (1976) 'Social Relations of Production and Consumption in the Human Service Occupations', *Monthly Review*, 28, 3, pp. 78–87.

STIMSON, G.V. (1974) 'Obeying doctor's orders: a view from the other side, *Social Science and Medicine*, 8, 2, pp. 97–104.

STIMSON, G.V. (1987) 'British Drug Policies in the 1980's: A Preliminary Analysis and Suggestions for Research', *British Journal of Addiction*, 82, 5 May, p. 477.

STIMSON, G.V., ALLDRITT, L., DOLAN, K. and DONOGHOE, M. (1988) 'Syringe Exchange Schemes for Drugs Users in England and Scotland', *British Medical Journal*, 196, pp. 1717–19.

STIMSON, G.V., ALLDRITT, L., DOLAN, K., DONOGHOE, M. and LART, R.A. (1988) *Injecting Equipment Exchange Schemes: Final Report*, London, Goldsmiths' College.

STIMSON, G.V. and OPPENHEIMER, E. (1982) *Heroin addiction: Treatment and Control in Britain*, London, Tavistock.

STIMSON, G. and WEBB, B. (1975) *Going to See the Doctor: The Consultation Process in General Practice*, London, RKP.

STOCKFORD, D. (1978) 'Social Services Provision', in WALKER, A. *Rural Poverty*, London, CPAG.

STOCKWELL, T. and CLEMENT, S. (1987) (Eds) *Helping the Problem Drinker: New Initiatives in Community Care*, Beckenham, Croom Helm.

STRATHERN, M. (1982) 'Kinship at the Cove: An Anthropology of Elmdon', in COHEN, A.P. (Ed.) *Belonging*, Manchester, Manchester University Press.

TAYLOR, P.J. (1977) *Distance Decay in Spatial Interaction*, Norwich, CATMG, 2 Geo Abstracts, Ltd.

TETHER, P. (1987) 'Preventing Alcohol Related Problems: The Local Dimension', in STOCKWELL and CLEMENT (Eds) *Helping the Problem Drinker: New Initiatives in Community Care*, Beckenham, Croom Helm.

TETHER, P. and ROBINSON, D. (1986) *Preventing Alcohol Problems: A Guide for Local Action*, London, Tavistock.

THOMAS, C.J. (1976) 'Sociospatial Variation and the Use of Services', in HERBERT, D.T. and JOHNSTON, R.J. (Eds) *Social Areas in Cities*, Vol. 2, Chichester, Wiley.

THOMPSON, I. (1983) 'The Ethical Debate', in GRANT, M. and RITSON, B. (Eds) *Alcohol: the Prevention Debate*, Beckenham, Croom Helm.

THOMPSON, J.B. (1988) 'Mass communication and modern culture: contribution to a critical theory of ideology', *Sociology*, 22, 3, pp. 359–83.

THOMPSON, P. (1983) *The Nature of Work: An Introduction to Debates on the Labour Process*, London, Macmillan.

THOROGOOD, N. (1988) *Health and the management of daily life amongst women of Afro-Caribbean origin living in Hackney*, University of London, unpublished PhD thesis.

THOROGOOD, N. (1989) 'Afro-Caribbean women's experience of the health service', *New Community*, 15, 3.

TOFFLER, A. (1980) *The Third Wave*, London, Pan Books.

TOWNSEND, P. and DAVIDSON, N. (1982) *Inequalities in Health: The Black Report*, Harmondsworth, Penguin.

TOWNSEND, P., DAVIDSON, N. and WHITEHEAD, M. (Eds) (1988) *Inequalities in Health*, Harmondsworth, Penguin.

TOWNSEND, P., PHILLIMORE, P. and BEATTIE, A. (1988) *Health and Deprivation: Inequality and the North*, Beckenham, Croom Helm.

TWIGG, J. (1986) *The Interface Between NHS and SSD: Home Helps, District Nurses and the Issue of Personal Care*, University of Kent, PSSRU.

TYDEMAN, P. (1983) 'Working in Safety, 150 Years of the Factory Inspectorate', *Employment Gazette*. 91, pp. 400–432.

TYRER, P. (1989) 'Risks of dependence on benzodiazepine drugs: the importance of patient selection', *British Medical Journal*, 298, 6666, pp. 102–5.

UNGERSON, C. (1983) 'Women and Caring: Skills, Tasks and Taboos', in Gamarnikow *et al.* (Eds) *The Public and the Private*, London, Heinemann.

UNGERSON, C. (1987) *Policy is Personal. Sex, Gender and Informal Care*, London, Tavistock.

VERBRUGGE, L.M. (1979) 'Marital Status and Health', *Journal of Marriage and the Family*, 41, pp. 267–85.

VERBRUGGE, L.M. (1983) 'Multiple roles and physical health of women and men', *Journal of Health and Social Behaviour*, 24, 1, pp. 16–30.

VAN THUNEN, J. (1966) 'Der Isolierte Staat' (1826), translated in HALL, P. (Ed.) *Thunen's Isolated State*, Oxford, Pergamon.

WADSWORTH, M.E.J. (1986) 'Serious illness in childhood and its association with later-life achievement', in WILKINSON, R. (Ed.) *Class and Health*, London, Tavistock.

WALDRON, I. (1980) 'Employment and women's health: an analysis of causal relationships', *International Journal of Health Studies*, 10, 2, pp. 435–54.

WALKER, A. (Ed.) (1978) *Rural Poverty*, London, CPAG.

WALLIS, R. and MORLEY, P. (Eds) (1976) *Marginal Medicine*, London, Peter Owen.

WALMSLEY, D.J. (1978) 'The influence of distance in hospital usage in rural New South Wales', *Australian Journal of Social Issues*, 13, pp. 72–81.

WALTERS, V. (1985) 'The Politics of Occupational Health and Safety', *The Canadian Review of Sociology and Anthropology*, 22, 1, pp. 57–79.

WARR, P. (1985) 'Twelve questions about unemployment and health,' in ROBERTS, B., FINNEGAN, R. and GALLIE, D. (Eds) *New Approaches to Economic Life*, Manchester, Manchester University Press.

WARR, P. and PARRY, G. (1982) 'Paid Employment and Women's Psychological Well-being', *Psychological Bulletin*, 91, 3, pp. 498–516.

WARREN, L. (1988) *Home Care and Elderly People, the Experiences of Home Helps and Elderly People in Salford*, unpublished PhD Thesis, University of Salford.

WARWICK, D. and LITTLEJOHN, G. (forthcoming) *Coal, Capital and Culture*, London, Routledge.

WATTERSON, A. (1986) 'Occupational Health and Illness: The Politics of Hazard Education', in RODMELL, S. and WATT, A. (Eds) *The Politics of Health Education*, London, Routledge and Kegan Paul.

WATTS, S. (1984) 'Practice View', in LISHMAN, J. (Ed.) *Social Work in Rural and Urban Areas*, Aberdeen, Aberdeen University Press.

WEBB, T., SCHILLING, R., BABB, D. and JACOBSON, B. (1987) *Health at Work?*, a Report on Health Promotion in the Workplace for the Health Education Council, London, Health Education Council/Authority.

WHITEHEAD, M. (1987) *The Health Divide: Inequalities in Health in the 1980s*, London, Health Education Council.

WIBBERLEY, G.P. (1978) 'Mobility and the Countryside', in CRESSWELL, R. (Ed.) *Rural Transport and Country Planning*, London, Leonard Hill.

WICKHAM, A. (1986) *Women and Training*, Milton Keynes, Open University Press.

WILKINSON, R. (1970) *The Prevention of Drinking Problems: Alcohol Control and Cultural Influences*, New York, Oxford University Press.

WILLMOTT, P. (1986) *Social Networks, Informal Care and Public Policy*, London, PSI.

WILLMOTT, P. (1987) *Friendship Networks and Social Support'*, London, PSI.

WILSON, P. (OPCS) (1980) *Drinking in England and Wales*, HMSO.

WILSON, R.A. and BOSWORTH, D. (1987) *New Forms and New Areas of Employment Growth*, Programme for Research and Action on the Development of the Labour Market: Final Report for the UK, OPEC.

WORLD HEALTH ORGANISATION (1948) *Official Record*, No. 2. (June).

WORLD HEALTH ORGANISATION (1980) *Problems Related to Alcohol Consumption*, N 650 Technical Report Series, Geneva, WHO.

WORLD HEALTH ORGANISATION (1981) *Global Strategy for Health for All by the Year 2000*, Geneva, WHO.

WRONG, D. (1963) 'Social inequality without social stratification', in HELLER, C.S. (Ed.) *Structural Social Inequality*, London, Collier Macmillan.

YATES, F. and HEBBLETHWAITE, D. (1985) 'Using Natural Resources for Preventing Drinking Problems', in HEATHER, N., ROBERTSON, I. and DAVIES, P. (Eds) *The Misuse of Alcohol*, Beckenham, Croom Helm.

YOUNG, K. and MILLS, L. (1980) *Public Policy Research*, London, SSRC.

Notes on Contributors

Pamela Abbott is a Senior Lecturer in Sociology and Social Policy at Polytechnic South West. Previous publications include *Community Care for Mentally Handicapped Children'*, 1987 (with Roger Sapsford); *Women and Social Class*, 1987 (with Roger Sapsford); *An Introduction to Sociology: Feminist Perspectives*, 1990 (with Claire Wallace).

Thomas Acton is a Senior Lecturer at Thames Polytechnic where he has worked since 1974. His major research interest is in Gypsies, but he has also published on South Chinese fisherfolk and in environmental health.

Sheila Allen is Pro-Vice Chancellor and Professor of Sociology at the University of Bradford.

Sara Arber is a Senior Lecturer in Sociology at the University of Surrey. Her current research is on inequalities in health stratification in later life and the care of the elderly. She is co-author of *Doing Secondary Analysis*, 1988.

Robin Bunton is Co-ordinator, Alcohol Concern Wales, a national charity working to reduce alcohol misuse. He has undertaken research in the areas of psychiatric education, community mental health programmes and health education campaigns.

Michael Bury is a Senior Lecturer in Sociology, Department of Social Policy and Social Science, Royal Holloway and Bedford New College, University of London. He is responsible for the MSc in Sociology with special reference to Medicine and has particular research interests in medical sociology, chronic illness and ageing.

Valerie Carroll was employed as a Research Assistant to the Social and Economic Life Initiative project by the Universities of Bradford and Leeds.

David Chambers is Principal Lecturer in the Environment at Thames Polytechnic. Prior to taking up his present appointment he worked as an environmental health officer. His research interests focus on the role of local authorities in the formulation and implementation of social policies, particularly housing urban renewal.

Norma Daykin is an Associate Lecturer in Social Policy in the Department of Nursing, Health and Applied Social Studies, Bristol Polytechnic. Her paper is based on a PhD thesis which is to be submitted to Bristol University.

Jonathan Gabe is a Lecturer in Sociology, General Practice Research Unit, Institute of Psychiatry, University of London. He is co-editor (with Paul Williams) of *Tranquillizers: Social, Psychological and Clinical Perspectives*, 1986, and has published in the areas of tranquillizer use, housing and mental health.

George Giarchi is Head of the Community Research Unit at Polytechnic South West. As a lecturer and researcher, he has concentrated his attention upon both rural studies and social gerontology. He is currently engaged in various projects for the elderly on behalf of Age Concern, and the Age Well Health Initiative.

Graham Hart is a Lecturer in Medical Sociology in the Academic Department of Genito-Urinary Medicine, University College and Middlesex School of Medicine, London. His research interests include health beliefs and behaviour of gay men in relation to AIDS, and the evaluation of a needle exchange scheme. He is editor of *AIDS: Social Representations, Social Practices*, 1989, and has recently contributed to the *Caring for Health: Dilemmas and Prospects* Open University course and *Readings for a New Public Health* (C.J. Martin and D.V. McQueen. Eds, 1989).

Gary Littlejohn is Reader in Comparative Sociology at the University of Bradford.

Geoff Payne is Assistant Director and Dean of the Faculty of Human Sciences at Polytechnic South West. He is author of *Employment and Opportunity*, 1987, and *Mobility and Change in Modern Society*, 1987, as well as articles on social mobility, social research and education.

Michael D. Peake was employed as Chest Consultant at Pontefract General Infirmary.

Ursula Sharma is a Senior Lecturer in the Department of Sociology and Anthropology, Keele University. Much of her research has been on gender and work in India and she has conducted extensive fieldwork in Indian villages and cities. Her recent research has concerned complementary health care in Britain, as perceived by both patients and practitioners.

Nicki Thorogood teaches Sociology of Health part-time at Middlesex Polytechnic and the Royal Free School of Medicine. She is also a development worker (job-share) for the City and Hackney Health Authority Young People's Project.

Lorna Warren is a Research Fellow at the Department of Sociological Studies, University of Sheffield where she is working with Alan Walker on a project to evaluate Neighbourhood Support Units and their role in the care of elderly people living at home.

Dennis Warwick is a Senior Lecturer in Sociology at the University of Leeds.

Caroline Welsh is employed as a temporary Research Assistant by the Universities of Bradford and Leeds.

Author Index

Subject Index

accidents 155, 157, 159, 160–2, 164
  see also occupational hazard
addiction 105, 119
Afro-Caribbean medicines 140–52
age 4, 5, 21–2, 31
AIDS 2, 8, 118, 119, 121, 123, 125, 126
alcohol 2, 8, 104–17, 148
  abuse 114
  misuse 9, 105, 108
alternative medicine 2, 4, 60, 127–52
  decision to use 132–7
  effectiveness 129–30
  users 127–9
amphetamines 120
  see also drugs

barbiturates 118
  see also drugs
benzodiazepines 87
  see also drugs
Black Report 3, 6, 37, 41, 50, 52, 172
body 90, 137, 147–8, 167
British Medical Association 129, 138
British Sociological Association 1, 10, 172
bush 141 ff
  see also Afro-Caribbean medicines

chiropractic 128
clients 77, 78, 128
  see also consumers
Committee on the Safety of Medicines 93

community 64
  care 61–2, 70–86, 106–7, 109–11, 115, 116
  physician 165, 167, 168, 170, 172
  see also locality
consumers 5, 6, 10, 65, 90, 129
Cornwall 59, 50–2, 64–8

day care centres 61
death 86, 118, 168
Department of Social Security 62
deprivation: *see* material deprivation
distance decay 63, 65, 69
domestic labour 41, 51, 55, 71, 74, 75, 85, 153
drugs 87–126, 131–2

educational qualifications 15–16, 73
elderly people 2, 4, 5, 59, 60, 62, 64, 70–86, 108, 111
environmental health 7, 21, 166–7, 170–74
  officers 167, 168, 170, 171, 173

epidemiology 1, 2, 12, 172

family roles 74–82, 86

General Household Survey 37, 43–4, 46–51, 54, 56, 112

199

Printed in the United Kingdom
by Lightning Source UK Ltd.
114702UKS00001B/35

9 781850 007876